John Tinkler
Chattanooga
1996

The Redress of Poetry

THE
REDRESS
OF
POETRY

SEAMUS
HEANEY

Farrar, Straus and Giroux

New York

Library of Congress Cataloging-in-Publication Data
Heaney, Seamus.
The redress of poetry / Seamus Heaney.
p.   cm.
1. English poetry—History and criticism. 2. American poetry—
History and criticism. 3. English poetry—Irish authors—History
and criticism.   I. Title.
PR503.H38   1995   821.009—dc20   95–19556   CIP

Grateful acknowledgment is made for permission to reproduce the
following: Excerpts from The Collected Prose of Elizabeth Bishop,
edited by Robert Giroux. Copyright © 1984 by Alice Methfessel.
Reprinted by permission of Farrar, Straus & Giroux, Inc. Excerpts
from The Complete Poems 1927–1979 of Elizabeth Bishop. Copyright
© 1979, 1983 by Alice Helen Methfessel. Reprinted by permission of
Farrar, Straus & Giroux, Inc. Extracts from Collected Poems of Dylan
Thomas (London, 1954), David Higham Associates. Extracts from
Complete Poems, 1920–76 of Hugh MacDiarmid, edited by Michael
Grieve and W. R. Aitken, Martin Brian & O'Keeffe Ltd. Extracts from
Frank O'Connor's translation of Brian Merriman's The Midnight
Court (Dublin, 1989), The O'Brien Press.

for Bernard and Heather O'Donoghue

Contents

Preface

The ten lectures reprinted here were first delivered in the course of my tenure as Professor of Poetry at Oxford between 1989 and 1994. It was an honour to be elected to the office and to be welcomed so wholeheartedly within the university. My predecessor, Peter Levi, wrote me a wonderful letter at the time, with all kinds of practical advice and an especially promising pen-and-ink sketch of the proper academic rig-out for Encaenia. It was typical of the good cheer and good reception I experienced in Oxford from the start, although I should also acknowledge here the warmth with which the appointment was greeted in Ireland. Perhaps the best example of the latter was a woman with a pram who was crossing the road at traffic lights in Omagh a couple of days after the result had been announced: she recognized me at the wheel of the car, gave me a quick – unsmiling – nod, a very definite thumbs-up, and then hurried smartly on about her business.

The Professor of Poetry is expected to deliver three public lectures each year: five of the fifteen I gave have been left out of this collection. A large part of one of them (on Louis MacNeice) is included in 'Frontiers of Writing' and one on Robert Frost (with specific reference to the theme of redress) is available in the twenty-fifth anniversary issue of *Salmagundi* (No. 88–89, Fall 1990–Winter 1991). The three contributed during my second year made up a triptych called 'Talking Shop': two of these were an extended treatment of concerns I deal with briefly in the Introduction to this book, and the third was a survey of the work of several younger Irish poets in the light of those same concerns. In the end, however, it seemed to me that that group of three was different in kind from the ten reprinted here, all of which focus upon a single work or a completed oeuvre by poets in the English, Irish and American canons.

The pieces that follow have been revised since they were delivered; there have been excisions and are one or two additions, but none of the arguments or judgements made on the original occasions has been altered. In some cases, important new books on the poets concerned appeared after the lectures were given – such as Brett Hillier's biography of Elizabeth Bishop, and Davis Coakley's book emphasizing the Irish dimension in Oscar Wilde – but their findings in general were a corroboration of the things I had been saying. In the case of 'Frontiers of Writing', however, I was definitely tempted to rewrite since it was delivered late in 1993, almost a year before the ceasefires by the Provisional IRA and the Loyalist paramilitaries, at a time when the mood in Britain and Ireland had been greatly darkened by bombing atrocities on the Shankhill Road and at Greysteel. I nevertheless decided to leave it unchanged because it had been deliberately composed as a concluding statement and also because many of the things I say there still hold good.

In the meantime, some of the lectures were repeated elsewhere and some of them have been published separately, beginning with 'The Redress of Poetry', which appeared as a pamphlet from Oxford University Press in 1990. 'Extending the Alphabet' was delivered in May 1993 as the E. J. Pratt Memorial Lecture at Memorial University in Newfoundland; 'Orpheus in Ireland' was published in The *Southern Review*, Vol. 32, No. 3, Summer 1995; 'John Clare's Prog' was included (as 'John Clare – A Bicentenary Lecture') in *John Clare in Context*, edited by Hugh Haughton, Adam Phillips and Geoffrey Summerfield, Cambridge University Press, 1994; 'Speranza in Reading' was given as the 1994 James McAuley Lecture in the University of Tasmania; 'A Torchlight Procession of One' was the R. I. Best Memorial Lecture, sponsored by the National Library of Ireland, in January 1993; 'Dylan the Durable?' was the 1992 Ben Belitt Lecture at Bennington College and appeared as a Bennington Chapbook; 'Joy or Night' was given as the W. D. Thomas Lecture at the University of Swansea in January 1993; and 'Frontiers of Writing' was carried in the first issue of *Bullan, An Irish Studies Journal*, published from St John's College, Oxford. Extracts from a number of the lectures appeared in *Harvard Review*. I am grateful to the sponsors of all these events and to the editors and publishers who saw the lectures into print in their original form. At a later stage, Christopher Reid and Jane Feaver, my editors at Faber and Faber, were as usual generous beyond measure with their gifts as readers and (re)writers.

My chief gratitude, however, must go to my friends in Oxford and to all those other 'hearers and hearteners of the work' who stayed the course. Since the experience of lecturing in the Examination Schools was not only honorific but daunting, it was always a relief to meet the supportive faces that one had met in the audience again, after the event, in the bar of the East Gate Hotel: bitter has never tasted sweeter. In more formal circumstances, the hospitality of the President and Fellows of Magdalen College and the President and Fellows of St John's made every visit a special occasion for my wife and myself: Anthony Smith gave us a home from home in the President's Lodgings at Magdalen and kept on finding ways to improve the surroundings in a suite that was already a joy to inhabit. I shall always remember the delight of waking up there on autumn mornings just as the sopranos of the college choir were beginning to run through their scales in the practice room below.

In Magdalen also I was untiringly guided and assisted in Oxford ways and means by Bernard O'Donoghue: whether it was a matter of accessing catalogues in the Bodleian or a play at Stratford, the Thames at Bablock Hithe or ballads in the Bullingdon Arms, he and his wife Heather were always to the fore, guarantors of the good cheer and good will that made my five years' stint as Professor such a happy experience.

Introduction

The first poem quoted in full in this book is George Herbert's 'The Pulley'; the last is one of my own, a twelve-line section from a sequence called 'Squarings'. The 'Squarings' poem tells the story of an apparition experienced by the monastic community in Clonmacnoise sometime during the Middle Ages: a crewman came down to them out of a visionary boat in the sky but could not stay and had to be helped back out of the human element because, as the abbot perceived, he would have drowned in it if he had remained. 'The Pulley' is a parable about God devising a way to keep the minds and aspirations of human beings turned towards the heavenly in spite of all the pleasures and penalties of being upon earth. Both poems are about the way consciousness can be alive to two different and contradictory dimensions of reality and still find a way of negotiating between them, but I did not notice this correspondence between their thematic and imaginative concerns until the whole book had been assembled in manuscript.

Once I saw the link, however, I was delighted. It confirmed my trust – the trust in which the subjects of these lectures were chosen – that a reliable critical course could be plotted by following a poetic sixth sense. In fact I now realize that the overall theme of the pieces collected here grew out of poetry I had been writing in the years preceding the summer of 1989 when my tenure at Oxford began. Poems and parables about crossing from the domain of the matter-of-fact into the domain of the imagined had been among the work that appeared in *The Haw Lantern* in 1987, and the Clonmacnoise poem was only one of several about being transported 'out to an other side' that had surfaced not long afterwards. What lay behind these poems was an interest in 'the frontier of writing' and, in fact, I was explicitly concerned with this idea in an early lecture (not reprinted here) which I gave at the beginning of my second year.

There I discussed Robert Frost's 'Directive' as an allegorical defence of poetry and since the terms of that discussion are echoed at various points in the following pages, I shall touch upon it again briefly by way of introduction. But before doing so, I want to bring up a passage by Robert Pinsky from his essay on 'Responsibilities of the Poet', because it meshes in general very interestingly with my own notion of 'the redress of poetry' and corroborates my reading of the Frost poem as being in some oblique but important way an apologia for all art. An artist, Pinsky writes,

needs not so much an audience, as to feel a need to answer, a promise to respond. The promise may be a contradiction, it may be unwanted, it may go unheeded . . . but it is owed, and the sense that it is owed is a basic requirement for the poet's good feeling about the art. This need to answer, as firm as a borrowed object or a cash debt, is the ground where the centaur walks.

This perception about the way art responds (and exercises its responsibility) has a special relevance in relation to the concluding section of 'Directive' in which the quester has been led beyond everything familiar – 'Back out of all this now too much for us' – to a deserted farmstead on a mountainside. This site Frost then presents as a locus of knowledge, a scene of instruction and revelation:

> First there's the children's house of make-believe,
> Some shattered dishes underneath a pine,
> The playthings in the playhouse of the children.
> Weep for what little things could make them glad.
> Then for the house that is no more a house,
> But only a belilaced cellar hole,
> Now slowly closing like a dent in dough.
> This was no playhouse but a house in earnest.
> Your destination and your destiny's
> A brook that was the water of the house,

Cold as a spring as yet so near its source,
Too lofty and original to rage.
(We know the valley streams that when aroused
Will leave their tatters hung on barb and thorn.)
I have kept hidden in the instep arch
Of an old cedar at the waterside
A broken drinking goblet like the Grail
Under a spell so the wrong ones can't find it,
So can't get saved, as Saint Mark says they mustn't.
(I stole the goblet from the children's playhouse.)
Here are your waters and your watering place.
Drink and be whole again beyond confusion.

What these lines are saying is that the games of make-believe which the children played in the playhouse were a kind of freely invented answer to everything experienced in the 'house in earnest' where (the tone makes this clear) life was lived in sorrow and in anger. Frost suggests, in fact, that the life endured by the occupants of the actual house finds its best memorial and expression in the 'house of make-believe'. He convinces us that the playhouse has the measure of the other house, that the entranced focus of the activity that took place as make-believe on one side of the yard was fit to match the meaning of what happened in earnest on the other side, and in doing so Frost further suggests that the imaginative transformation of human life is the means by which we can most truly grasp and comprehend it. What Virgil called *lacrimae rerum*, the tears of things, can be absorbed and re-experienced in the playthings in the playhouse – or in the words of the poem. Furthermore, the poem is like the broken drinking goblet stolen from the playhouse and dipped in the mountain stream because it too offers a clarification, a fleeting glimpse of a potential order of things 'beyond confusion', a glimpse that has to be its own reward. The poem provides a draught of the clear water of transformed understanding and fills the reader with a momentary sense of freedom and wholeness.

Moreover, it is in the space between the farmhouse and the playhouse that one discovers what I've called 'the frontier of writing', the line that divides the actual conditions of our daily lives from the imaginative representation of those conditions in literature, and divides also the world of social speech from the world of poetic language. And that dividing line is the real subject of Thomas Hardy's bewitching poem 'Afterwards'. Hardy may have begun this poem with the intention of writing about his imminent disappearance from the familiar world, but his ultimate achievement was to transform the familiar into something rich and strange:

When the Present has latched its postern behind my tremulous
    stay,
  And the May month flaps its glad green leaves like wings,
Delicate-filmed as new-spun silk, will the neighbours say,
  'He was a man who used to notice such things'?

If it be in the dusk when, like an eyelid's soundless blink,
  The dewfall-hawk comes crossing the shades to alight
Upon the wind-warped upland thorn, a gazer may think,
  'To him this must have been a familiar sight.'

If I pass during some nocturnal blackness, mothy and warm,
  When the hedgehog travels furtively over the lawn,
One may say, 'He strove that such innocent creatures should
    come to no harm,
  But he could do little for them; and now he is gone.'

If, when hearing that I have been stilled at last, they stand at the
    door,
  Watching the full-starred heavens that winter sees,
Will this thought rise on those who will meet my face no more,
  'He was one who had an eye for such mysteries'?

And will any say when my bell of quittance is heard in the
    gloom,
  And a crossing breeze cuts a pause in its outrollings,

Till they rise again, as they were a new bell's boom,
'He hears it not now, but used to notice such things'?

In one way, this is an expression of solidarity with the ordinary
world where people stand around after the news of a death,
wistful rather than desolate, and repeat the conventional decen-
cies. But in the end, the poem is more given over to the extraordinary than to the ordinary, more dedicated to the world-
renewing potential of the imagined response than to the adequacy of the social one. For part of the time, the reader is
confined to the company of the neighbours where all that is on
offer is conventional wisdom in untransfigured phrases. But
then consciousness is given access to a dimension beyond the
frontier where an overbrimming, totally resourceful expressive-
ness becomes suddenly available; and this entry into a condition
of illuminated rightness becomes an entry into poetry itself.

'He was a man who used to notice such things,' say the neighbours, on this side of the frontier. 'Which things?' asks the
reader, and from the other side the poem answers, 'The May
month flaps its glad green leaves like wings, / Delicate-filmed as
new-spun silk.' 'To him this must have been a familiar sight,'
say the neighbours. 'What must have been a familiar sight?'
asks the reader. 'The dusk, when, like an eyelid's soundless
blink, / The dewfall-hawk comes crossing the shades to alight /
Upon the wind-warped upland thorn', says the poem.
'Anything else?' says the reader. 'Blackness, mothy and warm',
says the poem. 'The full-starred heavens that winter sees', things
like that. 'My God!' says the reader.

The poem, in fact, is a showing forth of the way that poetry
brings human existence into a fuller life. It is obviously less
extravagant in its rhetoric than, say, Rilke's 'Sonnets to Orpheus', but it is no less fully alive to the excitements and transformations which poetic activity promotes. In fact, we could even
bend to our purpose here the words which conclude Rilke's first
sonnet in the Orpheus sequence; we could say that the opening
lines of each of the five stanzas of 'Afterwards' 'make a temple

deep inside our hearing', a temple which stands on the other side of the divide created by the passage of the god of poetry himself.

But poetry does not need to invoke a god to sanction its workings: its truth, as William Wordsworth asserted, does not stand upon 'external testimony but [is] carried live into the heart by passion; truth which is its own testimony, which gives competence and confidence to the tribunal to which it appeals, and receives them from that same tribunal.' Admittedly, Wordsworth is not very specific about the composition of that ultimate tribunal and its seat is anyhow likely to have been moved nowadays from 'the heart' to some more theoretically secure address; but it nevertheless survives as the tribunal whose reality all responsible poetry depends upon and the one through which its redress is mediated.

The Redress of Poetry

The Redress of Poetry

Professors of poetry, apologists for it, practitioners of it, from Sir Philip Sidney to Wallace Stevens, all sooner or later are tempted to show how poetry's existence as a form of art relates to our existence as citizens of society – how it is 'of present use'. Behind such defences and justifications, at any number of removes, stands Plato, calling into question whatever special prerogatives or useful influences poetry would claim for itself within the *polis*. Yet Plato's world of ideal forms also provides the court of appeal through which poetic imagination seeks to redress whatever is wrong or exacerbating in the prevailing conditions. Moreover, 'useful' or 'practical' responses to those same conditions are derived from imagined standards too: poetic fictions, the dream of alternative worlds, enable governments and revolutionaries as well. It's just that governments and revolutionaries would compel society to take on the shape of their imagining, whereas poets are typically more concerned to conjure with their own and their readers' sense of what is possible or desirable or, indeed, imaginable. The nobility of poetry, says Wallace Stevens, 'is a violence from within that protects us from a violence without'. It is the imagination pressing back against the pressure of reality.

Stevens, as he reaches this conclusion in his essay 'The Noble Rider and the Sounds of Words', is anxious to insist that his own words are intended to be more than merely sonorous, and his anxiety is understandable. It is as if he were imagining and responding to the outcry of some disaffected heckler in the crowd of those whom Tony Harrison calls 'the rhubarbarians', one crying out against the mystification of art and its appropriation by the grandees of aesthetics. 'In our time', the heckler protests, echoing something he has read somewhere, 'the destiny of man presents itself in political terms.' And in his understanding, and in the understanding of most people who protest against the ascription to poetry of any metaphysical force, those terms are going to derive from the politics of subversion, of redressal, of affirming that which is denied voice. Our heckler, in other words, will want poetry to be more than an imagined response to conditions in the world; he or she will urgently want to know why it should not be an applied art, harnessed to movements which attempt to alleviate those conditions by direct action.

The heckler, therefore, is going to have little sympathy with Wallace Stevens when he declares the poet to be a potent figure because the poet 'creates the world to which we turn incessantly and without knowing it, and . . . gives life to the supreme fictions without which we are unable to conceive of [that world]' – meaning that if our given experience is a labyrinth, its impassability can still be countered by the poet's imagining some equivalent of the labyrinth and presenting himself and us with a vivid experience of it. Such an operation does not intervene in the actual but by offering consciousness a chance to recognize its predicaments, foreknow its capacities and rehearse its comebacks in all kinds of venturesome ways, it does constitute a beneficent event, for poet and audience alike. It offers a response to reality which has a liberating and verifying effect upon the individual spirit, and yet I can see how such a function would be deemed insufficient by a political activist. For the activist, there is going to be no point in envisaging an order which is comprehensive of events but not in itself productive of new events. Engaged parties are not going to be grateful for a mere image – no matter how inventive or original – of the field of force of which they are a part. They will always want the redress of poetry to be an exercise of leverage on behalf of *their* point of view; they will require the entire weight of the thing to come down on their side of the scales.

So, if you are an English poet at the Front during World War I, the pressure will be on you to contribute to the war effort, preferably by dehumanizing the face of the enemy. If you are an

Irish poet in the wake of the 1916 executions, the pressure will be to revile the tyranny of the executing power. If you are an American poet at the height of the Vietnam War, the official expectation will be for you to wave the flag rhetorically. In these cases, to see the German soldier as a friend and secret sharer, to see the British government as a body who might keep faith, to see the South-East Asian expedition as an imperial betrayal, to do any of these things is to add a complication where the general desire is for a simplification.

Such countervailing gestures frustrate the common expectation of solidarity, but they do have political force. Their very power to exacerbate is one guarantee of their effectiveness. They are particular instances of a law which Simone Weil announced with typical extremity and succinctness in her book *Gravity and Grace*. She writes there:

If we know in what way society is unbalanced, we must do what we can to add weight to the lighter scale ... we must have formed a conception of equilibrium and be ever ready to change sides like justice, 'that fugitive from the camp of conquerors'.

Clearly, this corresponds to deep structures of thought and feeling derived from centuries of Christian teaching and from Christ's paradoxical identification with the plight of the wretched. And in so far as poetry is an extension and refinement of the mind's extreme recognitions, and of language's most unexpected apprehensions, it too manifests the workings of Weil's law.

'Obedience to the force of gravity. The greatest sin.' So Simone Weil also writes in *Gravity and Grace*. Indeed her whole book is informed by the idea of counterweighting, of balancing out the forces, of redress – tilting the scales of reality towards some transcendent equilibrium. And in the activity of poetry too, there is a tendency to place a counter-reality in the scales – a reality which may be only imagined but which nevertheless has weight because it is imagined within the gravitational pull of the actual and can therefore hold its own and

3

balance out against the historical situation. This redressing effect of poetry comes from its being a glimpsed alternative, a revelation of potential that is denied or constantly threatened by circumstances. And sometimes, of course, it happens that such a revelation, once enshrined in the poem, remains as a standard for the poet, so that he or she must then submit to the strain of bearing witness in his or her own life to the plane of consciousness established in the poem.

In this century, especially, from Wilfred Owen to Irina Ratushinskaya, there have been many poets who from principle, in solitude, and without any guarantee of success, were drawn by the logic of their work to disobey the force of gravity. These figures have become the types of an action that gains value in proportion to its immediate practical ineffectiveness. In their case, the espousal of that which critics used to call 'vision' or 'moral commitment' grew exorbitant and carried them beyond the charmed circle of artistic space and further, beyond domestic privacy, social conformity, and minimal ethical expectation, into the solitary role of the witness. Characteristically, figures of such spiritual stamina incline to understate the heroic aspect of their achievement and insist upon the strictly artistic discipline at the heart of their vocation. Yet the fact remains that for the writers I have mentioned, and others like them – Osip Mandelstam and Czeslaw Milosz, for instance – the redress of poetry comes to represent something like an exercise of the virtue of hope as it is understood by Václav Havel. Indeed, what Havel has to say about hope can also be said about poetry: it is

a state of mind, not a state of the world. Either we have hope within us or we don't; it is a dimension of the soul, and it's not essentially dependent on some particular observation of the world or estimate of the situation ... It is an orientation of the spirit, an orientation of the heart; it transcends the world that is immediately experienced, and is anchored somewhere beyond its horizons. I don't think you can explain it as a mere derivative of something here, of some movement, or of some favourable signs in the world. I feel that its deepest roots are in

4

the transcendental, just as the roots of human responsibility are . . . It is not the conviction that something will turn out well, but the certainty that something makes sense, regardless of how it turns out.

Of course, when a contemporary lifts a pen or gazes into the dead-pan cloudiness of a word processor, considerations like these are well in the background. When Douglas Dunn sits down at his desk with its view above the Tay Estuary or Anne Stevenson sees one of her chosen landscapes flash upon her inward eye, neither is immediately haunted by the big questions of poetics. All these accumulated pressures and issues are felt as an abiding anxiety but they do not enter as guiding factors within the writing process itself. The movement is from delight to wisdom and not vice versa. The felicity of a cadence, the chain reaction of a rhyme, the pleasuring of an etymology, such things can proceed happily and as it were autistically, in an area of mental operations cordoned off by and from the critical sense. Indeed, if one recalls W. H. Auden's famous trinity of poetic faculties – making, judging, and knowing – the making faculty seems in this light to have a kind of free pass that enables it to range beyond the jurisdiction of the other two.

It is only right that this should be the case. Poetry cannot afford to lose its fundamentally self-delighting inventiveness, its joy in being a process of language as well as a representation of things in the world. To put it in W. B. Yeats's terms, the will must not usurp the work of the imagination. And while this may seem something of a truism, it is nevertheless worth repeating in a late-twentieth-century context of politically approved themes, post-colonial backlash and 'silence-breaking' writing of all kinds. In these circumstances, poetry is understandably pressed to give voice to much that has hitherto been denied expression in the ethnic, social, sexual and political life. Which is to say that its power as a mode of redress in the first sense – as agent for proclaiming and correcting injustices – is being appealed to constantly. But in discharging this function, poets are in danger of slighting another imperative, namely, to redress poetry *as* poetry, to set it up as its own category, an eminence established and a pressure exercised by distinctly linguistic means.

Not that it is not possible to have a poetry which consciously seeks to promote cultural and political change and yet can still manage to operate with the fullest artistic integrity. The history of Irish poetry over the last 150 years is in itself sufficient demonstration that a motive for poetry can be grounded to a greater or lesser degree in programmes with a national purpose. Obviously, patriotic or propagandist intent is far from being a guarantee of poetic success, but in emergent cultures the struggle of an individual consciousness towards affirmation and distinctness may be analogous, if not coterminous, with a collective straining towards self-definition; there is a mutual susceptibility between the formation of a new tradition and the self-fashioning of individual talent. Yeats, for example, began with a desire 'to write short lyrics or poetic drama where every speech would be short and concentrated', but, typically, he endowed this personal stylistic ambition with national significance by relating it to 'an Irish preference for a swift current' and contrasting it with 'the English mind ... meditative, rich, deliberate', which 'may remember the Thames valley'.

At such moments of redefinition, however, there are complicating factors at work. What is involved, after all, is the replacement of ideas of literary excellence derived from modes of expression originally taken to be canonical and unquestionable. Writers have to start out as readers, and before they put pen to paper, even the most disaffected of them will have internalized the norms and forms of the tradition from which they wish to secede. Whether they are feminists rebelling against the patriarchy of language or nativists in full cry with the local accents of their vernacular, whether they write Anglo-Irish or Afro-English or Lallans, writers of what has been called 'nation language' will have been wrong-footed by the fact that their own literary formation was based upon models of excellence taken from the English language and its literature. They will have been predisposed to accommodate themselves to the consciousness which subjugated them. Naturally, black poets from Trinidad or Lagos and working-class writers from Newcastle or Glasgow will be found arguing that their education in Shakespeare or Keats was little more than an exercise in alienating them from their authentic experience, devalorizing their vernacular and destabilizing their instinctual at-homeness in their own non-textual worlds: but the truth of that argument should not obliterate other truths about language and self-valorization which I shall come to presently.

In any movement towards liberation, it will be necessary to deny the normative authority of the dominant language or literary tradition. At a special moment in the Irish Literary Revival, this was precisely the course adopted by Thomas MacDonagh, Professor of English at the Royal University in Dublin, whose book on *Literature in Ireland* was published in 1916, the very year he was executed as one of the leaders of the Easter Rising. With more seismic consequences, it was also the course adopted by James Joyce. But MacDonagh knew the intricacies and delicacies of the English lyric inheritance which he was calling into question, to the extent of having written a book on the metrics of Thomas Campion. And Joyce, for all his hauteur about the British Empire and the English novel, was helpless to resist the appeal of, for example, the songs and airs of the Elizabethans. Neither MacDonagh nor Joyce considered it necessary to proscribe within his reader's memory the riches of the Anglophone culture whose authority each was, in his own way, compelled to challenge. Neither denied his susceptibility to the totally persuasive word in order to prove the purity of his resistance to an imperial hegemony. Which is why both these figures are instructive when we come to consider the scope and function of poetry in the world. They remind us that its integrity is not to be impugned just because at any given moment it happens to be a refraction of some discredited cultural or political system.

Poetry, let us say, whether it belongs to an old political

dispensation or aspires to express a new one, has to be a working model of inclusive consciousness. It should not simplify. Its projections and inventions should be a match for the complex reality which surrounds it and out of which it is generated. *The Divine Comedy* is a great example of this kind of total adequacy, but a haiku may also constitute a satisfactory comeback by the mind to the facts of the matter. As long as the coordinates of the imagined thing correspond to those of the world that we live in and endure, poetry is fulfilling its counterweighting function. It becomes another truth to which we can have recourse, before which we can know ourselves in a more fully empowered way. In fact, to read poetry of this totally adequate kind is to experience something bracing and memorable, something capable of increasing in value over the whole course of a lifetime.

There is nothing exaggerated about such a claim. Jorge Luis Borges, for example, makes a similar point about what happens between the poem and the reader:

The taste of the apple (states Berkeley) lies in the contact of the fruit with the palate, not in the fruit itself; in a similar way (I would say) poetry lies in the meeting of poem and reader, not in the lines of symbols printed on pages of a book. What is essential is . . . the thrill, the almost physical emotion that comes with each reading.

Borges goes on to be more precise about the nature of that thrill or 'physical emotion' and suggests that it fulfils the continual need we experience to 'recover a past or prefigure a future' – a formulation, incidentally, which has a suggestive truth at the communal as well as at the personal level.

The issue is clarified further if we go back to Borges's first book of poems, and his note of introduction:

If in the following pages there is some successful verse or other, may the reader forgive me the audacity of having written it before him. We are all one; our inconsequential minds are much alike, and circumstances so influence us that it is something of an accident that you are the reader and I the writer – the unsure, ardent writer – of my verses.

Disingenuous as this may be, it nevertheless touches on something so common that it is in danger of being ignored. Borges is talking about the fluid, exhilarating moment which lies at the heart of any memorable reading, the undisappointed joy of finding that everything holds up and answers the desire that it awakens. At such moments, the delight of having all one's faculties simultaneously provoked and gratified is like gaining an upper hand over all that is contingent and (as Borges says) 'inconsequential'. There is a sensation both of arrival and of prospect, so that one does indeed seem to 'recover a past' and 'prefigure a future', and thereby to complete the circle of one's being. When this happens, we have a distinct sensation that (to borrow a phrase from George Seferis's notebooks) poetry is 'strong enough to help'; it is then that its redress grows palpable.

I would like to spend the rest of the available time in celebrating one such undisappointing poet. For three centuries and more, George Herbert exemplified the body heat of a healthy Anglican life. John Donne might be permitted his fever and chills, Henry Vaughan indulged for his Welsh mysticism, and Richard Crashaw condoned in spite of a torrid Catholicism; but George Herbert's daylight sanity and vigour, his *via media* between preciousness and vulgarity, promoted the ideal mental and emotional climate.

This may be a misrepresentation of the Herbert known to scholars and specialized readers, the poet whose 'tickle points of wit' were in fact subtle addresses to Calvinist divergences of doctrine within the Church of England, but I do not think it misrepresents the general impression of him which a sympathetic literate audience carries around. Herbert's work, moreover – so essential to the tradition of English lyric, so domiciled within a native culture and voice, so conscripted as a manifestation of the desirable English temperament – was long understood to embody the civilities and beliefs which England, through the operations of its colonial power, sought to impose upon other peoples. But in the end, my point has to be this: even the most imposed-upon colonial will discern in the clear element of Herbert's poetry a true paradigm of the shape of things, psychologically, politically, metaphorically and, if one wants to proceed that far, metaphysically. Even here, between marginalized reader and privileged poet, the Borgesian circularity applies. Herbert's work, in other words, is an example of that fully realized poetry I have attempted to define, a poetry where the co-ordinates of the imagined thing correspond to and allow us to contemplate the complex burden of our own experience.

His poems are wise and witty transformations of the ups and downs of his pulley-like sympathies. His wit, indeed, is as integral to his world view as his religious faith. All the antitheses which exercised him and upon which he exercised his mind – creator/creature, heaven/earth, soul/body, eternity/time, life/ death, Christ/man, grace/guilt, virtue/sin, divine love/courtly love – all these antitheses were commonly available through the cosmology and theology of the Church of England in the early seventeenth century, and the drama of Herbert's poems is played out wholly in terms of the Christian story and liturgy. But such antithetical pairings are experienced more immediately as emotional dilemmas than as doctrinal cruces: they are functions of the poet's mind as it moves across the frontier of writing, out of homiletics and apologetics into poetry, upon the impulses and reflexes of awakened language. At an elementary level, some grasp of the poems' basic conceptual and theological machinery is, of course, necessary, but what Borges calls 'the almost physical emotion that comes with each reading' derives from the superfluity of the poems' language-life and their structural animation. What might be called the DNA pattern of Herbert's imagination is fundamentally a matter of up-down, criss-cross motion, reversals effected with such symmetry that they are experienced as culminations, tensions so thoroughly exercised and traced home that they return the system to relaxation, dialogues so sinuous that they end with speakers ready to start again, sometimes from diametrically opposed premises. The wonder is that poems which seem so perfectly set to become perpetual-motion machines can find ways of closure and escape from their own unfaltering kinesis.

It is tempting to use the word 'balance' here, but to use it too soon would preclude sufficient acknowledgement of the volatile aspect of the Herbertian scales, the fluidity of all about the fulcrum, and the sensitivity of the arms to leverage by wit or wisdom equally. In fact, wit/wisdom may turn out to be the central antithesis, because it is in the delights of Herbert's witty making that the gravity of his judging and knowing works itself in – and then works itself out. At its best, this play of mind is heuristic. It may have illustrative force in relation to the truths of religion, but it is also doing the work of art: personal force is being moved through an aesthetic distance, and in a space where anything can happen the longed-for may occur by way of the unforeseen, or may be balked by the limitations of the usual.

In Herbert's 'The Pulley', for example, a pun on the word 'rest' is executed in slow motion. As in the operation of a pulley, one of the word's semantic loads – 'rest' in the sense of repose – is gradually let down, but as it reaches the limit of its descent into the reader's understanding, another meaning – 'rest' in the sense of 'remainder' or 'left-over' – begins to rise. At the end, equilibrium has been restored to the system, both by the argument and by the rhythm and rhyme, as 'rest' and 'breast' come together in a gratifying closure. But as with any pulley system, the moment of equilibrium is tentative and capable of a renewed dynamism. The poem can be read as a mimetic rendering of any pulley-like exchange of forces, but equally it presents itself as an allegory of the relationship between humanity and the Godhead, a humanity whose hearts, in St Augustine's phrase, 'are restless till they rest in Thee'.

The Pulley

When God at first made man,
Having a glasse of blessings standing by;

Let us (said he) poure on him all we can:
Let the worlds riches, which dispersed lie,
    Contract into a span.

    So strength first made a way;
Then beauty flow'd, then wisdome, honour, pleasure:
When almost all was out, God made a stay,
Perceiving that alone of all his treasure
    Rest in the bottome lay.

    For if I should (said he)
Bestow this jewell also on my creature,
He would adore my gifts in stead of me,
And rest in Nature, not the God of Nature.
    So both should losers be.

    Yet let him keep the rest,
But keep them with repining restlessnesse:
Let him be rich and wearie, that at least,
If goodnesse lead him not, yet wearinesse
    May tosse him to my breast.

Perhaps this poem does not immediately strike us as what has
been called 'big-league poetry'. Its pitch is low, it proceeds
about its business without histrionics, and the sureness of its
progress invests it with an underplayed self-containment. It is,
in fact, a little more sober than many of Herbert's poems. Nowhere does it evince the catch in the breath that occurs with
happy frequency elsewhere in his work. It does not have those
surprising local effects of lyric joy which remind us how available this poet once felt himself to be to a more erotic genre, how
capable he would have been of a delicious squandering had he
not made sacred poetry his whole vocation. But if 'The Pulley'
is subdued to its demure purpose, it still generates that compensatory pressure which all realized works exert against the surrounding inconsequentiality. In its unforced way, it does contain
within itself the co-ordinates and contradictions of experience,
and would be as comprehensible within the cosmology of Yin

and Yang as it is amenable to the dialectic of thesis, antithesis, and synthesis.

Herbert's most celebrated poem, 'The Collar', illustrates much more dramatically than 'The Pulley' all that I have been claiming for him. The dance of lexical possibilities in the title; the way in which the poem changes partners with the meanings of 'collar', as an article of clerical clothing and a fit of anger; the reversal of emotional states from affront to assuagement; the technical relish of postponing stanzaic composure until the last four lines – it is all as Seferis wants poetry to be, 'strong enough', and can be hung out on the imaginative arm of the balance to take the strain of our knowledge of things as they are:

> Away; Take Heed:
> I will abroad.
> Call in thy deaths head there: tie up thy fears.
> He that forbears
> To suit and serve his need,
> Deserves his load.
> But as I rav'd and grew more fierce and wilde
> At every word,
> Methoughts I heard one calling, *Childe*:
> And I reply'd, *My Lord*.

This poem has a wonderful logical and psychological self-sufficiency. It is so formally replete that it tempts me to quote from Wallace Stevens again: 'a poet's words are of things that do not exist without the words.' And yet 'The Collar' has an applicability beyond its own vivid occasion, and could be read at certain historical moments as a way of comprehending ironies and reversals more extensive than the personal crisis which it records. Which is to say that as a form of art it does relate very definitely to our existence as citizens of society. When the terrorists sit down at the negotiating-table, when the newly independent state enters history still being administered by the old colonial civil service, then the reversal which the poem traces is merely being projected upon a more extensive and populous screen.

This is why references to Herbert's simplicity can often come across as too simple themselves. His poems, of course, exhibit an attractive forthrightness; his articulation has an exhilarating clarity about it and gives the reader the airy sensation of invigilating from a superior plane. But neither the lucidity of presentation nor the even tenor of voice should diminish our respect for the tried quality of Herbert's intelligence. Even that immaculate ballet of courtesy and equilibrium in 'Love III' represents a grounded strength as well as a perfect tact. This country parson may not have gone to the *Gulag* for his faith, but he possesses a sort of Russian down-to-earthness, a readiness that would not be found wanting:

> Love bade me welcome: yet my soul drew back,
>   Guiltie of dust and sinne.
> But quick-ey'd Love, observing me grow slack
>   From my first entrance in,
> Drew nearer to me, sweetly questioning,
>   If I lack'd anything.
>
> A guest, I answer'd, worthy to be here:
>   Love said, You shall be he.
> I the unkinde, ungratefull? Ah my deare,
>   I cannot look on thee.
> Love took my hand, and smiling did reply,
>   Who made the eyes but I?
>
> Truth Lord, but I have marr'd them: let my shame
>   Go where it doth deserve.
> And know you not, sayes Love, who bore the blame?
>   My deare, then I will serve.
> You must sit down, sayes Love, and taste my meat:
>   So I did sit and eat.

*

The OED has four entries for 'redress' as a noun, and I began by calling upon the first sense which it provides: 'Reparation of, satisfaction or compensation for, a wrong sustained or the loss resulting from this.' For 'redress' as a verb the dictionary gives fifteen separate entries, all of them subdivided two or three times, and almost all of the usages noted as obsolete. I have also taken account of the first of these obsolete meanings, which is given as, 'To set (a person or a thing) upright again; to raise again to an erect position. Also *fig.* to set up again, restore, re-establish.'

But in following these rather sober extensions of the word, in considering poetry's possible service to programmes of cultural and political realignment, or in reaffirming poetry as an up-right, resistant, and self-bracing entity within the general flux and flex of language, I don't want to give the impression that its force must always be exercised in earnest, morally premeditated ways. On the contrary, I want to profess the surprise of poetry as well as its reliability; I want to celebrate its given, unforesee-able thereness, the way it enters our field of vision and animates our physical and intelligent being in much the same way as those bird-shapes stencilled on the transparent surfaces of glass walls or windows must suddenly enter the vision and change the direction of the real birds' flight. In a flash the shapes register and transmit their unmistakable presence, so the birds veer off instinctively. An image of the living creatures has induced a totally salubrious swerve in the creatures themselves. And this natural, heady diversion is also something induced by poetry and reminds me of a further (obsolete) meaning of 'redress', with which I would conclude, a meaning which comes in entry four of the verb, subsection (*b*): '*Hunting.* To bring back (the hounds or deer) to the proper course.' In this 'redress' there is no hint of ethical obligation; it is more a matter of finding a course for the breakaway of innate capacity, a course where something unhindered, yet directed, can sweep ahead into its full potential.

Herbert, for all his inclination to hold to the *via media* – at the line between exhaustion and unappeasability – provides us constantly with those unforeseen images and stanzas that send our reader's mind sweeping and veering away in delighted reflex:

> Lovely enchanting language, sugar-cane,
> Hony of roses, whither wilt thou flie?

Such an apostrophe, from his poem 'The Forerunners', is surely just the kind of apostrophe we would like poetry to call from us. That impulsive straining towards felicity – which we get in the 'window-songs' line of 'Dullness', for example – is a *sine qua non* of lyric power:

> Where are my lines then? my approaches? views?
> Where are my window-songs?
> Lovers are still pretending, and ev'n wrongs
> Sharpen their Muse.

For all his sacerdotal fragrance, Herbert never fully quelled this more profane *tendresse* in himself and his idiom, and the traces of that older, amorous, dandyish self are among the best rewards of his work. The confirmations bestowed by proportion and pace and measure are undeniably essential to his achievement, and there is a fundamental strength about the way his winding forms and woven metaphors match the toils of consciousness; but it is when the spirit is called extravagantly beyond the course that the usual life plots for it, when outcry or rhapsody is wrung from it as it flies in upon some unexpected image of its own solitude and distinctness, it is then that Herbert's work exemplifies the redress of poetry at its most exquisite.

24 October 1989

Extending the Alphabet:
On Christopher Marlowe's
'Hero and Leander'

It will soon be the 400th anniversary of the death by stab-
bing of Christopher Marlowe at a tavern in Deptford. The minutes of the coroner's inquest tell how he and three other men
spent the afternoon of 30 May 1593 'in quiet sort' in a room of
the inn, and how after supper a dispute arose about the bill –
the famous 'reckoning'. Marlowe is then said to have made a
sudden attack on one of his companions, a character called
Ingram Friser, who fought back and killed the poet with his
knife in self-defence.

The story has always had a slightly sinister feel to it, something to do with the mystery that hangs over those four companions withdrawn quietly out of the early summer day, the stealth
of their privacy, the hovering possibility of underhand ex-
changes or undercover deeds. And, of course, the fascination of
the event was every bit as potent for Marlowe's contemporaries,
for it did not escape their notice that the whole thing had been
vaguely foreshadowed in the dramatist's own writing. At the
conclusion of his play *Doctor Faustus*, for example, the Chorus
speaks these famous lines which combine the inexorability of
high poetry with the melodrama of popular preaching:

> Cut is the branch that might have grown full straight,
> And burnèd is Apollo's laurel-bough,
> That sometime grew within this learned man.
> Faustus is gone: regard his hellish fall,
> Whose fiendful fortune may exhort the wise,
> Only to wonder at unlawful things,
> Whose deepness doth entice such forward wits
> To practise more than heavenly power permits.

Given the disconsolate note of this passage and its significant placing as the curtain line of the play, it is no wonder that it was read as Marlowe's own self-epitaph and was seized upon after his murder in much the same way as the late poems of Sylvia Plath were seized upon after her suicide. Both deaths made sensational news and resulted in the poets becoming legendary figures: their tragic ends were seen to have been implicit in their writings all along. Preachers even rigged the Marlowe knifing so that it presented an instructive symmetry; they gave out that the dagger that killed him had been his own and that the fatal wound had been in his head, the very seat of the talent which had made him one of those damnably 'forward wits'. It was only to be expected, therefore, that the Chorus's lament for an overweening intellectual cut off in his prime should have been understood afterwards as a sort of prediction. To a hot-breathed public, high on murder gossip that carried with it the mingled whiff of religious, sexual and political scandal, the note of doom was not only audible: it was ominous and prophetic of Marlowe's fate.

That fate, moreover, had been predicted by others besides himself. Robert Greene's death-bed pamphlet, *Greene's Groats-worth of Wit bought with a Million of Repentance*, had been written nine months before Marlowe was stabbed at Deptford. The pamphlet is most famous for its attack on Shakespeare, but before Greene takes his side-swipe at the 'upstart crow', he has already warned a number of his peers about their own destinies, and although he does not use Marlowe's name, there is no doubt that the 'tragedian' being singled out in his deeply minatory address is indeed the same scandalous, atheistical, and morally reprehensible university wit, associate of Sir Walter Raleigh and student of the School of Night. Marlowe's intellectual effrontery, in other words, had been enough to put the wind up a man on his death-bed, and take a repentant sinner's mind off his own predicament – which is to say that the figure Marlowe cut in the minds of his contemporaries in the late 1580s and early 1590s was utterly exciting. The carouser who had been gaoled for a couple of weeks after being on the

spot at a fatal street-fight, the university student who had tasted
the thrills of espionage among the Catholic recusants of Reims,
the blasphemer who seemed to be out to break every taboo and
to transgress extravagantly in the realms of both religion and
sex – this figure, a star in his late twenties, a kind of cross
between Oscar Wilde and Jack the Ripper, moved in an aura of
glamorous immorality and political danger and was so riveting
and marked that the dying Greene felt free to finger him as the
next to go.

And, of course, the danger was not just an aura. Atheism and
blasphemy could be as fatal in late-sixteenth-century London as
anti-revolutionary sympathies were in Moscow in the 1930s.
Marlowe was denounced to the Privy Council, and the deposi-
tions of the informers have survived. Even if they are perused
with the suspicion that such documents always warrant, they
still conjure up the image of a man operating at full tilt, both
exhilarated and inflammatory. The whole performance was one
of great daring, and the reports of it still transmit something of
its original subversive headiness, partly exhibitionistic, partly
intellectually driven, but altogether inevitable and unstoppable.

In Marlowe's case, therefore, as in Plath's, the daring of the
work and the transgressions which it encompassed were the
first things to be emphasized in the aftermath of their deaths. Its
ironies and complications were relatively neglected; what got
highlighted were the points where it conformed to current expectations generated by the extreme behaviour of the writer. In
Plath's case, the image of victimized woman was immediately in
place as a consequence of her tragic suicide; in Marlowe's, it
was the image of the sinner's fall, of divine retribution for blas-
phemous presumptions. In each instance, the work was read
with more regard to what the posthumously created stereotype
might have been expected to produce than what the writer actually delivered. *Doctor Faustus*, for example, was regarded for a
very long time as a casebook of humanist 'overreaching' before
it was reconsidered as an anatomy of Christian despair. And
Plath was celebrated as the author of the vindictive 'Daddy' and

the morgue-cold 'Edge' whilst other more positively inspired works were ignored.

It is hardly news to be reminded of all this. Original poets can obviously sustain a variety of interpretations and answer to very different times and needs. What remains mysterious, however, is the source of that original strength, the very fact of poetic power itself, the way its unpredictability gets converted into inevitability once it has manifested itself, the way a generation recognizes that they are in the presence of one of the great unfettered events which constitute a definite stage in the history of poetry. It is the manifestation of this power in Marlowe's verse, in the first language-life of the poetry itself, that I wish to praise. If I begin by acknowledging that the conditions of a poet's reception and the history of subsequent responses to his or her work do indeed become a part of the work's force and meaning, it is only to indicate that I am as aware as the next person that the import of poetry is affected by several different agencies. But I remain convinced by what my own reading experience tells me: namely, that some works transmit an immediately persuasive signal and retain a unique staying power over a lifetime. Some works continue to combine the sensation of liberation with that of consolidation; having once cleared a new space on the literary and psychic ground, they go on to offer, at each re-reading, the satisfaction of a foundation being touched and the excitement of an energy being released.

I couldn't have put it that way thirty-four years ago when I first heard Professor Terence Spencer read from Marlowe's *Tamburlaine*. I was then a First Arts student at Queen's University, Belfast, sharing the benches of a lecture hall with others like me, the wary, needy sons and daughters of 1950s Ulster, all of us recent escapees from the sixth-form grind. Rumour had it that the professor had been a Shakespearean actor, which in itself was enough to engender a mood of suppressed anticipation. Certainly, when he appeared, he wasn't into playing down the drive and flourish of the big lines. He stalked to the podium, adjusted his gown, profiled himself a little theatrically and pitched into the prologue to *Tamburlaine* like a long-jumper going for the record:

> From jigging veins of rhyming mother-wits,
> And such conceits as clownage keeps in pay,
> We'll lead you to the stately tent of war,
> Where you shall hear the Scythian Tamburlaine
> Threatening the world with high astounding terms,
> And scourging kingdoms with his conquering sword.
> View but his picture in this tragic glass,
> And then applaud his fortunes as you please.

And then we were off:

> Then sit thou down, divine Zenocrate;
> And here we crown thee Queen of Persia,
> And all the kingdoms and dominions
> That late the power of Tamburlaine subdu'd.
> As Juno, when the giants were suppress'd,
> That darted mountains at her brother Jove,
> So looks my love, shadowing in her brows
> Triumphs and trophies for my victories;
> Or as Latona's daughter, bent to arms,
> Adding more courage to my conquering mind.
> To gratify the sweet Zenocrate,
> Egyptians, Moors, and men of Asia,
> From Barbary unto the Western India,
> Shall pay a yearly tribute to thy sire;
> And from the bounds of Afric to the banks
> Of Ganges shall his mighty arm extend.

It was impossible not to be carried away by the sheer rhetorical power of this work, and difficult not to share the headiness of the English Renaissance moment as it declared itself in the un-trammelled climb of Marlowe's verse. And even though I have learned to place this poetry's expansionist drive in the context of nascent English imperialism, I am still grateful for the enlargements it offered, the soaring orchestration, the roll-call of place names and of figures from classical mythology. It was a fundamentally pleasurable experience that need not be reneged on for the sake of any subsequent political correctness.

Ought I to have been less ready to be carried away? Maybe I should have been taught to beware of the military push of the thing, and been reminded that this English pentameter marched in step with the invading English armies of the late Tudor period – those who in the 1580s and 1590s were systematically preparing the conquest of Gaelic Ireland and the future plantation of Ulster in the 1620s. Yet the movement of the lines was so heady and the rhetoric so thrilling that the temptation to go with it proved irresistible. What I want to do here, therefore, is to find a way of reaffirming the value and rights of Marlowe's poetry in our own post-colonial time. When resistance to works from the canonical 'centre' has replaced formal appreciation as the predominant approach to literary study, it is necessary to find a way of treating the marvellously aspiring note of his work as something more than a set of discourses to be unmasked. When the word 'humanist' has become almost a term of abuse, it is necessary to consider whether we would want to have Marlowe's whole keyboard of classical reference demeaned. Surely it is still possible to take cognizance of the unpredictable artistic excellence of Marlowe's plays and poems while acknowledging that they are bound up with a particular moment of English history, and are thereby implicated with the late-Tudor project of national consolidation at home and colonization abroad. There's no doubt, for example, that an up-to-the-minute commentator would be inclined to regard the Virgilian longueurs of Marlowe's early play *Dido Queen of Carthage* as a covert endorsement of the expeditionary drives beginning to take shape in late-sixteenth-century England. Aeneas's mission to found a new Troy, from which he is not to be deflected by the power and distraction of love itself, undoubtedly corroborates in imaginative terms the historical effort that would soon go into the founding of a New England and a London Derry.

Obviously, then, when I re-read *Edward II* for this lecture, I was not only aware of the way it could be adapted by British film-maker Derek Jarman as a liberationist masquerade, and turned into a contemporary parable about the suppression of homosexual love. I was also conscious of the banishment to Ireland of Gaveston, the King's favourite, as something more than a shift of plot. Inevitably, in the present intellectual climate, it was hard not to read in Gaveston's relegation to the status of non-person an equal relegation of Ireland to the status of non-place. By its inclusion within the realm of English influence, late-medieval Ireland had become at once an annexe of the civil conquerors and the locus of a barbarism that had to be held at bay. One of the accusations against King Edward, after all, was that

> The wild O'Neill, with swarms of Irish kerns
> Lives uncontrolled within the English pale.

This wild O'Neill was not the one whose rebellious armies would later drive Edmund Spenser off his 3,000-acre estate in County Cork, an estate which Spenser took over round about the time of the play's production in London, and which had been confiscated from the Irish Earl of Desmond in the aftermath of the recent English campaign in Munster. When Spenser settled in Kilcolman, it was in a country almost depopulated by slaughter and famine. Within the previous half-year an estimated 30,000 men, women and children had perished; Spenser himself, indeed, when acting as secretary to Lord Grey, had witnessed massacre on a large and systematic scale at Smerwick Harbour, where 600 Spaniards and Irish had been butchered. And, needless to say, it was also at Smerwick that Sir Walter Raleigh had performed as one of Queen Elizabeth's captains was expected to and, in the words of the old *Spenser Handbook*, 'had done rough work for Lord Grey'.

We have been forced to cast a suspicious eye on the

pretensions of Renaissance humanism by having its sacred texts placed in the context of their authors' participation in such brutally oppressive escapades; we have been rightly instructed about the ways that native populations and indigenous cultures disappear in the course of these civilizing enterprises, and we have learnt how the values and language of the conqueror demolish and marginalize native values and institutions, rendering them barbarous, subhuman, and altogether beyond the pale of cultivated sympathy or regard. But even so, it still seems an abdication of literary responsibility to be swayed by these desperately overdue correctives to a point where imaginative literature is read simply and solely as a function of an oppressive discourse, or as a reprehensible masking. When it comes to poetic composition, one has to allow for the presence, even for the pre-eminence, of what Wordsworth called 'the grand elementary principle of pleasure', and that pleasure comes from the doing-in-language of certain things. One has to allow for the fact that, in the words of Ezra Pound:

the thing that matters in art is a sort of energy, something more or less like electricity or radio activity, a force transfusing, welding and unifying. A force rather like water when it spurts up through very bright sand and sets it in swift motion. You may make what image you like.

Pound's image does not preclude art's implication in the structures and shifts of power at any given moment, but it does suggest a salubrious role for it within the body politic; and another image which the Czech poet Miroslav Holub uses about theatre may also be adduced here. Holub sees the function of drama, and so by extension the function of poetry and of the arts in general, as being analogous to that of the immunity system within the human body. Which is to say that the creative spirit remains positively recalcitrant in face of the negative evidence, reminding the indicative mood of history that it has been written in by force and written in over the good optative mood of human potential.

This reminding, this work of immunity building, is effected

by intrinsically artistic means, for it is obvious that poetry's answer to the world is not given only in terms of the content of its statements. It is given perhaps even more emphatically in terms of metre and syntax, of tone and musical truenesc; and it is given also by its need to go emotionally and artistically 'above the brim', beyond the established norms. These things are the artistic manifestation of that affirming spiritual flame which W. H. Auden wanted the good person and the good poet to show, a manifestation which has less to do with argument or edification than with the fact and effort of articulation itself. And this is why I want to focus my remarks upon Marlowe with a consideration of his utterly delightful poem 'Hero and Leander', a work happily in love with its own inventions, written at the height of the young master's powers, a work which exercises itself entirely within the playhouse of erotic narrative in the tradition of the Latin poet Ovid, but which remains responsive to and transformative of the real pains of love as they are experienced in 'the house in earnest'.

The story of Leander's love for Hero was told by the Greek poet Musaeus and Marlowe's version takes off from the Greek original, although it famously does not tell the whole story. It was left incomplete at his death, but its incompleteness is not the only reason why Marlowe's poem is generally agreed to be a late work. George Chapman may have rounded out the first 800-odd lines of the narrative, yet his longer and graver treatment of the second half of the story is really no more mature than Marlowe's treatment of the first half. It's just that Marlowe's lines are without that earnestness which we too automatically associate with the word 'mature'. Everything in the early stages of the romance suited his gifts – Leander's physical beauty and erotic susceptibility, Hero's delicious combination of chastity and sexuality, Leander's swimming to Hero across the Hellespont and their first rapturous love-making. Chapman then took up the post-coital consequences of it all: Leander's return to Abydos where the goddess Ceremony appears to him and constrains him to due marriage with Hero, Hero's turmoil and eventual preparation for their wedding, and finally, after several digressions and postponements, the climactic incident of Leander's drowning and Hero's sacrificing of herself for love. In Chapman's words:

> She fell on her love's bosom, hugg'd it fast
> And with Leander's name she breathed her last.
> Neptune for pity in his arms did take them,
> Flung them into the air, and did awake them
> Like two sweet-birds, surnamed th'Acanthides,
> Which we call thistle-warps, that near no seas
> Dare ever come, but still in couples fly
> And feed on thistle-tops, to testify
> The hardness of their first life in their last:
> The first in thorns of love, and sorrows past.

In the poem as we have it, it is Marlowe who presents the account of the couple's first life when Hero appears as 'Venus' nun' and Leander is her infatuated slave, yet it is hard to find any intimation of the thorn and thistle side of things in Marlowe's version of their situation. What we get instead in the first two sestiads is a rapturous, permissive atmosphere, a *tír-na-n-óg* where the line between playfulness and transgression is at first confused and then suspended until all the inner partitions of the psyche have been opened. Bisexual cajolement, an indulgent recognition of the predatory within the amatory, a gift for transforming the louche and the lax into a nice stylistic decorum – it all goes to prove that Marlowe does indeed deserve the title, 'forward wit', though not in the damning sense in which the Chorus applied the term to Doctor Faustus.

Here, for example, is Marlowe's description of the décor in Venus's temple at Sestos:

> Of crystal shining fair the pavement was;
> The town of Sestos called it Venus glass.
> There might you see the gods in sundry shapes
> Committing heady riots, incest, rapes:

For know that underneath this radiant floor
Was Danae's statue in a brazen tower,
Jove slyly stealing from his sister's bed
To dally with Idalian Ganymede,
Or for his love Europa bellowing loud
Or tumbling with the rainbow in a cloud;
Blood-quaffing Mars, heaving the iron net
Which limping Vulcan and his cyclops set;
Love kindling fire, to burn such towns as Troy;
Sylvanus weeping for the lovely boy
That now is turned into a cypress tree,
Under whose shade the wood gods love to be.

It would be hard to remain a nun of any sort, never mind a nun of Venus, in such an environment; and so indeed it proves to be in Hero's case. But this catalogue of amatory exploits only shows Marlowe limbering up. The poem goes on to deal more delicately and deliciously with the whole matter of sexual attraction and in this regard 'Hero and Leander' is a boldly liberating work; in it the language of desire, the limits of the possible and the inventions of imagination combine to give a supple and mature image of human life. It is comic in tone but not gullible in perception. It abandons the tragic and heroic pitch of the plays but still manages to keep faith with their project of going over the top. The poetry of 'Hero and Leander' is less sonorous than that of *Tamburlaine*, less shot through by dread and lament than that of *Doctor Faustus*. As other commentators have pointed out, it is nearer to the note of Gaveston's infatuated daydreams in *Edward II*, and truer thereby to the hedonistic and homoerotic impulses that seem to have been so powerful an element in Marlowe's own sensibility.

In 'Hero and Leander' all his energy and subversiveness seem to get transformed into relish and artifice. Obviously, there's a difference of scale between the minor epic and the five-act play, but what is instructive is the way in which the poem encompasses by purely lyrical means much of the complexity and project of the plays. And the project of the plays can be represented to some extent by an analogy first proposed by the South African writer André Brink in relation to the role of writers in a repressed society. People in such societies, according to Brink, typically employ only a portion of the alphabet that is available to them as human beings. In matters of race or sex or religion, citizens will confine the range of their discourse to a band of allowable usages between, say, A and M. This will be a more or less conscious act of self-censorship, as much a collusion as a consensus. So it then becomes the writer's task to expose this state of affairs, to extend the resources of expression up to perhaps N or V, and thereby both to affront and to enlighten. We might say, therefore, that in his plays Christopher Marlowe pursued this extension of the humanist alphabet in a more or less confrontational way, and that his overreaching heroes represent a deliberately scandalous approach. But in the lyric and narrative poetry, the approach is by seduction, and the new subversive letters which he would add to the alphabet of human expression become part of what Harry Levin has called a 'rhetoric of enticement'. In the poems, he beguiles rather than confronts. Take, for instance, lines from the very start of the poem, which begin by describing the extraordinarily ingenious workmanship that adorned Hero's footwear, and then go on to elaborate and linger fondly in their own erotic daydreams. They are typical of a persistent and very attractive note in Marlowe's writing:

> Buskins of shells all silvered used she,
> And branched with blushing coral to the knee,
> Where sparrows perched, of hollow pearl and gold,
> Such as the world would wonder to behold:
> Those with sweet water oft her handmaid fills,
> Which as she went would chirrup through the bills.
> Some say for her the fairest Cupid pined,
> And looking in her face was strooken blind.

> But this is true, so like was one the other,
> As he imagined Hero was his mother;
> And oftentimes into her bosom flew,
> About her naked neck his bare arms threw,
> And laid his childish head upon her breast,
> And with still panting rocked, there took his rest.
> So lovely fair was Hero, Venus' nun.

Admittedly, this 'rhetoric of enticement' is a very fine development of Marlowe's art. In the plays, his mighty line is typically less subtle, and far more percussive. In *Tamburlaine*, for example, the reader or audience is in thrall to the poetic equivalent of a dynamo-hum, a kind of potent undermusic. It is a sound which both exhilarates and empowers, as if the words are at one and the same time being set free and held on course along some high flight-path. When he is writing at full tilt for the stage, Marlowe's lines possess the lift and drag of orbit, a promise that entropy can be kept at bay for as long as invention can exercise itself. And this is not just a matter of musicality. It has equally to do with the stamina of his taunting intelligence, since what keeps the metre at full stretch is not only the energy of the beat but an extra propulsion that comes from what Yeats once called 'a powerful and passionate syntax':

> The thirst of reign and sweetness of a crown,
> That caus'd the eldest son of heavenly Ops
> To thrust his doting father from his chair,
> And place himself in the imperial heaven,
> Mov'd me to manage arms against thy state.
> What better precedent than mighty Jove?
> Nature, that fram'd us of four elements
> Warring within our breasts for regiment,
> Doth teach us all to have aspiring minds:
> Our souls, whose faculties can comprehend
> The wondrous architecture of the world,
> And measure every wandering planet's course,
> Still climbing after knowledge infinite,

And always moving as the restless spheres,
Will us to wear ourselves, and never rest,
Until we reach the ripest fruit of all,
That perfect bliss and sole felicity,
The sweet fruition of an earthly crown.

Infectious as it is, however, this dramatic blank verse turns out to be a less sinuous instrument than the rhyming couplet of 'Hero and Leander'. Marlowe's development of a suppler, almost Chaucerean way with the line is obviously linked to his early translation of Ovid's *Amores*, done while he was a student. These episodes from the Imperial Roman *vie de bohème* are virtuoso work, and deserve far more attention than they tend to get. They have wiliness and sexiness and scholastic panache, and would be as much at home among the cleveralites of James Joyce's university wits in *A Portrait of the Artist as a Young Man* as they must have been among the scholars of sixteenth-century Cambridge. But when we come to the art of 'Hero and Leander', we are closer to the world of 'Anna Livia Plurabelle', to the hithering-thithering whims of a self-possessed mind, a mind that knows both the penalties of life and its invitations, one closer to the spirit of carnival than to the shock tactics of agitprop.

Here, for example, is Leander arriving at Hero's tower for the second time – and lucky to be there, having survived the lusty attentions of Neptune as he swam the Hellespont. (Neptune had mistaken him for Ganymede, in a wonderful bit of underwater innuendo that I shall return to.) Meanwhile:

By this, Leander being near the land,
Cast down his weary feet, and felt the sand.
Breathless albeit he were, he rested not
Till to the solitary tower he got,
And knocked, and called, at which celestial noise
The longing heart of Hero much more joys
Than nymphs and shepherds when the timbrel rings,
Or crooked dolphin when the sailor sings.

She stayed not for her robes, but straight arose,
And drunk with gladness to the door she goes,
Where seeing a naked man, she screeched for fear
(Such sights as this to tender maids are rare;)
And ran into the dark herself to hide . . .
Rich jewels in the dark are soonest spied:
Unto her he was led, or rather drawn,
By those white limbs, which sparkled through the lawn.
The nearer that he came, the more she fled,
And seeking refuge, slipped into her bed.
Whereon Leander sitting thus began,
Through numbing cold, all feeble, faint and wan:
'If not for love, yet, love, for pity sake,
Me in thy bed and maiden bosom take;
At least vouchsafe these arms some little room,
Who, hoping to embrace thee, cheerly swum.
This head was beat with many a churlish billow,
And therefore let it rest upon thy pillow.'
Herewith affrighted Hero shrunk away,
And in her lukewarm place Leander lay,
Whose lively heat, like fire from heaven fet,
Would animate gross clay, and higher set
The drooping thoughts of base declining souls
Than dreary Mars carousing nectar bowls.
His hands he cast upon her like a snare;
She, overcome with shame and sallow fear,
Like chaste Diana when Actaeon spied her,
Being suddenly betrayed, dived down to hide her.
And as her silver body downward went,
With both her hands she made the bed a tent,
And in her own mind thought herself secure,
O'ercast with dim and darksome coverture.
And now she lets him whisper in her ear,
Flatter, entreat, promise, protest and swear,
Yet ever as he greedily assayed
To touch those dainties, she the harpy played,

31

And every limb did as a soldier stout
Defend the fort, and keep the foeman out.

It may be a bit of a let-down to follow this scene with a technical comment, but something that Ezra Pound said about Marlowe's Ovid translations is even more pertinent to the writing here. In his 'Notes on Elizabethan Classicists' Pound ventures the following opinion about Marlowe's use of the couplet:

The reader, if he can divert his thought from matter to manner, may well wonder how much the eighteenth-century authors have added, or if they added anything save a sort of faculty for systematization of product, a power to repeat certain effects regularly and at will.

There is more spontaneity than system, for sure, in the lines I have just quoted: the eighteenth-century might have managed the feminine rhyme on 'billow' and 'pillow', but the lukewarm place that Leander slips into under the bedclothes was probably never warmed again in exactly the right way until Molly Bloom jingled the bedsprings more than three hundred years later. In the meantime Keats might generate an equivalent body heat and Byron might dodge with equal speed through the rhymes, but the Marlovian combination of laid-back wit and sensuous indulgence would remain unique.

This writing prompts one to revise another line of Yeats's and to say that here 'there's *nothing* ails our colt'. Marlowe's Pegasus has bolted free of the five-act harness and sports himself in a manner at once strenuous and unconstrained. The digressions and ornamental effects which the Ovidian genre more or less requires turn out to be ideal romping spaces. This poetry is in great fettle. It is nimble yet it is by no means lightweight: if you break into its path, you'll come up against enough observation and premeditated meaning to knock you sideways. Just consider, for example, how solidly the images of stripped athletes and gold ingots contribute to the crucial momentum of these famous lines, a momentum that gives the final couplet its irresistible proverbial clinch:

It lies not in our power to love or hate,
For will in us is overruled by fate.
When two are stripped, long ere the course begin
We wish that one should lose, the other win;
And one especially do we affect
Of two gold ingots like in each respect.
The reason no man knows: let it suffice,
What we behold is censured by our eyes.
Where both deliberate, the love is slight;
Who ever loved, that loved not at first sight?

The verse here is like a thick cable being paid out wittily by an intelligence that is nevertheless the very opposite of thick-witted. In fact, I am reminded of Joseph Brodsky's remarks about intonation in poetry, which appear in his recent introduction to the work of Aleksandr Kushner: 'In a poem,' Brodsky writes, 'the testimony to spiritual tension is intonation; or, more accurately, intonation in a poem – and not in a poem only – stands for the motion of the soul.' The motion of the soul, then, in 'Hero and Leander' is forward towards liberation and beatitude, but it is a motion countered by an implicit acknowledgement of repression and constraint. This dialectic is expressed formally by the co-existence of a supple voice within a strict metrical pattern, and tonally by a note that is modulating constantly between the scampish and the plangent. Consider, for example, the episode I referred to earlier, in which the god Neptune appears as a befuddled old sensualist, mistaking Leander for Ganymede and then immediately going on to the sexual equivalent of automatic pilot – into a kind of subaqueous cruising gear. This interlude proves to be more successful in extending the alphabet of the permissible (both in the area of sexual behaviour and in the literary treatment of it) than the more head-on effort made in *Edward II*. The 'Hero and Leander' episode is more explicit in its presentation of amorous play than we might have expected, and yet the androgynous merriment of it all was already implicit in the earliest description of Leander in the First Sestiad. In fact, what gives 'Hero and Leander' its special power as a liberating document is its freedom from any intention to coerce or affront. The reader is enticed towards a tolerant attitude by having his or her sexual preferences toyed with and having the opposite preference discreetly insinuated at the same time. Here, for example, Marlowe serves notice in a subliminal way that Leander is destined to encounter other loves besides Hero's:

> His body was as straight as Circe's wand;
> Jove might have sipped out nectar from his hand.
> Even as delicious meat is to the taste,
> So was his neck in touching, and surpassed
> The white of Pelops' shoulder. I could tell ye
> How smooth his breast was, and how white his belly,
> And whose immortal fingers did imprint
> That heavenly path with many a curious dint
> That runs along his back, but my rude pen
> Can hardly blazon forth the loves of men,
> Much less of powerful gods: let it suffice
> That my slack muse sings of Leander's eyes,
> Those orient cheeks and lips, exceeding his
> That leapt into the water for a kiss
> Of his own shadow, and despising many,
> Died ere he could enjoy the love of any.
> Had wild Hippolytus Leander seen,
> Enamoured of his beauty had he been;
> His presence made the rudest peasant melt,
> That in the vast uplandish country dwelt.
> The barbarous Thracian soldier, moved with nought,
> Was moved with him, and for his favour sought.

I seem to remember being told as a student that Marlowe's plays were short on humour; but the strength of these lines depends precisely upon a very engaging combination of humour and eroticism. And, of course, these androgynous frolics at the start of the poem are the narrative equivalent of showing a revolver in the first scene of a play: they are going to have to go off with a bang later on. Which is exactly what happens in the Second Sestiad when Leander plunges into the Hellespont, and is sighted by the cruising sea-god, Neptune, and mistaken by him for Ganymede, a youth whom we can fairly call, I suppose, Jove's 'minion'.

> The lusty god embraced him, called him love,
> And swore he never should return to Jove.
> But when he knew it was not Ganymede,
> For under water he was almost dead,
> He heaved him up, and looking on his face,
> Beat down the bold waves with his triple mace,
> Which mounted up, intending to have kissed him,
> And fell in drops like tears because they missed him.
> Leander being up, began to swim,
> And, looking back, saw Neptune follow him;
> Whereat aghast, the poor soul 'gan to cry,
> 'O let me visit Hero ere I die.'
> The god put Helle's bracelet on his arm,
> And swore the sea should never do him harm.
> He clapped his plump cheeks, with his tresses played,
> And smiling wantonly, his love bewrayed.
> He watched his arms, and as they opened wide
> At every stroke, betwixt them he would slide
> And steal a kiss, and then run out and dance,
> And as he turned, cast many a lustful glance,
> And throw him gaudy toys to please his eye,
> And dive into the water, and there pry
> Upon his breast, his thighs, and every limb,
> And up again, and close beside him swim,
> And talk of love. Leander made reply,
> 'You are deceived, I am no woman, I.'

The double-takes and *double entendres* of Shakespeare's Romantic comedies, with their cross-dressers all at sexual cross-purposes, are implicit in this writing; and the maturity I commended earlier is present not as moral *gravitas* but as a fully attained artistic mastery, the casual technical virtuosity of the poetry being the equivalent of a happy inner freedom in the poet. Marlowe is involved here in a show-off performance, operating with real spontaneity and affection, in control of a far greater range of expression than he was at the beginning of his stage career. Obviously, as I've remarked already, the intonation of 'Hero and Leander' is not as ominous or stricken as the great scenes of *Doctor Faustus*, yet it does issue from a kind of seasoned knowledge that is almost unshockable, certainly undupable, but still not altogether disenchanted. Its psychological realism insists that too much should not be expected from people, or from life in general, while its artistic virtuosity insists that too much is the least we should expect. The poem is at one and the same time a structure of sounds and sweet airs that give delight and hurt not, a tongue-in-cheek love story and an intimation of a far more generous and desirable way of being alive in the world.

In his *Defence of Poesy*, Sir Philip Sidney linked the creative act of the poet with the pursuit of virtue, 'since our erected wit maketh us know what perfection is, and yet our infected will keepeth us from reaching unto it.' There is, of course, something too simple, perhaps even too phallocentric about that account of the matter, and no honest reader of poems, then or now, would see moral improvement or, for that matter, political education, as the end and purpose of his or her absorption in a poetic text. There's more phenomenological accuracy in John Keats's notion that poetry surprises by a fine excess, although it's worth remembering that by 'excess' Keats did not mean just a sensuous overabundance of description. What he also had in mind was a general gift for outstripping the reader's expectation, an inventiveness that cannot settle for the conventional notion that enough is enough, but always wants to extend the alphabet of emotional and technical expression. Even a poem as tonally sombre as, say, 'Tintern Abbey' is doing something surprising and excessive, getting further back and deeper in than the poet knew it would, the poet being nevertheless still ready to go with it, to rise to the rhythmic and rhetorical occasion.

At these moments there is always a kind of homoeopathic benefit for the reader in experiencing the shifts and extensions which constitute the life of a poem. An exuberant rhythm, a display of metrical virtuosity, some rising intellectual ground successfully surmounted – experiencing things like these gratifies and furthers the range of the mind's and the body's pleasures, and helps the reader to obey the old command: *nosce teipsum*. Know thyself. If I may quote a stanza from an occasional poem of my own:

> This is how poems help us live.
> They match the meshes in the sieve
> Life puts us through; they take and give
>   Our proper measure
> And prove themselves most transitive
>   When they give pleasure.

Sidney too was concerned with this tonic effect of poetry when he spoke in his *Defence* of 'the . . . forcibleness or *Energia* (as the Greeks call it) of the writer'; and it is this original forcibleness, this sensation of clear water springing through sand, that makes work like Marlowe's 'Hero and Leander' so valuable and guarantees its safe passage through a world of accusing ideologies and impugned ideals.

19 November 1991

Orpheus in Ireland:
On Brian Merriman's
The Midnight Court

Joseph Brodsky once suggested that the highest goal human beings can set before themselves is the creation of civilization. What Brodsky had in mind was much the same thing, I assume, as W. B. Yeats had in mind when he spoke about the 'profane perfection of mankind', a perfection which for Yeats depended on something that he called, in another context, 'the spiritual intellect's great work'. In fact, in their own extravagant and undaunted ways, what both poets were really talking about was the central, epoch-making role that is always available in the world to poetry and the poet.

To occupy this role, of course, it is not necessary for the poet to cut a figure in the world. Emily Dickinson and Gerard Manley Hopkins contributed to the construction of a desirable civilization without ever establishing themselves as particularly notable presences in the minds of their contemporaries. And the same could be said of Brian Merriman, author of *Cúirt an Mheán-Oíche* (*The Midnight Court*), a poem written in the Irish language in 1780, a poem from beyond the Pale in all senses, but especially the literal sense. In Ireland, the Pale was that area around Dublin where the English language and an Anglocentric culture had been longest established, but Merriman lived and wrote in the province of Munster, where the Gaelic ethos continued to retain a considerable influence right down into the late eighteenth century. It was in Munster, for example, that another late great poem of the Irish language appeared at almost the same moment as *The Midnight Court*. This was the extraordinary lamentation raised by Eibhlín Dhubh Ní Chonaill over the corpse of her husband Art O'Laoghaire, an Irish captain whom English soldiers killed at Carriginima in Co. Cork in 1774. *Caoineadh Airt Uí Laoghaire* was a spontaneous keen uttered by a bereft widow, a poem that surged up out of an oral tradition and a mourning rite as old as Homer. It was also a poem that spoke out of and on behalf of the oppressed native Catholic population of Ireland, a Gaelic majority placed legally beyond the pale of official Anglo-Irish life by the operation of the Penal Laws – laws which forbade Catholics access to higher education and the professions, and severely curtailed their rights to own property, laws which were as scandalous in their day as the system of apartheid has been in ours.

Even so, Eibhlín Dhubh's poem was not primarily a political rallying cry. It was an outburst both heartbroken and formal, a howl of sorrow and a triumph of rhetoric. It was also a poem that proclaimed for almost the last time the integrity of the Gaelic order and the ordained place of poetry within that order, a place where there was a fortifying consonance between the personal and the communal voice. No wonder Peter Levi chose to focus on *Caoineadh Airt Uí Laoghaire* in his inaugural lecture as Professor of Poetry when he spoke about poetry's immemorial office to lament the dead. And no wonder, either, that it was from the family of such an impassioned silence-breaker that the great political silence-breaker of early-nineteenth-century Ireland emerged. Daniel O'Connell was a nephew of Eibhlín Dhubh, and Daniel O'Connell was also the man who in 1829 achieved Catholic Emancipation for Ireland and earned himself the title of 'The Liberator', then and in times to come.

If we were to think of sexual politics as opposed to national politics, we might well award the same title to Brian Merriman, for although his poem belonged in several important respects to the Irish past and to the literary conventions of medieval Europe, it can also be read as a tremor of the future. Certainly, as a text to be either repressed or promoted, it has featured significantly within the Irish literary tradition for more than 200 years. Here I want to give an outline of the story it tells and then give some account of ways it has been read at different critical moments during the course of this century in Ireland. I also want to argue that within a category which we might call 'world literature', the poem has been insufficiently recognized as one of the most original and unexpected achievements of the eighteenth century; it is a comic work, vitally linked to its Irish time and place, but I shall try to amplify its claims by setting it within a European perspective that is even longer than the usual medieval one. In doing so, I shall also be suggesting that *The Midnight Court* contributes not only to the vitality of Irish culture but to the creation of that whole civilization which the poets in their un-messianic way have always managed to envisage and augment.

The poet in question here lived between 1749 and 1805, but the other facts known about him are few. He was born in Co. Clare, probably into what we would nowadays call a single-parent family. Eventually he acquired a stepfather when his mother got married and settled in Feakle, where the poet himself would later teach a school and cultivate a small farm. His name appears, for example, in the records of a Dublin agricultural society in 1797, when he won two prizes for his flax crops. Also in 1797, he married and five or six years later moved with his young family to the nearby city of Limerick. And it was in Limerick, at the early age of fifty-six, that he died suddenly on 27 July 1805, an event noted in the *General Advertiser and Limerick Gazette* in a manner that gave little indication of what his real life-work had been: 'Died on Saturday morning in Old Clare Street, after a few hours illness, Mr. Bryan Merryman, teacher of Mathematics, etc.'

Merriman's poem, of course, is now the best-known thing about him. The large number of nineteenth-century manuscripts and twentieth-century translations are impressive evidence of its popularity from the beginning, and its relevance to contemporary issues is as lively now as it was in East Clare in the 1780s. What we are talking about is a work of just over a thousand lines, written in a hammer-and-tongs vernacular, in buoyant couplets, a poem which is to some extent a parody of aspects of conventional Gaelic poetry and to some extent a transformation of them. It is a dream vision: the poet is discovered in an idealized landscape in the neighbourhood of Lough Graney where he promptly falls asleep and is peremptorily assailed by a dreadful female grotesque, a bailiff who summonses him to a court that is in midnight session somewhere in the Feakle district. The president of the court is the fairy queen of Munster, Aoibheall of Craglee, and even though its location is very firmly in the local world of Co. Clare, the setting does have an otherworldly radiance about it. Aoibheall is the guardian spirit of the country and guarantor among other things of its women's rights to sexual fulfilment and equality, and it is she who has organized this special sitting – special not only because it is a woman's court, but also because it is fair and just and incorruptible, a dream court which momentarily redresses the actual penal system under which the native population have to endure. But even so, Merriman, it must be said, exhibits very little interest in protesting against the prevailing political conditions. These are simply and scornfully noted as he quickly proceeds to the heart of his poetical matter, which is more psycho-sexual than national-patriotic.

And here perhaps it is worth noting a distinction which critics used to make in the case of poems like *The Canterbury Tales* and *The Divine Comedy* where it makes sense to separate Chaucer or Dante as the authors of the poem from Chaucer or Dante as characters within their own compositions. Merriman also writes himself in as a participant in his own narrative, and we can say about him as a character in the poem what T. S. Eliot said about Tiresias in *The Waste Land*, namely, 'what [he] witnesses is the substance of the poem'. What Merriman (the character) witnesses, then, is a debate between a young woman and an old man, a debate that is eventually adjudicated by Aoibheall; and Aoibheall's verdict on the case implicates him in the action and exposes him to accusation and punishment by the vindicated women.

The poem can be divided into three main parts. First (as I've just outlined) comes a description of the setting and the summons, during which the bailiff deplores the condition of the country and focuses with particular rancour on the failure of young and marriageable men (including the poet) to mate or marry with the available and passionately languishing women. Then comes the main body of the work, the courtroom drama itself, which is composed of three long speeches. The first of these is a tirade by a young woman who complains of being sexually neglected and then goes on to boast vigorously and convincingly of her own attributes and aptitudes as a sexual creature. Here is my translation of the opening of this central section, beginning with Merriman's description of the court itself:

And there (I am sure) lit torches showed
A handsome, grand, well-built abode,
A stately, steadfast, glittering space,
Accessible and commodious.
And I saw a lovely vision woman
Ensconced on the bench of law and freedom,
And saw her fierce, fleet guard of honour
Rank upon rank in throngs around her.
I saw then too rooms filling full,
Crowding with women from wall to wall,
And saw this other heavenly beauty
With her lazy eye, on her dignity,
Seductive, pouting, with curling locks,
Biding her time in the witness box.
Her hair spilled down, loosed tress on tress,
And a hurt expression marked her face;
She was full of fight, with a glinting eye,
Hot on the boil, ill-set and angry –
Yet for all her spasms, she couldn't speak
For her hefts and huffing had made her weak.
She looked like death or a living death wish
She was so cried out; but straight as a rush,
She stood to the fore as a witness stands

Flailing and wailing and wringing hands.
And she kept it up; she raved and screeched
Till sighing restored her powers of speech.
Then her downlook went, her colour rose,
She dried her eyes and commenced as follows:
'A thousand welcomes! And bless Your Highness!
Aoibheall of Crag, our prophetess!
Our daylight's light, our moon forever,
Our hope of life when the weeping's over!
O head of all the hosted sisters,
Thomond can thole no more! Assist us!
My cause, my case, the reason why
My plea's prolonged so endlessly
Until I'm raving and round the twist
Like a maenad whirled in a swirl of mist –
The reason why is the unattached
And unprovided for, unmatched
Women I know, like flowers in a bed
Nobody's dibbled or mulched or weeded
Or trimmed or watered or ever tended;
So here they are, unhusbanded,
Unasked, untouched, beyond conception –
And, needless to say, I'm no exception.
I'm scorched and tossed, a sorry case
Of nerves and drives and neediness,
Depressed, obsessed, awake at night,
Unused, unsoothed, disconsolate,
A throbbing ache, a dumb discord,
My mind and bed like a kneading board.
O Warden of the Crag, incline!
Observe the plight of Ireland's women,
For if things go on like this, then fuck it!
The men will have to be abducted!'

Why, she goes on to ask, do men have to marry hags and harri-
dans when she and her like are throbbing with need? For it

43

should be said that this poem is not about romantic love but about sexual appetite and wasted sexual opportunity. Professor Sean O'Tuama, one of the poem's most informed critics, makes this point and quotes to good effect an observation by Johan Huizinga. O'Tuama sees in *The Midnight Court* a survival of unofficial, uncourtly, medieval genres which proceeded untouched by the sentiment of the troubadours, and he enriches his account of the poem by reference to Huizinga's claim that

We should picture two layers of civilization superimposed, co-existing though contradictory. Side by side with the courtly style of literary and rather recent origin, the primitive forms of erotic life kept all their force . . .

The Midnight Court does have this primitive basis and nowhere is the melding of the archaic, the erotic and the realistic more evident than at that point in the young woman's first speech when she lists the places she paraded, the fashions she wore and the various superstitious rites she performed in order to attract the attention of a man. The following translation is by Frank O'Connor, from a version first published in 1945 and banned for a while by the Censorship Board of the Irish Free State – although there would seem to be nothing in these particular lines that they could have objected to:

> My hair was washed and combed and powdered,
> My coif like snow and stiffly laundered;
> I'd a little white hood with ribbon and ruff
> On a spotty dress of the finest stuff
> With facings to show off the line
> Of a cardinal cloak the colour of wine,
> A cambric apron filled with showers
> Of fruit and birds and trees and flowers,
> Neatly fitting, expensive shoes
> And the highest of heels pegged up with screws,
> Silken gloves and all in spangles
> Of brooches, buckles, rings and bangles.

And you mustn't imagine I've been shy,
The sort that slinks with a downcast eye,
Solitary, lonesome, cold and wild,
Like a mountainy girl or an only child.
I tossed my cap at the crowds of the races
And kept my head in the toughest places . . .

But I'm wasting my time on a wild-goose chase,
And my spirit is gone – and that's my case!
After all my hopes and sulks and passions,
All my aping of styles and fashions,
All the times that my cards were spread
And my hands were read and my cups were read,
Every old rhyme, pishrogue and rune,
Crescent, full moon and harvest moon,
Whit and All Souls and the First of May,
I've nothing to show for all they say.
Every night as I went to bed
I'd a stocking of apples under my head,
I fasted three canonical hours
To try and come round the heavenly powers,
I washed my shift where the stream ran deep
To hear my lover's voice in sleep;
Often I swept the woodstack bare,
Burned bits of my frock, my nails, my hair,
Up the chimney stuck the flail,
Slept with a spade without avail;
Hid my wool in the limekiln late
And my distaff behind the churchyard gate;
Flax in the road to halt coach and carriage,
And haycocks stuffed with heads of cabbage,
And night and day on the proper occasions
Invoked Old Nick and all his legions,
But 'twas all no good and I'm broken-hearted
For here I am at the place I started,
And that is the cause of all my tears,

Fast in the rope of the rushing years
With age and want in lessening span
And death at the end and no hopes of a man.

As soon as the young woman ends her complaint – with a threat to use black magic if her luck doesn't turn – a fierce old man springs into the witness box. He speaks with demented rage about his own marriage to a young woman like the one who has just quit pleading. He had been the victim of a conspiracy; on the wedding night, he discovered he had brought to bed a wife already pregnant and long notorious for her promiscuity and venereal capacities. Marriage, he says, should be abandoned; children born out of wedlock are far more healthy and vigorous anyhow; doesn't he have his wife's bastard to prove it? And he furthermore insists that the evidence of the previous witness is totally suspect, for she is as untrustworthy and duplicitous as the woman he married. Snarlygob is Frank O'Connor's name for this vigorous ancient and the name sits well with the venomous realism of the lines where he contrasts the living conditions from which the young woman witness has sprung with the finery she now parades in because of sexual favours rendered:

Now tell us the truth and don't be shy,
How long are you eating your dinner dry?
A meal of spuds without butter or milk
And the dirt in layers beneath your silk.
Bragging and gab becomes your like
But I know just where you sleep at night,
And blanket or quilt you never saw
But a strip of old mat and a bundle of straw
In a dirty old hut without a seat
And slime that slashes about your feet,
A carpet of weeds from door to wall
And the hens inscribing their tracks on all;
The rafters in with a broken back
And the brown rain lashing through every crack –
'Twas there you learned to look so fine;

Now, may we ask how you came by the style?
We all admired the way you spoke –
But whisper, treasure, who paid for the cloak?
A sparrow with you would die of hunger –
How did you come by all the grandeur,
All the tassels and all the lace?
Would you have us believe they were got in grace?
The frock made a hole in somebody's pocket,
And it wasn't yourself that paid for the jacket,
But leaving that and the rest aside,
Tell us, just how did the shoes arrive?

The 'treasure' comes back at him, of course, and gives as good as she has got. In a brilliant plea for sympathy for all women like the one spancelled to Snarlygob and his ilk, she reels off an indignant and marvellously specific list of his inadequacies as a lover and of his wife's attempts to overcome them. Why, she then asks in desperation, are the clergy not allowed to marry? Aren't some of the most bullish and ebullient men in the country going round in clerical clothes? Don't they leave their mark here and there in houses and families already? Why not give them their sexual heads and free them from their vows of celibacy? And so on. The main body of the poem ends on this powerful subversive note, and the witnesses step back to hear the verdict from Aoibheall. But since this verdict and its enactment are what I want to talk about at the end of the lecture, I shall postpone discussion of it for now except to say that Merriman, the character in the poem, is subject to Aoibheall's sentence as well and is convicted with all the rest of Ireland's males of insufficient amorous drive and a failure of conjugal will.

I have been quoting in English because my own familiarity with the poem comes from reading it in translation. And anyone who wants to get to know it can find representative passages in the standard anthologies of Irish verse – Brendan Kennelly's *Penguin Book of Irish Verse* prints O'Connor's version, John Montague's *Faber Book of Irish Verse* gives examples of the treatment of different parts of the work by different translators, and Thomas Kinsella has his own abbreviated and forthright version of the poem in the *Oxford Book of Irish Verse* which he edited. In the Republic of Ireland, of course, most people learn the opening lines at school in the original Irish. Yet, even in translation, it is easy to appreciate the fact that *Cúirt an Mheán-Oíche* has a totally invigorating way with language. In some places, to be sure, there is a copiousness that amounts to overload and parody in the Irish vocabulary; but elsewhere it exhibits an abundance which is the fine surprising excess of poetic genius in full flight.

It is parody, however, that is most in evidence near the beginning of the poem, in the description of the bailiff who enters the scene not only as her astonishing self – 'Bony and huge, a terrible hallion' – but also as a send-up. Merriman's first audience would have recognized her as a burlesque version of the visionary beauty who is a constant feature of an Irish poetic genre called the *aisling*. *Aisling* means vision and the *aisling* genre evolved in Ireland during the late seventeenth and eighteenth centuries; mostly it was a kind of Jacobite dream, a political fantasy about the future liberation of Ireland by the Stuarts, a compensatory response to the traumatic defeat which the native Gaelic order had suffered in the wake of the Cromwellian and Williamite campaigns. Typically, an *aisling* begins with the poet encountering in his dream-vision a woman whose beauty drives him to diction and description of the most ardent sort; the woman is, of course, an image of Ireland, an allegorical representation of the country's subject state, and she goes on to tell of her rape by the foreigner, or her thraldom to the heretic, or whatever. But in the end she consoles herself and the poet by prophesying that her release will be effected by a young prince from overseas.

Merriman's bailiff is, among other things, a blast of surrealistic ridicule directed at such a fantasy. She comes on as both a literary and a political corrective to self-deception. She is a form of overkill whose purpose is to undermine. She directs attention to the demeaned realities of the here and now rather than deflecting the imagination into consoling reverie. But at the same time, she is also a manifestation of that fine excess which gives the poem its immense panache. Here is my version of her entry on the unsuspecting scene:

> Leafy branches were all around me,
> Shooting grasses and growths abounded;
> There were green plants climbing and worts and weeds
> That would gladden your mind and clear your head.
> I was tired out, dead sleepy and slack,
> So I lay at my length on the flat of my back
> With my head well propped, my limbs at ease
> In a nest in a ditch beside the trees . . .
>
> But my rest was short for next there comes
> A sound from the ground like the roll of drums,
> A wind from the north, a furious rout
> And the lough in a sulphurous thunderlight.
> And then comes looming into view
> And steering towards me along the bay
> This hefty menacing dangerwoman,
> Bony and huge, a terrible hallion.
> Her height, I'd say, to the nearest measure,
> Was six or seven yards or more,
> With a swatch of her shawl all japs and glar
> Streeling behind in the muck and clabber.
> It was awe-inspiring just to see her,
> So hatchet-faced and scarred and sour –
> With her ganting gums and her mouth in a twist
> She'd have put the wind up man or beast.
> And Lord of Fates! Her hand was a vice
> Clamped on a towering staff or mace
> With a spike on top and a flange of brass
> That indicated her bailiff's powers.
>
> Her words were grim when she got started.

49

'Get up,' she said, 'and on your feet!
What do you think gives you the right
To shun the crowds and the sitting court?
A court of justice, truly founded,
And not the usual rigged charade,
But a fair and clement court of women
Of the gentlest stock and regimen.
The Irish race should be grateful always
For such a bench, agreed and wise,
In session now two days and a night
In the spacious fort on Graney Height . . .

To add to which, the whole assembly
Decreed on the Bible this very day:
The youth has failed, declined, gone fallow –
A censure, sir, that pertains to you.
In living memory, with birthrates fallen
And marriage in Ireland on the wane,
The country's life has been dissipated,
Pillage and death have worn it out.
Blame arrogant kings, blame emigration,
But it's you and your spunkless generation –
You're a source blocked off that won't refill.
You have failed your women, one and all.

The Midnight Court has a demonstrable relevance to the Ireland of its day, and in fact the poem has in recent decades been as much the locus of comment by social historians and folklorists as by literary critics; yet while this realism is one of its strengths, it is hard to feel that Merriman wrote in a realistic spirit. Admittedly, the comic phantasmagoria does constitute a definite, exhilarated retort to economic conditions and matrimonial patterns in East Clare in the late eighteenth century; but it would be hard to argue that the poem represents an act of civic concern on the poet's part. Indeed, one of the great triumphs of The Midnight Court as a creative achievement is that it feels utterly unconstrained. There's an animating buzz of topicality in its inventions, but in no way does it read like a dated document; and this is in large measure because the court set-up represents not a submission to the conditions of Merriman's world but a creative victory over them.

Merriman, in other words, did not devise the courtroom as a method of presenting evidence about the state of the sex-war in Co. Clare or about the social and economic impediments to early marriage. You can imagine a documentary film team or an Open University sociology unit assembling the results of its research and questionnaires, and then hitting upon the idea of a court case as a way of clarifying the topic. But with Merriman, as with any creative writer, the process is reversed. The image came first and then the evidence supplied itself almost as a kind of spontaneous reflex. For Merriman, the courtroom was not a method, but a stroke of genius; its real virtue lay in the way it released the flood of the poet's inventiveness.

Swift, for example, said that once he had thought of big men and little men, the whole of *Gulliver's Travels* was already more or less written; and something similar could have been claimed by Merriman when he hit upon the idea of burlesquing the *aisling* and the court of love, since this conception not only got his poem running but quickly sent it flying into vernacular overdrive. Professor Sean O'Tuama is both convincing and illuminating when he argues that Merriman was indeed working within this medieval literary convention of the love court, enshrined most influentially in Jean de Meun's treatment of it in the *Roman de la Rose* and then dispersed in ballads and other more or less popular forms throughout Europe and England and Norman and Gaelic Ireland. O'Tuama shows that the young woman's second speech is a kind of *chanson de la malmariée*, a form of lover's complaint which turns up all over the place 'in French, Italian, Scottish and indeed Irish popular literature'; that the praise of bastards is to be found in *King Lear* and in Richard Savage's poem *The Bastard*, published in Dublin in 1728; and so on. Yet even O'Tuama cannot quite bring the scholarly record into satisfactory alignment with the imaginative origin of the poem. Every attempt to link Merriman directly to a literary source, he admits, has to operate on a hypothesis, and yet he believes that the evidence does prove that the medieval themes were transmuted by Merriman into what he calls 'a new demonic comic creation which is absolutely eighteenth century'.

The court, then, is more a carnival where Merriman's imagination runs riot than a judicial inquiry into the rights and wrongs of the sexual mores of East Clare in the 1770s. Moreover, Merriman's most effective agent in summoning the volubility which distinguishes the whole proceedings is neither the bailiff who strides so commandingly into the poet's dream nor the bailiff's staff with its official insignia; the true motive force is the couplet which gives the poem its metrical norm and its distinctive music:

> Ba gnáth me ag siúl le ciumhais na h-abhann
> Ar bháinseach úr is an drúcht go trom,
> In aice na gcoillte i gcoim an tsléibhe
> Gan mhairg gan mhoill ar shoilse an lae.

It is not that anything about these lines is especially original in point of language or technique, it's more that they establish a melody. They strike a tuning fork and immediately a whole orchestra of possibility comes awake in the poet's ear and in the language itself. Another great unfettered event gets under way. Another unpredictable poetic intervention changes the contours of poetry itself. And it is this mixture of extravagance and inevitability which distinguishes *Cúirt an Mhéan-Oíche* and makes it more than a gallery of rural sexual stereotypes. Obviously, the success of the poem has also to do with the forceful pressure of urgent, credible human voices, and with the huge inherent interest of the sexual game itself; much is at issue, and yet it is not only the perennial relevance of the theme which guarantees the poem's ongoing appeal. What makes it a work that can still 'engross the present and dominate memory' is Merriman's vital gift for 'the stylistic arrangements of experience'.

Not that anyone would ever want to deny the importance and interest of the whole liberating hullabaloo that the poem raises about sexual matters. Or perhaps I should say gender matters, since gender rather than sex is where the flashpoint of the argument comes nowadays, and the poem's centrality to this debate is yet another example of the way it is able to subsume into itself the social and intellectual preoccupations of different periods and to answer them by divulging new and timely meanings. If, therefore, we are prepared to make an artificial distinction between the poem's socio-political quotient and its artistic quotient, we could argue that during the first half of the century and more, *Cúirt an Mheán-Oíche* was important because it sponsored a libertarian and adversarial stance against the repressive conditions which prevailed during those years in Irish life, public and private. And we could further argue that in more recent times its importance has shifted: from being an ally in the war against sexual repression and a censorship obsessed with sexual morality, the poem has become a paradigm of the war initiated by the women's movement for women's empowerment, their restoration to the centre of language and consciousness and thereby also to the centre of all the institutions and functionings of society.

This shifting and salubrious relationship between the poem and its world can be illustrated by looking very briefly at its reception and interpretation at three different moments over the last hundred years. Seventy years ago, for example, when the Irish critic and cultural nationalist Daniel Corkery gave his account of it in *The Hidden Ireland*, he was fairly eager to play down Merriman's send-up of clerical celibacy and his advocacy of unconstrained heterosexual activity between consenting adults. Rather than saluting these extravagances as fantastic possibilities to be savoured in a spirit of hilarity and transgression, Corkery spoke with a certain primness of the poem's treatment of 'curious questions' and attributed the pagan force of the thing to its ideas as such. It was as if he were anxious not to find the poet guilty of some form of un-Irish activity. Corkery inclined therefore to blame what he called the poem's 'irreligious ideas' on foreign influences, and he favoured the old academic notion that these ideas came from Voltaire and Rousseau, and that Merriman had picked them up through reading the books of these Enlightenment *philosophes* in the houses of the gentry he was supposed to have been so fond of visiting. Yet Corkery could not help recognizing that the poem's subversiveness derives in large measure from a native strain of paganism surviving unregenerate at different levels in Irish popular culture. But he fudged the issue, presumably because it would have been an embarrassment for a propagandist of the new self-Gaelicizing Irish Free State to discover in the older Gaelic literature too gleeful an endorsement of anti-clerical attitudes and too robust a promulgation of the basic desirability of promiscuous sexual behaviour.

Conditions have changed dramatically since Corkery's book appeared in 1924. The literary and moral constraints have clearly eased when an Irish-language woman poet like Nuala Ni Dhomhnall can publish in Ireland, with an Irish publisher and to Irish acclaim, a poem like 'Féar Suaithinseach' which implies that it is the sanctified male priest who is in need of the healing ministrations of the sexual woman and not the other way around; or when in another poem called 'Gan do Chuid Eadaigh', she expresses what might be called naked delight in imagining in erotic detail the body of a lover stripped of his clothes.

But even if Merriman's poem can be read nowadays as a precursor of these free treatments of sexuality, and can be seen as one of a line of precursors that includes James Joyce's *Ulysses* and, indeed, Frank O'Connor's 1945 translation of *The Midnight Court* itself, it is still not immune to moralistic criticism of a more recent kind. The poem still stands in danger of being accused for different reasons under the terms of a new feminist consensus. For example, I discovered that the political activist Mairin de Burca described it some thirteen years ago as 'sexist rubbish'. She did concede that men may mean well, but she nevertheless maintained that they 'cannot write intelligently about women's oppression'. This in itself sounds like a bit of sexist rubbish; and I would certainly argue that Brian Merriman should be immune to the common feminist castigation of Irish men poets for representing women (and Ireland) in the passive, submissive roles of maiden and mother. In fact, Merriman deserves a specially lenient hearing in the women's court, if only for having envisaged his own prosecution ahead of time and for having provided the outline of a case against himself. He was surely something of a progressive when it came to the representation of women. He gave them bodies and brains and let them speak as if they lived by them. He revised and implicitly criticized the *aisling* genre by burlesquing its idealized, victimized maiden in the figure of the beam-limbed bailiff; and he gave to the other young flesh-and-blood *speirbhean* in the witness box a transfusion of emotional and rhetorical energy long denied to women by poets who had preceded him.

Still, the fact that the poem is now probably read more in English translations than in the original Irish has by no means lessened the impression of *machismo* which surrounds it in the mind of the general reader. Of these translations, Frank O'Connor's is probably the best and the best known, and since its emphatic bawdiness was meant to challenge the censor as much as it was meant to delight the reader, O'Connor very deliberately upped the sexual ante in a distinctly male idiom. In an introduction to the first 1945 edition of this version, he admits that there are qualities in the Irish which his own English, for better or worse, had tended to coarsen:

As always, when he deals with women's human needs, [Merriman] puts real tenderness and beauty into the writing. My English cannot give the delicacy and fragrance of a line like *Ag súil trím chola le cogar ó'm cheile.* There is nothing remarkable about it . . . no extravagance of imagery or language which you can translate; it is a pure classical beauty of vowels and consonants which you either hear or do not hear.

This amounts to an admission by O'Connor that in his translation the surface noise of his own provocative anti-puritanical agenda is going to be more audible than the under-music of the women's voices; which means that those aspects of the poem most likely to offend a contemporary feminist are highlighted rather than mitigated by his treatment of them in English. A sensitized reader nowadays, man or woman, is going to be more uneasy than O'Connor ever was about, for example, the picture of the young woman setting her cap so assiduously for a man, or about the normative status which the poem – in spite of its subversive intent – grants to the state of marriage. So even though from a feminist viewpoint there has to be something admirable about the way Aiobheall of Craglee regulates the world of the poem (like a woman president in charge of the court and the country, a kind of *aisling* promise of Mary Robinson); and though there is a redemptive realism in the young witness's revelation that women can be every bit as sexually capable and cupidinous as men, it is nevertheless true that the poem places much emphasis on woman as a kind of human brooder and mostly ignores her potential as a being independent of her sexual attributes and her reproductive apparatus.

But all of this has to be understood in the context of the poem's overall drive to celebrate the creaturely over the ethereal in human beings, male or female. As Gearóid Ó Cruadhlaoidh has argued, Merriman sees the country's deliverance and the return of fertility and prosperity for all in the restoration of 'the basic, healthy, animal, life instinct of the mature, adult individual man and woman, free from conventional guilt.' And it is this same impulse to lift all kinds of bans and to break what Merriman's contemporary, William Blake, called 'the mind-forged manacles', it is this anti-establishment animus which gives the original its great panache, even though it also gives a slightly too pronounced strut to O'Connor's English. His intention was to taunt, to affront the prudes and goad the censorship board. And in this respect O'Connor was also influenced, I am certain, by the example of Yeats. He had known Yeats and worked with him closely during the 1930s, when

many of Yeats's own poems had the sort of upfront histrionic sexuality and confrontational drive which distinguish
O'Connor's translation. Indeed we are almost certain to meet
Crazy Jane on the road to O'Connor's midnight court. His purpose was to raise hackles, so he was prepared for his English
to make slightly more of a racket than the Irish might have
warranted.

All I'm doing here, of course, is stating the obvious thing;
namely, that the loss of subtlety O'Connor noted in his own
translations had to do with the gain in audibility which he
needed if the poem was to do its work of protest in the world
that he inhabited. And with this example of what we might call
O'Connor's Hibernia-harrowing enterprise, I hope I have given
sufficient illustration of what I meant when I said in the beginning – perhaps a bit too rhetorically – that *The Midnight Court*
had a role to play in the construction of a desirable civilization.
Without impairment to its artistic integrity, it has continued to
sustain the praise and the blame of generations of commentators
and the interpretations of different translators, and in so doing it
has promoted those workings of the spirit and exercises of the
intelligence which are good and desirable ends in themselves.

Before I conclude, however, I want to read the poem (as I
promised I would) in an old poetic context rather than a new
political one. This reading suggested itself because I have been
recently involved in a project where I was commissioned to
translate the story of Orpheus and Eurydice as it appears in
Ovid's *Metamorphoses*. At the end of the story, when Orpheus
has looked back and lost Eurydice to death all over again, Ovid
says:

> The sun passed through the house
> Of Pisces three times then, and Orpheus
> Withdrew and turned away from loving women –
> Perhaps because there only could be one
> Eurydice, or because the shock of loss
> Had changed his very nature. Nonetheless,

> Many women loved him and, denied
> Or not, adored.

Naturally I detected a faint, distant parallel between the situation of this classical poet figure, desired by those he has spurned, and the eighteenth-century Irish poet as he appears at the end of *Cúirt an Mheán-Oíche*, arraigned for still being a virgin when the country is full of women who'd be only too glad to ease him of his virtue. And the parallel was reinforced when I realized that the portrait of Merriman as the jocund poet, playing his tunes the length and breadth of the country – the portrait which appears at the end of the Irish poem – is another manifestation of the traditional image of Orpheus as master poet of the lyre, the patron and sponsor of music and song. But what transposed the parallel from a minor to a major key was a further recognition of the way that the *death* of Orpheus, as related by both Ovid and Virgil before him, provides an acoustic where the end of *Cúirt an Mheán-Oíche* can be heard to new effect and where, indeed, some of the critical objections which have been voiced against the final section of the poem can be made sense of in a new way.

Both Frank O'Connor and Sean O'Tuama are uneasy, for example, about the lack of poetic climax, the relatively conventional thinking and the relatively temperate tone of Aoibheall's final judgement. In his definitive 1981 account of the poem in *Irish University Review*, O'Tuama writes:

It is quite probable, then, that the *Court of Love* apparatus finally ended up more a hindrance than a help. Some more irrational or surrealistic type of concluding structure might have helped Merriman to reveal more climactically his dark, archaic feelings.

What happens at the end of *Cúirt an Mheán-Oíche* is that Aoibheall, the fairy president of the bench, gives a verdict in which she decrees that unmarried males of twenty-one and over are to be taken by women, tied to a tree beside a headstone in Feakle graveyard, and thoroughly whipped. She also decrees that the worn-out, sexually incapable husbands of sexually vigorous women should connive in the action when their wives take younger lovers, and should provide the legal cover of a family name when the children arrive. She prophesies furthermore that a time will come when Rome will permit the Catholic clergy to marry, and ends with a passionate if slightly moralistic outburst against male sexual braggarts who are as inadequate as they are scandalous. Then, after Aoibheall has delivered her verdict, the young woman plaintiff turns on the poet and rallies the women against him as a typical male offender; and finally, just as they are all about to put Aoibheall's sentence into action, the thing comes abruptly to an end as the poet starts up, awake and saved. Here are the final lines of the young woman's speech and the conclusion of the poem:

> 'So hear me now, long-suffering judge!
> My own long hurt and ingrown grudge
> Have me desolated. I hereby claim
> A woman's right to punish him.
> And you, dear women, you must assist.
> So rope him, Una, and all the rest –
> Anna, Maura – take hold and bind him.
> Double twist his arms behind him.
> Remember all the sentence called for
> And execute it to the letter.
> Maeve and Sive and Sheila! Maureen!
> Knot the rope till it tears the skin.
> Let Mr Brian take what we give,
> Let him have it. Flay him alive
> And don't draw back when you're drawing blood.
> Test all of your whips against his manhood.
> Cut deep. No mercy. Make him squeal.
> Leave him in strips from head to heel
> Until every single mother's son
> In the land of Ireland learns the lesson.
>
> And it only seems both right and fitting
> To note the date of this special sitting

So calm your nerves and start computing:
A thousand minus a hundred and ten –
Take what that gives you, double it, then
Your product's the year.' She'd lifted her pen
And her hand was poised to ratify
The fate that was looking me straight in the eye.
She was writing it down, the household guard
Sat at attention, staring hard
As I stared back. Then my dreaming ceased
And I started up, awake, released.

It is true that it is a blithe conclusion to a potentially baleful situation. What O'Tuama calls the archaic feelings are efficiently aborted by the dream convention, yet there is a lingering sense that the nightmare scenario is truer to the psychic realities than the daylight world to which the poet is returned in the final couplet. Even the partial vengeance J. M. Synge allows Pegeen Mike and her cohorts to practise upon Christy Mahon at the end of *The Playboy of the Western World* is more genuinely scaresome than the actions carried out by Merriman's court. The good humour of it all can be explained, of course, by Merriman's very healthy sense of proportion and by the requirements of the Court of Love convention. But an archaic beast has indeed stirred under the poem's surface and the reader experiences a vague need to see it unleashed into action – another way of saying that the Merriman poem has a mythic potency which its comic mode deflects and defuses. The myth in question is, of course, the myth of Orpheus, which Ovid renders fully in his account of the dismemberment of the bard at the hands of the frenzied maenads:

They circled him, still using as their weapons
Staffs they had twined with leaves and tipped with cones
That were never meant for duty such as this.
Some pelted him with clods, some stripped the branches
To scourge him raw, some stoned him with flintstones.
But as their frenzy peaked, they chanced upon

Far deadlier implements.

> Near at hand
> Oxen in yokes pulled ploughshares through the ground
> And sturdy farmers sweated as they dug –
> Only to flee across their drills and rigs
> When they saw the horde advancing. They downed tools
> So there for the taking on the empty fields
> Lay hoes and heavy mattocks and long spades.
> The oxen lowered their horns, the squealing maenads
> Cut them to pieces, then turned to rend the bard . . .

Ovid provides one possible explanation for this feral behaviour of the maenads by saying that after the loss of Eurydice Orpheus had spurned the love of women and turned his amorous attention to young boys, the implication being that the maenads' action is a form of heterosexual revenge upon homosexual activity. But however we interpret the Latin or the Irish stories in relation to the sexual politics of their times, it seems to me that Merriman's poem is backlit in an especially illuminating way if it is read in relation to the much more violent outcome of the Orpheus episode in Ovid's *Metamorphoses*. Not only does its central action – namely, the summoning and arraignment of the male poet by a court of aggrieved women – take on a new resonance; but the perceived weaknesses of its conclusion are put into perspective and the poem's claim to be considered in the context of what I called world literature is greatly enhanced. The poem remains, of course, what any vital work has to be, a response to the local conditions; but it becomes something more. Its power is augmented by being located within the force-field of an archetype. The phallocentrism of its surface discourse can be re-read as an aspect of male anxiety about suppressed female power, both sexual and political; and the weakness of its conclusion, namely the deflection of the threat to Brian, this tidy outcome can be seen as the price that the satirical eighteenth-century mind was prepared to pay in order to keep the psychosexual demons of the unconscious at bay for a while longer.

Still, given the down-to-earthness of this poem's cast of characters and the directness of their speech, this would be a rather elevated note to end on. Perhaps I can convey the ongoing reality of the poem's life more simply by recollecting a Saturday evening last August when I had the privilege of unveiling a memorial to Brian Merriman on the shore of Lough Graney in Co. Clare, where the opening scene of *The Midnight Court* is set. The memorial is a large stone quarried from a hill overlooking the lake, and the opening lines are carved on it in Irish. The people who attended the ceremony were almost all from the local district, and they were eager to point out the exact corner of the nearby field where the poet had run his hedge-school, and the spot on the lough shore where he had fallen asleep and had his vision. This was and is the first circle within which Merriman's poem flourished and continues to flourish. Later that evening, for example, in a marquee a couple of miles farther down the road, we attended a performance by the Druid Theatre Company from Galway in which the poem was given a dramatic presentation with all the boost and blast-off that song and music and topical allusion could provide. Again, hundreds of local people were in the tent, shouting and taking sides like a football crowd as the old man and the young woman battled it out and the president of the court gave her judgement. The psychosexual demons were no longer at bay but rampant and fully recognized, so that the audience, at the end of the performance, came away from the experience every bit as accused and absolved as the poet himself at the end of his poem. The 'profane perfection of mankind' was going ahead and civilization was being kept on course: in a ceremony that was entirely convincing and contemporary, Orpheus had been re-membered in Ireland.

21 October 1993

John Clare's Prog

Prog: *Gain or profit in a bargain; booty.*

Almost thirty years ago, in a poem called 'Follower', I wrote about myself as a child dragging along behind my father when he was out ploughing. The poem began:

My father worked with a horse-plough,

and unremarkable as this may have been as a line of verse, it was still the result of some revision. In fact, I had deliberately suppressed the one touch of individuality that had appeared in the first version. Originally I had written:

My father *wrought* with a horse-plough,

because until relatively recently that verb was the common one in the speech of mid-Ulster. Country people used the word 'wrought' naturally and almost exclusively when they talked about a person labouring with certain tools or animals, and it always carried a sense of wholehearted commitment to the task. You wrought with horses or with a scythe or with a plough; and you might also have wrought at hay or at flax or at bricklaying. So the word implied solidarity with speakers of the South Derry vernacular and a readiness to stand one's linguistic ground: why, then, did I end up going for the more pallid and expected alternative 'worked'?

The answer is, I suppose, because I thought twice. And once you think twice about a local usage you have been displaced from it, and your right to it has been contested by the official linguistic censor with whom another part of you is secretly in league. You have been translated from the land of unselfconsciousness to the suburbs of the *mot juste*. This is, of course, a very distinguished neighbourhood and contains important citizens like Mr Joyce, persons who sound equally at home in their hearth speech and their acquired language, persons who seem to have obliterated altogether the line between self-conscious and unselfconscious usage, and to have established uncensored access to every coffer of the word-hoard. But this spontaneous multivocal proficiency is as far beyond most writers as un-broken residence within the first idiom of a hermetically sealed, univocal home place. Our language may indeed be our world, but our writing, unless we happen to belong with the multitudi-nous geniuses like Joyce or Shakespeare, or with those whom we might call the monoglot geniuses – like John Clare – our writing is unlikely ever to be entirely co-extensive with that world.

Clare, we might say, wrought at language but did not become over-wrought about it. Early in his literary career, he had what is called success. His first 1820 volume, *Poems Descriptive of Rural Life and Scenery*, was reprinted; he went from Helpston to London; he met the well-known writers of the day; he had respect and learned something about the literary milieu. And then, notoriously, the fashion changed, the celebrity dwindled, the publications got spaced out and were less and less noticed until he ended up in Northamptonshire Asylum for the last twenty years of his life, having spent his late thirties and forties in mental confusion, economic distress and poetic neglect. It was only in 1978, for example, that a publisher brought out the extraordinarily copious collection entitled *The Mid-Summer Cushion* which Clare had ready for printing in the 1830s.

All regrettably true. But for the purposes of re-reading him today, we might express this truth in a different way and say that, after an initial brush with the censor, Clare refused to co-operate. The story of his career, in other words, can be ex-pressed as follows. Once upon a time John Clare was lured to the edge of his word-horizon and his tonal horizon, looked about him eagerly, tried out a few new words and accents and then, wilfully and intelligently, withdrew and dug in his local heels. Henceforth, he declared, I shall not think twice. It is this wilful strength of Clare's that I want to talk about, how it manifests itself and constitutes the distinctive power of his poetry. And I want to say something also about what his example can mean to poets at the present time, on the eve of his bicentenary year, in social and linguistic conditions of a far more volatile and various sort than those that prevailed when he was negotiating the personal, poetic and historical crises of his prime.

Like all readers, I am indebted to John Barrell's diagnosis of Clare's strengths and complications, in so far as it reveals him as a poet who possessed a secure local idiom but operated within the range of an official literary tradition. And previous to Barrell's work, of course, I read Clare in editions by Geoffrey Summerfield and Eric Robinson. In fact, my only regret in talking about Clare here today is that Geoffrey Summerfield is no longer alive to know about it. His sudden death in February 1991 was a great loss, and not only in the field of Clare studies. But it is some compensation to have his recent Penguin *Selected Clare* which, taken together with other recent editions by R. K. R. Thornton, Eric Robinson and David Powell, have given us Clare's works in all their unpunctuated vigour. This modern editorial effort has prepared the way for a wider recognition of the foundedness of Clare's voice and the sureness of his instinct in cleaving to his original 'sound of sense'. His unmistakable signature is written in most distinctively and sounded forth most spontaneously in the scores of fourteen-line poems which Clare wrote about small incidents involving the flora and fauna of rural Northamptonshire. Some of these poems are indeed conventional sonnets, with an octave and a turn and a sestet, or with some gesture either to that Petrarchan shape or to the Shakespearean one. But many of them are like the one I'm going to read now, seven couplets wound up like clockwork and then set free to scoot merrily through their foreclosed motions. He seemed to write this kind of poem as naturally as he breathed:

> I found a ball of grass among the hay
> And proged it as I passed and went away
> And when I looked I fancied something stirred

And turned agen and hoped to catch the bird
When out an old mouse bolted in the wheat
With all her young ones hanging at her teats
She looked so odd and so grotesque to me
I ran and wondered what the thing could be
And pushed the knapweed bunches where I stood
When the mouse hurried from the crawling brood
The young ones squeaked and when I went away
She found her nest again among the hay
The water oer the pebbles scarce could run
And broad old cesspools glittered in the sun

Clare progged the ball of grass. With equal metrical ease and lexical efficiency, he could have poked it, or with some slight readjustment of the pentameter, he could have prodded it. But had he done either of these things, both he and his readers would have been distanced in a minimal yet essential way from the here-and-nowness, or there-and-thenness, of what happened. I am reminded of a remark made once by an Irish diplomat with regard to the wording of a certain document. 'This,' he said, 'is a minor point of major importance.' In a similar way, the successful outcome of any work of art depends upon the seeming effortlessness and surefingeredness with which such minor points are both established and despatched. To take another instance, there is in this poem a very instructive use of the preposition 'at' rather than the more expected 'from' or 'on', in the couplet:

When out an old mouse bolted in the wheat
With all her young ones hanging at her teats . . .

'Hanging on' would have had certain pathetic, anthropomorphic associations that would have weakened the objective clarity of the whole presentation; 'hanging from' would have rendered the baby mice far too passive; 'hanging at' suggests 'catching at' and itself catches the sudden desperate tiny tightening of the mouse-jaws, and so conveys a reaction that is both biologically automatic and instinctively affectionate. (There is also an echo, of course, of the phrase 'at the teat'). But the real strength, once again, is the way the idiom has sprung into its place in the line without any trace of choice or forethought on the poet's part; and in this it partakes of the poem's overall virtue, which is its notational speed. The couplets hurry in upon themselves as fast as pencil-strokes in an excited drawing and, as in the act of drawing, there is no anxiety about lines repeating and intersecting with the trajectory of other lines. This is why the 'ands' and 'whens' and self-contained couplets and end-stopped movement of the lines do not irk as they might. They are clearly a function of the perception rather than a fault of the execution. They are eager to grab a part of the action. They are both a prerequisite and a consequence of one kind of accuracy and immediacy, as delightful in their compulsively accelerating way as the beautiful deceleration of the two final lines:

> The water oer the pebbles scarce could run
> And broad old cesspools glittered in the sun.

Once again, what is achieved in this couplet is not a self-conscious effect but a complete absorption. The eye of the writing is concentrated utterly upon what is before it, but also allows what is before it deep access to what is behind it. The eye, at any rate, does not lift to see what effect it is having upon the reader; and this typical combination of deep-dreaming in-placeness and wide-lens attentiveness in the writing is mirrored by the cesspools as they glitter within the sun. They too combine a deep-lodged, hydraulic locatedness within the district with a totally receptive adjustment to the light and heat of solar distances.

And yet, innocent as the poet's eye may seem, it is worth stressing the point that his poem is as surely made of words as any by Mallarmé. It has a special realism and reliability because it is a naturalist's observation, but neither the simplicity of its utterance nor the solidity of its content line by line should prevent its being regarded as a poetic achievement of rare finesse and integrity. In fact, in the water that is scarcely fit to run over

the pebbles there is to be found an analogue for the thirst or
ache at the core of Clare's poetry. This ache comes from his
standing at the frontier of writing, in a gap between the unmistakably palpable world he inhabits and another world,
reached for and available only to awakened language.

The kind of excellence I have been praising in 'The Mouse's
Nest' was not quite allowed for by the critical language Clare
inherited from the eighteenth century. He wrote more richly
and strangely than he could have told himself. There is an eerie
distance between the materiality of what I have just been discuss-
ing and the abstract primness of the following, also by Clare:

> A pleasing image to its page conferred
> In living character and breathing word
> Becomes a landscape heard and felt and seen
> Sunshine and shade one harmonizing green . . .
> Thus truth to nature as the true sublime
> Stands a mount atlas overpeering time

These lines come from a verse-essay called 'Shadows of Taste'
and they reveal Clare outside the borders of his first world,
rehearsing the new language and aligning himself with the new
perspectives of a world beyond. The footwork here is more
self-conscious and the carriage of the verse more urban than
anything in the sonnet about the mouse's nest, and it would
therefore have been more acceptable to his first reading public.
Naturally enough, his 1820 volume of *Poems Descriptive of
Rural Life and Scenery* was influenced by the modes of landscape writing established by Goldsmith and Thomson and Gray
and Collins. In order to cross the line from his unwriting self to
his writing identity, Clare had to proceed upon the moving stair
of those styles which were the current styles. An early poem to
his native village of Helpston, for example, speaks with the
unmistakable accents of Goldsmith's *Deserted Village*:

> Hail humble Helpstone where thy valies spread
> And thy mean village lifts its lowly head

Unknown to grandeur and unknown to fame
No minstrel boasting to advance thy name

and so on. And here is another passage, again taken from
'Shadows of Taste', which reveals him as an equally resourceful
mimic when it comes to projecting the voice of Alexander
Pope:

Styles with fashions vary – tawdry chaste
Have had their votaries which each fancied taste
From Donns old homely gold whose broken feet
Jostles the readers patience from its seat
To Popes smooth rhymes that regularly play
In music stated periods all the way
That starts and closes starts again and times
Its tuning gammut true as minster chimes
From those old fashions stranger metres flow
Half prose half verse that stagger as they go
One line starts smooth and then for room perplext
Elbows along and knocks against the next
And half its neighbour where a pause marks time
There the clause ends what follows is for rhyme

This is really laid-back stuff. For all his reputation as a peas-
ant poet, Clare had mastered the repertoire of prescribed
styles and skills: nowadays a poet as capable and informed as
this would probably be headhunted to teach a graduate work-
shop in versification. The point is, however, that Clare's later,
less conventionally correct and less (so to speak) tasteful
forays into poetic utterance should really be understood as
the redress of poetry in the third sense in which I used the
term in my inaugural lecture. This was a sense that came
from the chase, where 'to redress' meant to bring the hounds
or the deer back to the proper course, and I associated this
meaning of the term with the breakout of innate capacity
which marks all true lyric activity.

The excitement of finding oneself suddenly at full tilt on the right path, of having picked up a scent and hit the trail, this kind of sprinting, hurdling joy manifests itself in scores of sonnets and short poems of exclamatory observation which Clare wrote all through his life, but especially in the 1820s and 1830s. And this is the part of his work I am singling out for special praise. Which is not to say that I want to decry the full-dress correctness of other writings by him. The combination of realism, moralism and metrical efficiency when he is on his best Augustan behaviour has to be saluted. These more sententious poems show Clare at work under the influence of the poetry-speak current in England in his day; it would have taken a talent, indeed, as educated and overbearing as Joyce's to have resisted the orthodoxies then governing nature writing. Some of these were famously expressed in a letter to Clare from his publisher, John Taylor. Taylor was being neither exploitative nor insensitive, but simply acting as a mouthpiece for received ideas about correct poetic behaviour, when he urged Clare to 'raise his view' and 'speak of the Appearances of Nature ... more philosophically.' But this is not the writing of Clare's which has worn best. Its excellence is, as I say, characteristic of its time; it moves fluently and adequately but it moves like water that flows over a mill-wheel without turning it.

On the other hand, the poems of Clare's that still make a catch in the breath and establish a positively bodily hold upon the reader are those in which the wheel of total recognition has been turned. At their most effective, Clare's pentameters engage not just the mechanical gears of a metre: at their most effective, they take hold also on the sprockets of our creatureliness. By which I only mean that on occasion a reader simply cannot help responding with immediate recognition to the pell-mell succession of vividly accurate impressions. No one of these is extraordinary in itself, nor is the resulting poem in any way spectacular. What distinguishes it is an unspectacular joy and totally alert love for the one-thing-after-anotherness of the world. Here, by way of illustration, is another one of Clare's sonnets in couplets – perhaps we should call them *supplets* – picked almost at random from the ones Clare wrote at Northborough during his early and middle forties:

> The old pond full of flags and fenced around
> With trees and bushes trailing to the ground
> The water weeds are all around the brink
> And one clear place where cattle go to drink
> From year to year the schoolboy thither steals
> And muddys round the place to catch the eels
> The cowboy often hiding from the flies
> Lies there and plaits the rushcap as he lies
> The hissing owl sits moping all the day
> And hears his song and never flies away
> The pinks nest hangs upon the branch so thin
> The young ones caw and seem as tumbling in
> While round them thrums the purple dragon flye
> And great white butter flye goes dancing bye

Rarely has the butteriness of a butterfly been so available. The insect has flown into the medium and survives forever there as a pother of lip movement and a set of substituted feet in the scansion of the line. And the old pond here is like the cesspool in 'The Mouse's Nest', in so far as it embodies for Clare not only the reality of all such places *as* places, with distinct characters and histories, but also their value as a set of memories and affections at the back of his mind. There is dreamwork going on here, as well as photography. The casual rightness and potency of the thing come from a level of engagement well below the visual; in fact, the whole poem acts as a reminder of how integrated and concentrated a poetic response can be. What is unstated can still be felt as a potent charge inside or behind an image or a cadence, and what lies behind the self-possession, the sureness of tone and grip on place in such a poem is Clare's great feat of endurance in the face of historical and personal crises.

So far, for example, I have not mentioned Clare's solidarity with the plight of the rural poor, or taken account of the Enclosure Act that affected Helpston in 1809; I have not commented upon the trauma of the poet's move from his native village at the age of thirty-nine to the nearby parish of Northborough; I have not enumerated his gradually more frequent depressions, lapses of memory, hallucinations and collapses into delusion when he imagined himself Lord Byron or the prizefighter Jack Randall; I have not dwelt upon the desperate love he felt for his childhood sweetheart Mary Joyce or his intermittent conviction that he was married to her as well as to his wedded wife, Martha Turner; nor have I alluded to his voluntary entry into Dr Allen's mental hospital in High Beach in Epping Forest in 1837 and his heartbreaking journey of escape out of there four years later in July 1841. But, if I have done none of these things, it is not because I believe that Clare did not suffer fantastically, fiercely and unrelievedly as a result of them, or that they are not fundamental to his sensibility and achievement as a poet.

On the contrary, the vigour of the poetry is linked to the fact that Clare was harrowed and stricken by personal and historical upheavals all the days of his life, until the two final suspended decades he spent in Northampton Asylum. The poems of these years have understandably been called the 'poems of John Clare's madness' and yet *as poems* they seem to me less terribly keyed than much that came before them. The torsions and distortions reached a climax in 1841, just before and after his escape from Epping Forest, and during the opening stages of his final commitment on 29 December of that year. These are the months when he wrote his two Byronic pastiches, *Child Harold* and *Don Juan*, the latter of which once more deploys in wonky but madly convincing ways Clare's old gift for mimicry. In this work, he assumes an antic disposition, taunting the reader with a highly aggressive and transgressive intelligence, making sexual and political hay and mayhem. Enigma and affront are precariously balanced, for example, when he turns his attention to his present whereabouts in Essex:

> There's Doctor Bottle, imp who deals in urine,
> A keeper of state-prisons for the queen

As great a man as is the Doge of Turin
And save in London is but seldom seen
Yclep'd old A-ll-n – mad-brained ladies curing
Some p-x-d like Flora and but seldom clean
The new road o'er the forest is the right one
To see red hell and, further on, the white one

This is good stuff but it is not quite Clare in his element. The work which simultaneously displays the greatest pressure, the greatest sureness and the greatest nonchalance comes in the main in poems written before Northampton. Obviously, nobody is going to deny the apocalyptic pathos of his most famous asylum poem – the one beginning 'I am – yet what I am none cares or knows' and including the line about 'the vast ship-wreck of my lifes esteems'; nor is anybody going to undervalue the bonus of indispensable songs and sonnets that belong to this period, especially the very late sonnet 'To John Clare' (and not forgetting either 'The Round Oak', 'The Yellowhammer', 'The Wood Anemonie', 'The flag top quivers in the breeze', 'The Thunder mutters louder and more loud', and others). But what crowns the lifetime's effort is the great outpouring in his early middle years of short verse about solitary figures in a landscape, or outcast figures, or threatened creatures, or lonely creatures, or birds and birds' nests, or dramatic weather changes, all of which manage to convey uncanny intimations of both vulnerability and staying power. By the very fact of having got themselves written, these poems manifest the efficacy of creative spirit in the face of all the adversity I noticed a moment ago; and they prove once again the truth of Keith Douglas's notion that the work of art inheres in 'stating some truth whose eternal quality exacts the same reverence as eternity itself.'

In this work, Clare is led towards the thing behind his voice and ear which Nadezhda Mandelstam called 'the nugget of harmony'. To locate this phonetic jewel, to hit upon and hold one's true note, is a most exacting and intuitive discipline, but it was particularly difficult for a writer like Clare, whose situation in the 1820s was to some extent the same as Christopher Murray Grieve's a hundred years later; which is to say that Clare, like Grieve, was operating within a received idiom that he half-knew was not the right one for him. Grieve dealt with the problem by inventing synthetic Scots and becoming Hugh Mac-Diarmid. Perhaps if Clare had changed his name to John Fen or Jack Prog, his wilfulness would have been more clarified and his awareness of what his poetry had to do would have been more pointed. Even so, one might say that MacDiarmid's theoretical passion in the 1920s fulfilled Clare's poetic intuition of the 1820s – although Clare's was always by far the surer voice, artistically speaking. Everything that MacDiarmid wrote about revitalizing the vernacular, all his aspirations to unblock linguistic access to a reservoir of common knowledge and unacknowledged potential, all his angry regret that English literature maintained 'a narrow ascendancy tradition instead of broad-basing itself on all the diverse cultural elements and splendid variety of languages and dialects, in the British Isles' – all this was a making explicit of what was implicit in much of Clare's practice. And I believe that MacDiarmid would also have recognized some affinity between himself and Clare when it came to the use of the ballad measure.

This was the one poetic beat that had sounded in the ears of both poets from the beginning, the measure in which personal and communal experience could enter each other as indissolubly as two streams, and it was the measure in which Clare's moral outrage got expressed most pungently. When, for example, in one of his most powerful poems, the quarry field known as Swordy Well begins to speak, we recognize immediately that Clare's voice is in a deep old groove and that he is hauling into vivid speech an awareness of injustice for which he has paid a personal price; yet it is also an awareness sanctioned by the bleak folk wisdom of the ballad tradition and by the high tragic understanding of life shared by the authors of *King Lear* and *The Book of Job*.

The 1809 Act of Parliament for the Enclosure of Helpston

74

had granted Swordy Well to the overseers of the roads in the parish. The field had thereby lost its independence and become like a pauper, dependent upon parish charity. In Clare's poem, what opens the channels of expression so exhilaratingly is the removal of every screen between the identity of the person and the identity of the place. 'The Lament of Swordy Well' is by no means as extraordinary an achievement as MacDiarmid's *A Drunk Man Looks at the Thistle,* but it still represents a thrilling integration of common idiom and visionary anger of the sort that MacDiarmid longed to reintroduce in Scotland. However, the main point I want to make about it is that the ballad stanza does for Clare what it would do for MacDiarmid; it places him at the centre of his world and keeps his voice on course like a plough in a furrow. Here are a few selected stanzas, where the assailed dignity of the pauper and the fate of the requisitioned ground are mutually expressive of each other's plight:

> I hold no hat to beg a mite
> Nor pick it up when thrown
> Nor limping leg I hold in sight
> But pray to keep my own
> Where profit gets his clutches in
> Theres little he will leave
> Gain stooping for a single pin
> Will stick it on his sleeve . . .
>
> Alas dependance thou'rt a brute
> Want only understands
> His feelings wither branch and root
> That falls in parish hands
> The muck that clouts the ploughman's shoe
> The moss that hides the stone
> Now Im become the parish due
> Is more then I can own . . .
>
> The silver springs grown naked dykes
> Scarce own a bunch of rushes

When grain got high the tasteless tykes
Grubbed up trees banks, and bushes
And me they turned me inside out
For sand and grit and stones
And turned my old green hills about
And pickt my very bones

These things that claim my own as theirs
Where born but yesterday
But ere I fell to town affairs
I were as proud as they
I kept my horses cows and sheep
And built the town below
Ere they had cat or dog to keep
And then to use me so . . .

The bees flye round in feeble rings
And find no blossom bye
Then thrum their almost weary winds
Upon the moss and die
Rabbits that find my hills turned o'er
Forsake my poor abode
They dread a workhouse like the poor
And nibble on the road . . .

Ive scare a nook to call my own
For things that creep or flye
The beetle hiding neath a stone
Does well to hurry bye
Stock cats my struggles every day
As bare as any road
He's sure to be in somethings way
If eer he stirs abroad . . .

The point of this poem, of course, and of another similar if gentler exercise in dramatic monologue called 'The Lamentations of Round Oak Water', is to make a point. Their social protest and their artistic effort are in perfect step. And if there is an emphatic thump to the metre, this is inherent in the convention: the broad effect comes with the genre. What I want to emphasize is that the ballad stanza kept Clare on the right road poetically by giving him a traditional tune to march to, if not exactly complete access to his own 'nugget of harmony'.

That nugget is something more elusive and more individual to a poet than anything comprised by a metre. In Clare's case, it is to be found mostly in the poems that we might call his short takes. These are quick little forays of surprising innocence and accuracy, poems where subjects such as the ones I mentioned earlier – creatures, country scenes and so on – pass in and out of language every bit as fluently as moods and impulses pass between the body and the weather itself. In these poems the nugget of harmony is not present as a virtuosity; the trueness of these 'supplets' has less to do with composed sweetness and nice modulation and deliberate technique than with a spontaneous at-homeness in speech itself. In fact, there is not a great deal of variety in the tunes of the poems, just as there never is any great variety of pitch in the cries that people let out at moments of spontaneous excitement – and the work I'm thinking of can be understood to constitute a succession of just such brief, intense, spontaneous outcries.

The poems about birds' nests belong to this category, especially ones like 'The Wryneck's Nest' and 'The Fern Owl's Nest'. Well-known snap-shot work such as 'Hares at Play' belong to it also; and little genre paintings like the sonnet on 'The Woodman'; and landscape poems such as 'Emmonsdale Heath'; and, in a deeper register, the short sonnet sequence about 'The Badger' and the sonnet-diptych about 'The Marten-Cat' and 'The Fox'. The desire to quote all of these is strong but the time is short and the texts are widely available. Here instead is an incidental example of the kind of excellence I have in mind, a fragment of sorts, just a stray stanza really, and yet its random swoop upon the momentary – its casually perfect close-ups on raindrops, for example – illustrates all over again the fact that the truth of art does lie in those minor points of major importance:

> The thunder mutters louder and more loud
> With quicker motion hay folks ply the rake
> Ready to bust slow sails the pitch black cloud
> And all the gang a bigger haycock make
> To sit beneath – the woodland winds awake
> The drops so large wet all thro' in an hour
> A tiney flood runs down the leaning rake
> In the sweet hay yet dry the hay folks cower
> And some beneath the waggon shun the shower

It's populous, it's unpretentious, it seems effortless, yet it is actually a triumph of compression that manages to combine the shapeliness of nine end-stopped, closed-off lines in rhyme with the totally active movements of clouds and haymakers and raindrops and waterlogged wind. In fact, the movements of the world are here an aspect of the movements of Clare's own vivid spirit; and the lines both illustrate and obey the Wordsworthian imperative that poetry should disclose in the workings of the universe analogues for the working of the human mind and soul. Just because Clare's poetry abounds in actualities, just because it is as full of precise delightful detail as a granary is full of grains, does not mean that it is doomed to pile up and sink down in its own materiality. On the contrary, that which is special and unique about it is its lambency, its skim-factor, its bobbing unencumbered motion. It is what Lawrence calls the poetry of the living present; and its persistent theme, under many guises, in different subjects and scenes and crises, is the awful necessity of the gift for keeping going and the lovely wonder that it can be maintained – a gift which is tutored by the instinctive cheer and courage of living creatures, and heartened by every fresh turn and return of things in the natural world. Clare is always cheering for the victim, always ready to pitch in on the side of whatever is tender and well disposed, or whatever is courageous and outnumbered – like the badger:

He turns about to face the loud uproar
And drives the rebels to their very doors
The frequent stone is hurled where eer they go
When badgers fight and every ones a foe
The dogs are clapt and urged to join the fray
The badger turns and drives them all away
Though scarcly half as big dimute and small
He fights with dogs for hours and beats them all
The heavy mastiff savage in the fray
Lies down and licks his feet and turns away
The bull-dog knows his match and waxes cold
The badger grins and never leaves his hold
He drives the crowd and follows at their heels
And bites them through. The drunkard swears and reels

Needless to say, in spite of my praise for these vivid shorter poems, I do not wish to underrate performances by Clare of greater rhetorical sweep and more sustained intellectual purpose. His ode 'To the Snipe', for instance, is something of a set-piece and exhibits the customary fit between word and thing – the quagmire overgrown 'with hassock tufts of sedge', and the moor with its 'spungy lap' – but what makes it a poem of classical force is the perfect posture it maintains as it moves energetically through the demands of a strict and complex stanza. There's something almost Marvellian about its despatch and articulation. Just because I set such store by Clare, the astonished admirer, doesn't mean I don't admire the more deliberately ambitious poet of lines like these:

Lover of swamps
The quagmire overgrown
With hassock tufts of sedge – where fear encamps
Around thy home alone

The trembling grass
Quakes from the human foot
Nor bears the weight of man to let him pass

Where he alone and mute

Sitteth at rest
In safety neath the clump
Of huge flag-forrest that thy haunts invest
Or some old sallow stump . . .

For here thy bill
Suited by wisdom good
Of rude unseemly length doth delve and drill
The gelid mass for food

'To the Snipe' is one kind of excellence, and there are others. Nobody would want to slight the balmier, plashier riches of a poem like 'The Summer Shower', or the set-pieces in *The Shepherd's Calendar*, or those other much praised and thematically central poems of the Northborough period like 'The Flitting' and 'Remembrances'. But it's possible to acknowledge the different orders of excellence which these poems represent and still choose to prize most in Clare's oeuvre that attribute which Tom Paulin characterized in another context as 'the now of utterance'.

Paulin has written on Clare most recently in an essay of brilliant advocacy in *Minotaur* (1992), his book about poetry and the nation state. But here I want to draw attention to the very suggestive remarks he made earlier in his introduction to *The Faber Book of Vernacular Verse* (1990), where he had this to say about Clare's texts as we now have them, restored to their original unpunctuated condition:

The restored texts of the poems embody an alternative social idea. With their lack of punctuation, freedom from standard spelling and charged demotic ripples, they become a form of Nation Language that rejects the polished urbanity of Official Standard.

And then, having alluded to the poet's 'Ranter's sense of being trapped within an unjust society and an authoritarian language', Paulin concludes that 'Clare dramatizes his experience of the class system and its codified language as exile and imprisonment in Babylon.' By implication, then Clare is a sponsor and a forerunner of modern poetry in post-colonial nation languages, poetry that springs from the difference and/or disaffection of those whose spoken tongue is an English which sets them at cultural and perhaps political odds with others in possession of that normative 'Official Standard'. Paulin's contention is that wherever the accents of exacerbation and orality enter a text, be it in Belfast or Brooklyn or Brixton, we are within earshot of Clare's influence and example. What was once regarded as Clare's out-of-stepness with the main trends has become his central relevance: as ever, the need for a new kind of poetry in the present has called into being precursors out of the past.

But still, when we look at Paulin's own poetry, and that of Les Murray, Liz Lochhead, Tony Harrison, Derek Walcott, Edward Kamau Brathwaite and many figures in the dub and reggae tradition, it becomes evident that nobody can any longer belong as innocently or entirely within the acoustic of a first local or focal language as Clare could – *focus* being, you remember, the Latin word for hearth. Nowadays, every isle – be it Aran or Orkney or Ireland or Trinidad – is full of broadcast noises, every ear full of media accents and expendable idioms. In the few nooks of dialect I have kept in touch with over the years, the first things children speak nowadays are more likely to be in imitation of TV jingles than of the tones of their parents. So what a poet takes from Clare in these conditions is not an antiquarian devotion to dialect or a nostalgia for folkways; rather, the instructive thing about Clare's practice is the way it shows the necessity for being forever at the ready, always in good linguistic shape, limber and fit to go intelligently with the impulse.

In the shorter poems I have been praising, Clare exhibits the same kind of self-galvanizing, gap-jumping life that sends poems by Tom Paulin and Les Murray catapulting and skimming off and over two or three different language levels. The kind of learned and local words that propel their poems and open them inward and forward, the whole unruly combination of phonetic jolts and associated sidewindings, all this obviously issues from a far more eclectic relish of language than Clare ever developed. Nevertheless, he would have been at home with the verve and impatience which the vocabulary of these poets manifests, their need to body-swerve past the censor and shoulder through decorum, to go on a poetic roll that can turn on occasion into a political rough ride.

Clare, in fact, inspires one to trust that poetry can break through the glissando of post-modernism and get stuck in the mud of real imaginative haulage work. He never heard Mandelstam's famous phrase about Acmeism being a 'nostalgia for world culture', but oddly enough, it makes sense to think of Clare in relation to the arrival of poetry in that longed-for place or state – an arrival which John Bayley has recently observed in the work of many gifted contemporaries. The dream of a world culture, after all, is a dream of a world where no language will be relegated, a world where the ancient rural province of Boeotia (which Les Murray has made an image for all the outback and dialect cultures of history) will be on an equal footing with the city-state of Athens; where not just Homer but Hesiod will have his due honour. Clare's poetry underwrites a vision like this, where one will never have to think twice about the cultural and linguistic expression of one's world on its own terms since nobody else's terms will be imposed as normative and official. To read him for the exotic flavours of an archaic diction and the picturesque vistas of a bucolic past is to miss the trust he instills in the possibility of a self-respecting future for all languages, an immense, creative volubility where human existence comes to life and has life more abundantly because it is now being expressed in its own self-gratifying and unhindered words.

20 October 1992

Speranza in Reading:
On 'The Ballad of Reading Gaol'

All women become like their mothers. That is their
tragedy. No man does. That's his.
> Oscar Wilde, *The Importance of Being Earnest*

In choosing the subjects for these lectures, I am not guided in
any very systematic way by the need to stick to an overall
theme. On every occasion, the *sine qua non* has been the
memory of an early reading that mutated over the years into a
definite loyalty to the poem or poet in question. At the same
time, I did want to clarify something about the way poetry
persists and operates as a mode of redress, the way it justifies its
readers' trust and vindicates itself by setting its 'fine excess' in
the balance against all of life's inadequacies, desolations and
atrocities; and I have grounded my convictions in every case
upon that sensation of rightness which is experienced once a
poem makes an indelible first impression in the ear and then
survives in the mind as a pleasure, a potency and even, occasionally, a principle.

All this was put far more simply and succinctly by Richard
Ellmann in his biography of Oscar Wilde when he concluded
his discussion of 'The Ballad of Reading Gaol' by saying, 'Once
read, it is never forgotten.' And in these plain words, Ellmann
summed up the experience of anyone who has ever come under
the sway of Wilde's haunting, problematical poem. My own
decision to talk about it has therefore much to do with my
having read it over thirty years ago in a large leather-bound
Book of Old Ballads, edited by – of all people – the gossip
columnist Beverley Nichols. I bought this tome second-hand in
Belfast, in Smithfield Market, while I was still a new graduate of
Queen's University, intent upon getting together the basic texts

of a poetry library. I bought it because I knew many of the poems in it already – 'The Wife of Usher's Well', 'Sir Patrick Spens', 'Thomas Rhymer' and so on – but also because of its full-page colour illustrations, the luxury binding and the large-scale format, all of which produced a kind of designer antiquity that I fell for. And there was also something engagingly old-fashioned about Nichols's motives for collecting the ballads in the first place. 'These poems', he wrote in his introduction,

are the very essence of the British spirit. They are to literature what the bloom of the heather is to the Scot, and the smell of the sea to the Englishman. All that is beautiful in the old word 'patriotism' . . . is latent in these gay and full-blooded measures.

Nichols actually went out of his way to elevate Wilde's ballad above those parts of his oeuvre which are less than 'full-blooded', and he was undoubtedly right to see a radical difference between the mannered, ironical style of almost everything else that Wilde wrote and the macabre atmosphere of lines like these:

> He did not wear his scarlet coat,
>   For blood and wine are red,
> And blood and wine were on his hands
>   When they found him with the dead,
> The poor dead woman whom he loved
>   And murdered in her bed.
>
> He walked amongst the Trial Men
>   In a suit of shabby grey;
> A cricket cap was on his head,
>   And his step seemed light and gay;
> But I never saw a man who looked
>   So wistfully at the day.
>
> I never saw a man who looked
>   With such a wistful eye
> Upon that little tent of blue

Which prisoners call the sky,
And at every drifting cloud that went
With sails of silver by.

I walked, with other souls in pain,
Within another ring,
And was wondering if the man had done
A great or little thing,
When a voice behind me whispered low,
'That fellow's got to swing.'

Thirty years on, I have a cooler sense of the poem and its limitations than I had when I first read it in that de luxe edition, yet something in me still responds to its peculiar undermusic, the gathering force of lamentation that is immediately audible in those opening lines. They conjure up a mood of distress that is inseparable from the thought of Oscar Wilde's disgrace, his negative transformation at the height of his fame from idol to ogre of the English cultural scene. The lines arise out of a shared experience of humiliation, as fact and fiction, art and life, combined in a way that the younger Wilde would have thoroughly disapproved of.

The fiction is that the poem is spoken by a prisoner who shares a peculiar sense of intimacy with a condemned murderer who is waiting to be hanged in Reading Gaol. The fact is that it was written shortly after Wilde's release from that gaol, but while he was still, psychologically, very much a convict: the author of the poem was no longer the Oscar of theatrical triumphs and dinners at the Café Royal but Convict C.3.3., and it was this prison number rather than Wilde's own name that appeared on the title page of the work when it was published. This was Wilde's way of indicating that he was now forever a secret sharer of the griefs and guilts of the doomed world of the gaol, and in the poem this gaol world becomes an aspect of the homosexual demi-monde that he had frequented so loftily and so lavishly when he had held sway a few years earlier as the culture hero of the hour. The erotic intimacy which pervades the writing every time the condemned man appears is a signal that Wilde was still imaginatively unreformed after his prison stint: his deepest sympathies lay with the tribe of outcasts, back somewhere in a world of rent-boys and rampant parties and long weekends with Lord Alfred Douglas, the world that had been exposed so mercilessly by the prosecution informers during Wilde's trials in 1895.

So I'm coming back to it here for its own sake, but also because of the nice coincidence of my having been connected with Oscar Wilde's old college during the past four years at Oxford. I too have enjoyed my time at Magdalen, but unlike Oscar, I have been unable to mislay my Irish accent. And this is probably just as well, since I want to talk about 'The Ballad of Reading Gaol' as the work of Wilde, the Irish writer, the poet who was his mother's son in the literary as well as the biological sense, son of Speranza, the nationalist poet, as well as of Lady Wilde, the *grande dame* of the salons: which is to say that I am going to look at the poet in the light of some recent post-colonial readings of Wilde by critics like Declan Kiberd and Terry Eagleton. Eagleton's play *Saint Oscar* is a bravura interpretation of Wilde's English career as both a consequence of his Irish background and an occlusion of it. *Saint Oscar* is full of a ventriloquistic inventiveness that enables the author not so much to sound Wilde's depths as to sound off his surfaces, tick him off by taking him off. It is a theatrical event where the catharsis is in the criticism, and where the subject, who once suffered the name of pervert in England, is made to revert to Ireland. Here, for example, is Oscar as Eagleton presents him at the time of his trial, making that most Irish of last stands, the speech from the dock:

I object to this trial on the grounds that no Irishman can receive a fair hearing in an English court because the Irish are figments of the English imagination. I am not really here; I am just one of your racial fantasies. You cannot manacle a fantasy. I do not believe in your morality and I do not believe in your truth. I have my own truth and morality which I call art. I am not on trial here because I am a pervert but because I am an artist, which in your book comes to much the same thing. You hold that a man is a man and a woman is a woman. I hold that nothing is ever purely itself, and that the point where it becomes so is known as death. I therefore demand to be defended by metaphysicians rather than by lawyers, and that my jury should be composed of my peers – namely, poets, perverts, vagrants and geniuses.

As it turns out, Eagleton's Oscar has had his wish granted, at least partially. Criticism of Wilde has entered a phase of relish and extravagance which he would surely have approved of. Declan Kiberd, in his 1984 Field Day pamphlet *Anglo-Irish Attitudes*, has just the right kind of verve:

Wilde saw that the image of the stage Irishman tells us more about English fears than Irish realities, just as the still vibrant Irish joke tells us far less about the Irishman's foolishness than about the Englishman's persistent and poignant desire to say something funny. In this case, Wilde opted to say something funny for the English, in a lifelong performance of Englishness which constituted a parody of the very notion. By becoming more English than the English themselves, Wilde was able to invert, and ultimately to challenge, all the time-honoured myths about Ireland.

My own point, therefore, could be stated as follows: that Oscar Wilde's 'Ballad of Reading Gaol' should end up in a book of ballads, published during the 1930s with the intention of boosting British patriotism, is the ultimate inversion, since the proper place for this poem would be in a book of Irish ballads, where it would appear as an example of that most disaffected of Irish genres, the gaol journal, a kind of writing popularized by the political defiance of John Mitchel's prison diaries in the nineteenth century and by the subversive volubility of Brendan Behan's *Borstal Boy* in the twentieth. In 'The Ballad of Reading Gaol', in other words, Oscar Wilde converted himself into the kind of propagandist poet his mother (the fiery Speranza) had been fifty years before, the kind of poet that he had gone to England to avoid becoming; and so one could argue that his *literary* tragedy was that he did become like his **mother,** embracing in the end a fervent rhetorical mode of writing which was bound to be artistically deleterious.

Wilde, of course, was the first to perceive the truth and piquancy of all this. While the poem was still in manuscript and he himself was still convalescent as a writer – only five months out of gaol, shaken and shaky, bereft of his old paradoxical brilliance – he wrote to Robert Ross:

The poem suffers under the difficulty of a divided aim in style. Some is realistic, some is romantic: some poetry, some propaganda . . . but as a whole I think the production is interesting: that it is interesting from more points than one is artistically to be regretted.

This is a most candid and exact piece of self-appraisal, so it may be that W. B. Yeats was right in imagining that, had Oscar lived, he would have revised the poem, and revised it down to the realistic, unromantic, unpropagandistic form in which he, Yeats, presented it to the world in 1936, in *The Oxford Book of Modern Verse*. Yeats preserved thirty-eight of the original 109 stanzas, and, in his own estimation, 'now that I have plucked from *The Ballad of Reading Gaol* its foreign feathers it shows a stark realism akin to that of Thomas Hardy, the contrary of all its author deliberately sought. I have plucked out even famous lines because, effective in themselves, put into the Ballad they become artificial, trivial, arbitrary; a work of art can but have one subject.'

For Yeats, that subject was the objective tale of a condemned man's last days and his impact upon the minds of his fellow convicts, in particular the convict who tells the tale. He is therefore ready to sacrifice some of the ballad's most famous stanzas because for him they are too insistent, making explicit what should be implicit. The autobiographical plea lurked too near the surface of these lines, for example, so they had to go:

> Yet each man kills the thing he loves,
>   By each let this be heard,
> Some do it with a bitter look,
>   Some with a flattering word.

The coward does it with a kiss,
The brave man with a sword!

The fever and power of this stanza derive from Wilde's sense that the condemned man is his double. Both had committed crimes of passion and so, for both, their sexuality and their offence were intimately allied; the poet, in other words, was also fastening upon the murderer as a figure through whom he could indulge in a vicarious exercise of self-castigation and self-pity, but Yeats was not prepared to allow this self-gratifying aspect of Wilde's writing to absorb attention. For Yeats, the proper object of that attention was the man who had actually killed his wife in a fit of jealousy and swung for it in Reading Gaol in July 1896. 'I have stood in judgment upon Wilde,' he wrote, 'bringing into light a great, or almost great poem.'

Yeats's version was comparatively objective and forthright, the work of an authoritative public poet, a Nobel Prize winner, 'the finished man among his enemies'; Wilde's original ballad was more compensatory and confiding, the work of an ex-convict on the run from English society, a writer whose most recent production had been the long, self-pitying, self-justifying letter to Lord Alfred Douglas known as *De Profundis*. Indeed, a note which Wilde called 'romantic' pervades that whole work; in spite of his determined effort at castigation, Wilde can never altogether allow the accuser in himself to become detached from the accused Bosie. There is a sort of relish in the recrimination, a self-cancelling release of balm along with the blame, a guilty savouring of the knowledge that he had demeaned himself by indulging for so long the perpetrator of the affronts he is now being driven to catalogue.

It would seem then that the composition of *De Profundis* contributed to the writing of 'The Ballad' in two ways. First of all, Wilde was only too aware that his vindictive résumé of Douglas's crimes against their love had been to some extent calculated to kill that love, and so the poem's famous refrain must partly derive from that bitter knowledge. And second, the

melody of recrimination which Wilde developed in the prose of
De Profundis was transposed into a new key in the verse that
followed a few months later. The banshee note which he struck
on his own behalf in the letter found an even more effective
pitch in the ballad when it came into play on behalf of Trooper
Charles Thomas Wooldridge, the man for whom the hangman
donned his gardening gloves exactly one year before Wilde took
up his pen in July 1897:

> Some love too little, some too long,
>   Some sell, and others buy;
> Some do the deed with many tears,
>   And some without a sigh:
> For each man kills the thing he loves,
>   Yet each man does not die.
>
> He does not die a death of shame
>   On a day of dark disgrace,
> Nor have a noose about his neck,
>   Nor a cloth upon his face,
> Nor drop feet foremost through the floor
>   Into an empty space.
>
> He does not sit with silent men
>   Who watch him night and day;
> Who watch him when he tries to weep,
>   And when he tries to pray;
> Who watch him lest himself should rob
>   The prison of its prey . . .
>
> He does not feel that sickening thirst
>   That sands one's throat, before
> The hangman with his gardener's gloves
>   Comes through the padded door,
> And binds one with three leathern thongs,
>   That the throat may thirst no more.

By keening the trooper, Wilde was keening himself, unrestrain-
edly and understandably; and the suffering man in him pre-

ferred not to recognize what the creating mind did surely know, namely, that for the purposes of his ballad, less would have been more. Indeed, the extent to which Wilde had been driven off his old aesthetic ground is evident from his remark that the length of the poem was necessary in order to shake confidence in the penal system. Coming from the man who had once declared that style, not sincerity, was the essential, and that the slightest hint of an ethical sympathy was an artistic flaw, this was a most unexpected piece of pleading, and another indication of how much Wilde's confidence in the prerogatives of his art had been shaken.

In bringing to light 'a great, or almost great poem', Yeats cast into the dark not only the propaganda but also those elements which Wilde himself recognized as being 'romantic', yet which he could not help including. And when Wilde says romantic, he is surely not speaking only – or mainly – in a literary historical sense, but is rather acknowledging that the poem springs from his own clandestine emotional life. Yeats, as I have suggested, would seem to have cut the famous line 'each man kills the thing he loves' because it surreptitiously privileged Wilde's own suffering in this regard. But Yeats wisely retained the stanzas in which the claustrophobic intensity of the gaol conditions and the psychological identification between speaker and condemned man work together to produce a haunting statement of the poem's central intuition. It is in these stanzas, in fact, that the intimation of collusion between speaker and condemned man is extended to a point where it implicates the reader as well. Wilde suggests that all of us are secret sharers, accomplices in some original sin of betrayal; and he further suggests that society represents this common pact of shame and cover-up, and that society acts hypocritically when it ostracizes and condemns those whom it brands as deviants. The deviant, in fact, is the true representative of the way people are:

> At last the dead man walked no more
> Amongst the Trial Men,

And I knew that he was standing up
  In the black dock's dreadful pen,
And that never would I see his face
  In God's sweet world again.

Like two doomed ships that pass in storm
  We had crossed each other's way:
But we made no sign, we said no word,
  We had no word to say;
For we did not meet in the holy night
  But in the shameful day.

A prison wall was round us both,
  Two outcast men we were:
The world had thrust us from its heart,
  And God from out His care:
And the iron gin that waits for Sin
  Had caught us in its snare.

What is powerful and attractive here is just what distinguishes all the best parts of the narrative, namely, a crossing of the Victorian convention of melodramatic recitation with matter far more personal and distressful. Wilde's own public humiliation is recalled with great economy in his invocation of the 'black dock's dreadful pen', and his preference for 'the holy night' over 'the shameful day' maintains a defence of the homoerotic life in face of the world's total rejection. Obviously, in one way, there is something entirely conventional about the subject of murder and retribution, the setting of gaol yard and gaol cell, the cast of warder and hangman and chaplain, the dreadful props of gallows and quicklimed grave – all of these things belong in the tradition of the broadside ballad. But they are also like the elements of a *fin de siècle* nightmare, recurrent terrors in the recurrent dream of this man who has *not* come through. For it has to be said that neither the protagonist of the ballad nor its narrator finds any absolution. The poem's true subject is entrapment, intimacy and collusion. In spite of the deliberate echoes of Dante, and the allusion to souls in pain enduring their allotted spell in the great gallery of purgation; and in spite of the way Christ is invoked near the end of the poem, as a redemptive force who will obliterate the mark of Cain from the guardsman's soul – in spite of these affirmative gestures, the poem can bestow no final liberation upon either the speaker or the condemned man, 'each in his numbered tomb', because the speaker *is* the condemned man. The ties that bind them, erotic and conspiratorial, survive the execution and will not admit of being loosened.

In a ballad like 'Barbara Allen', for example, the traditional image of roses and briars entwined in a true lovers' knot resolves the tragedy of the lovers by subsuming them into the salubrious diurnal processes of nature, but when this image appears in Wilde's poem, it resolves nothing:

> But neither milk-white rose nor red
> > May bloom in prison-air;
> The shard, the pebble, and the flint,
> > Are what they give us there:
> For flowers have been known to heal
> > A common man's despair.

> So never will wine-red rose or white,
> > Petal by petal, fall
> On that stretch of mud and sand that lies
> > By the hideous prison-wall,
> To tell the men who tramp the yard
> > That God's Son died for all.

Wilde's roses are spectral blooms, more suggestive of a cursed than a blessed condition. They bind rather than absolve the living and the dead. They are like the red lips in Wilfred Owen's accusatory poem 'Red Lips Are Not So Red', another work where a conventionally romantic image is being made to serve a disturbingly subversive purpose. When Owen wrote of the casualties in Flanders that 'Red lips are not so red / As the stained stones kissed by the English dead', he robbed the lips of their romantic mystique in much the same way as Wilde leached the traditional consolation out of the roses.

Indeed, Wilde's situation in Reading Gaol as poet and witness prefigured the case of those poets who found themselves condemned to the horror of the trenches during World War One. His physical experience of conditions in a Victorian prison, his exposure to a brutality in the lower depths which was matched only by the complacency and impassiveness to be found at higher levels, his recognition of how ruthlessly society covered up its atrocious base, all this put into question the categories of Art and Beauty which had been the fixed stars of his life up to that point. Like much twentieth-century war poetry, 'The Ballad of Reading Gaol' was written in order to warn and it could almost have carried as an epigraph a famous sentence from Owen's draft introduction in which he declared: 'Above all, I am not concerned with Poetry.' It could almost have carried this epigraph, but not quite, because 'Poetry' in the old nineties sense had not been abandoned by Wilde, and kept cutting into the minatory tones of the core poem like a Muzak station broadcasting on a different wavelength. It's hardly fair to quote from these weaker parts, but it is nevertheless instructive. Here, for example, is Wilde evoking the nightmare mood endured by prisoners in the gaol once they knew a hanging was about to take place. 'The Crooked Shapes of terror crouched,/ In the corners where we lay', says the speaker, and goes on:

> They glided past, they glided fast
> Like travellers in a mist.
> They mocked the moon in a rigadoon
> Of delicate turn and twist,
> And with formal pace and loathsome grace
> The phantoms kept their tryst.
>
> With mop and mow we saw them go,
> Slim shadows hand in hand:
> About, about, in ghastly rout

They trod a saraband:
And the dammed grotesques made arabesques,
Like wind upon the sand.

Wilde liked to think of the ballad as the cry of Marsyas, but this sounds like the strings of Mantovani. It is closer to being an elaboration of the melodies of Coleridge's 'Rime of the Ancient Mariner' than a response to the screams of the flogged prisoner that Wilde had heard coming from the basement of Reading Gaol on 15 May 1897, three days before his own release. The victim was a half-demented soldier whom the doctors regarded as a malingerer and whom some visiting justices had consequently sentenced to twenty-four lashes. Wilde was naturally deeply affected by this, and by the sight of three children waiting to be assigned to their cells at about that same time. They had been convicted of snaring rabbits and were unable to pay their fines. 'I would have saved them if I could', Lord Byron had said in similar circumstances. Wilde did a bit better; he wrote on their behalf to the *Daily Chronicle* and endeavoured to have the fines paid. But the spectacle of children being consigned to gaol just as he was about to emerge must have brought back the trauma and humiliation of his own early experience of the penal system and quickened the ethical impulse behind the ballad.

During his trials in 1895, Wilde had been magnificent in the dock and had conducted himself with as much dramatic style as any Irish patriot ever did; but he was savagely trampled upon by the system and was to endure far more merciless and spirit-breaking treatment than a convicted felon like John Mitchel, for example, who was at least treated as a civilized adult by the authorities on his prison ship. In Wilde's case, nothing was mitigated. He was issued with prison clothes. He ate porridge and bread and suet pudding in insufficient quantities. He slept on a plank bed. He walked the treadmill. He picked oakum. He had no writing materials, no books. He suffered from diarrhoea. He suffered from earache. Insomnia and hunger reduced him to a

physical wreck. He wept easily and was for months in a state of
nervous collapse, at the mercy of brutal warders who exercised
their authority with petty ferocity:

> We tore the tarry rope to shreds
>   With blunt and bleeding nails;
> We rubbed the doors, and scrubbed the floors,
>   And cleaned the shining rails:
> And, rank by rank, we soaped the plank,
>   And clattered with the pails.
>
> We sewed the sacks, we broke the stones,
>   We turned the dusty drill:
> We banged the tins, and bawled the hymns,
>   And sweated on the mill:
> But in the heart of every man
>   Terror was lying still.
>
> So still it lay that every day
>   Crawled like a weed-clogged wave:
> And we forgot the bitter lot
>   That waits for fool and knave,
> Till once, as we tramped in from work,
>   We passed an open grave.
>
> With yawning mouth the yellow hole
>   Gaped for a living thing;
> The very mud cried out for blood
>   To the thirsty asphalte ring:
> As we knew that ere one dawn grew fair
>   Some prisoner had to swing.
>
> Right in we went, with soul intent
>   On Death and Dread and Doom:
> The hangman, with his little bag,
>   Went shuffling through the gloom:
> And each man trembled as he crept
>   Into his numbered tomb.

'The Ballad of Reading Gaol' is Wilde's poem of human solidarity, his attempt to produce, in Kafka's great phrase, a book that would be an axe to break the frozen sea in each of us. But the literary fact of the matter is that the axe which is still capable of shattering the surfaces of convention is neither the realistic ballad which Yeats fashioned nor the original romantic plea from which he extracted it; it is rather the hard-edged, unpathetic prose that Wilde created in dialogues like 'The Decay of Lying' and dramas like *The Importance of Being Earnest*. His brilliant paradoxes, his over-the-topness at knocking the bottom out of things, the rightness of his wrong-footing, all that exhilarated high-wire word-play, all that freedom to affront and exult in his own uniqueness – that was Wilde's true path towards solidarity. The lighter his touch, the more devastating his effect. When he walked on air, he was on solid ground. But when he stepped on earth to help the plight of lesser mortals, he became Oisin rather than Oscar. His strength dwindled and his distinction vanished. He became like other men. He became one of the chain-gang poets, a broken shadow of the brilliant littérateur who had once written that 'Lying, the telling of beautiful untrue things, is the proper aim of Art.' By the time he wrote the ballad, however, his aim had come to be the telling of the ugly true things:

> The vilest deeds like poison weeds,
>   Bloom well in prison air;
> It is only what is good in Man
>   That wastes and withers there:
> Pale Anguish keeps the heavy gate,
>   And the Warder is Despair.
>
> For they starve the little frightened child
>   Till it weeps both night and day:
> And they scourge the weak and flog the fool,
>   And gibe the old and grey,
> And some grow mad, and all grow bad,
>   And none a word may say.

Each living cell in which we dwell
Is a foul and dark latrine,
And the fetid breath of living Death
Chokes up each grated screen,
And all, but Lust, is turned to dust
In Humanity's machine.

All the same, if the propagandist ballad is not Oscar Wilde's proper genre, it is still a kind of writing which was naturally available to him from the start. His mother, Jane Francesca Elgee, had begun her writing career in Dublin in the 1840s with a series of fiery patriotic poems published in the *Dublin Magazine*. Writing under the pseudonym of 'Speranza' and under the impression that her family name, Elgee, meant that she was descended from the Alighieri family – as in Dante Alighieri – the future Lady Wilde composed poems that proclaimed a heartfelt sympathy for the plight of the famine victims in Ireland and a firebrand's enthusiasm for the cause of rebellion against British rule. Speranza herself, of course, was from a well-to-do Dublin Unionist background, so her association with Charles Gavan Duffy and other activists and intellectuals in the circle was already an act of rebellion, an embrace of the forbidden other which foreshadowed her son's more extreme rejection of the conventional pieties. And Oscar in his turn was very much in favour of the company she had kept. In a lecture which he gave in San Francisco in 1882 during his famous American tour, he was emphatic about his admiration for those revolutionaries of 1848. His lecture notes survive and contain declarations like the following:

As regards these men of forty-eight, I look on their work with peculiar reverence and love, for I was indeed trained by my mother to love and reverence them, as a catholic child is the saints of the calendar. The earliest hero of my childhood was Smith O'Brien, whom I remember well – tall and stately with a dignity of one who had fought for a noble idea and the sadness of one who had failed . . . John Mitchel, too, on his return to Ireland I saw, at my father's table with his eagle eye and impassioned manner. Charles Gavan Duffy is one of my friends in

London, and the poets among them were men who made lives noble poems also ... The greatest of them all, and one of the best poets of this century in Europe was, I need not say, Thomas Davis. Born in the year 1814 at Mallow in County Cork, before he was thirty years of age, he and the other young men of the *Nation* newspaper had, to use Father Burke's eloquent words, created 'by sheer power of Irish intellect, by sheer strength of Irish genius, a national poetry and a national literature which no other nation can equal.'

It would have been no surprise if, after this, Wilde had gone on to write a poem of his own called 'To Ireland in the Coming Times', where he might have wanted himself to be accounted, like Yeats, 'one / With Davis, Mangan, Ferguson' and recognized as the 'True brother of a company / That sang to sweeten Ireland's wrong, / Ballad and story, rann and song.' But it was surely the very deep-seatedness of Wilde's familiarity with nineteenth-century Irish patriotic poetry that made him less susceptible to it as a mode of expression. Yeats was converted to Irish themes by the sudden glamour and admirable literary intelligence of John O'Leary, but for Wilde these themes were always a given, if passed-over, element in his heritage. And, of course, he was every bit as aware as Yeats ever was of the artistic inadequacies of the work done by the *Nation* poets, an awareness he veiled very graciously in San Francisco when it came to reading poems by Speranza herself:

Of the quality of Speranza's poems I, perhaps, should not speak, for criticism is disarmed before love, but I am content to abide by the verdict of the nation, which has so welcomed her genius and understood the song – noticeably for its strength and simplicity – that ballad of my mother's on 'The Trial of The Brothers Sheares' in '98.

This ballad about the trial of two brothers Wilde then proceeded to read and, in the light of all we know today, it was a most significant choice. Yet even at the time of the San Francisco reading, in 1882, long before Wilde's own trials, it must already have had a special personal meaning for him. It had been placed first, after all, in Lady Wilde's first collection of poems when it appeared in 1864. Oscar was then ten years of age and would have been deeply susceptible to the dedication page of the volume which read, 'Dedicated to my sons Willie and Oscar Wilde'; the page also carried the following quotation:

> I made them indeed
> Speak plain the word country. I taught them no doubt
> That a country's a thing men should die for at need.

In a book dedicated to them with such patriotic fervour, Oscar and Willie could hardly have failed to take to heart a poem actually called 'The Brothers', positioned so unignorably at the front of the collection. In it, the two protagonists are awaiting sentence for their part in the rebellion:

> They are pale, but it is not fear that whitens
>   On each proud, high brow,
> For the triumph of the martyr's glory brightens
>   Around them even now . . .

> IV
> Before them, shrinking, cowering, scarcely human,
>   The base informer bends,
> Who, Judas-like, could sell the blood of true men
>   While he clasped their hand as friends.

Clearly, it is not such a long poetic step from this story of the betrayal of noble youth by the handclasp of a friend to a realization that 'each man kills the thing he loves'; nor is it possible to ignore the correspondence between this fictional court with its sentenced brother and informer witness – between this and the actual court where the testimony of rent boys would be crucial in securing the conviction of one of the brothers to whom Speranza's ballad was so pointedly addressed. I am suggesting, in other words, that Oscar's bearing, years later, in the 'black dock's dreadful pen' may well have been affected by the noble demeanour of the character in his mother's poem.

Moreover, Lady Wilde's example in life was every bit as passionate and unworldly as her exempla in literature. Not only did she approve of Oscar's staying in England to face the scandal of trial after his first suit against Queensberry; she had herself behaved with a similar lack of regard for her personal freedom during two crucial trials in her own earlier life. On each of those occasions her conduct combined, in an admirable way, the honourable and the histrionic. The circumstances of these trials were outlined in detail by Terence de Vere White in his excellent 1967 book called *The Parents of Oscar Wilde* and they were also, of course, placed succinctly and suggestively in context by Richard Ellmann in his biography. Suffice it to say that on two celebrated occasions, first in 1848 during the political trials of her journalist associates at the *Nation* and then in 1864 during a libel action which highlighted her husband's reputation as a sexual adventurer, Lady Wilde had behaved with great style. On the former occasion, in an attempt to implicate herself and exonerate the accused editors, she had intervened in the court's proceedings from the public gallery and declared her responsibility in the crime they were accused of, a declaration which the court chose to ignore; then again, during the libel action, she had established an unassailable level of hauteur when she said that she regarded all the scandal surrounding her husband as a fabrication. And on the occasion of Sir William's death she showed a similar capacity for loyalty, decorum and panache when she allowed a veiled woman, obviously the mother of one of Sir William's illegitimate children, to come to pay her respects in the Wilde house.

I called this lecture 'Speranza in Reading' because I wanted to draw attention to these parallels and foreshadowings and coincidences of style and behaviour between mother and son. It's not that there is anything new in noticing the resemblance; it's just that, by recalling it, the provenance of the ballad is illuminated even if its stylistic faults are not extenuated. But I also wanted to talk about the 'The Ballad of Reading Gaol' because it represents a kind of work not usually discussed within the academy. Its effects are probably deemed too broad, its popularity too misplaced, its status within Wilde's oeuvre too insecure to warrant serious consideration. And yet, for all that, the poem does give credence to the idea of poetry as a mode of redress. In it, Wilde the aesthete was stripped of his dandy's clothes to become Wilde the convict; the Dives of the coteries was compelled to know life as the Lazarus of the underworld. The master of the light touch came to submit to the heaviness of being and came, as a result, to leave his fingerprints on a great subject.

That image of fingerprints is another of Richard Ellmann's contributions to our appreciation of the poem, and one of his most illuminating, since it suggests that the poem works by stealth and succeeds in implicating the reader as accomplice, *hypocrite lecteur, mon semblable, mon frère*. Wilde summonses the guilty thing in the self as well as in society: the poem not only condemns the penal system but also insinuates that each reader is guilty within the cell of his or her secret being. The relatively objective ballad which Yeats excerpted from the original does have a powerful and passionate quality of the kind that he himself would have aimed for; but the ballad which Wilde wrote, while it is more self-indulgent and confiding, lodges a plea and generates a sympathy which are uniquely disturbing.

26 October 1993

A Torchlight Procession of One:
On Hugh MacDiarmid

Christopher Murray Grieve took the pseudonym Hugh Mac-
Diarmid in 1922 and between then and his death in 1978
turned himself into one of the most excessive writers of the
twentieth century. His *Complete Poems*, in two volumes, run to
some 1500 pages and represent only a fraction of his total
output; the prose is more voluminous still, for MacDiarmid was
a journalist and controversialist from his teenage years and
made his living by producing copy for newspapers and under-
taking commissions for a variety of full-length books. The work
as a whole reveals a disconcerting unevenness, but the quality
of his best poetry and the historic importance of his whole
endeavour mean that MacDiarmid deserves more attention
than he has received outside his native Scotland.

MacDiarmid's position in Scottish literature and culture is in
many respects analogous to that of Yeats in Ireland, and the
liberationist ambitions of Irish writers were always of great
importance to him. His linguistic overweening was hugely
encouraged by the example of Joyce, whilst Yeats and other
post-Revival writers continued to be highly influential in his
programme of cultural nationalism. One could even say that
MacDiarmid achieved for Scotland what the combined efforts
of the Gaelic League and the Literary Revival achieved for
Ireland: first of all, he effected a reorientation of attitudes to the
country's two indigenous languages, the Scots Gaelic of the
Highlands and Islands and the vernacular Scots of the Borders
and Lowlands. And secondly, MacDiarmid also more or less
singlehandedly created a literature in one of these languages,
and acted as an inspiration for the poet who was to change the
course of poetry in the other.

In the 1920s, MacDiarmid himself emerged fully fledged as a

writer of lyric genius in the language he had invented and which he called Synthetic Scots; in the 1930s, his friendship with Sorley MacLean helped MacLean to fare forward and become the redemptive genius of modern poetry in Gaelic. Within the contemporary conditions, in other words, MacDiarmid demonstrated the artistic possibilities of the indigenous speech and in so doing brought to the fore what he called 'lapsed or unrealized qualities' in the two linguistic heritages which corresponded 'to "unconscious" elements in a distinctive Scottish psychology'. All in all, his practice and example have had an inestimable influence on the history of Scottish writing in particular, and Scottish culture in general over the last fifty years. There is a demonstrable link between MacDiarmid's act of cultural resistance in the Scotland of the 1920s and the literary self-possession of writers such as Alasdair Gray, Tom Leonard, Liz Lochhead and James Kelman in the 1980s and 1990s. He prepared the ground for a Scottish literature that would be self-critical and experimental in relation to its own inherited forms and idioms, but one that would also be stimulated by developments elsewhere in world literature.

MacDiarmid, then, was an inspirational writer whose artistic achievement remains problematic. He was a communist and a nationalist, a propagandist and a plagiarist, a drinker and a messer, and he carried out all these roles with immense panache. He made enemies with as much flair as he made friends. He was a Stalinist and a chauvinist, he was Anglophobic and arrogant, but the very excessiveness which he constantly manifested, the exorbitant quality that marked everything he did, also charged his positive achievements and gave them real staying power. To put it another way, MacDiarmid possessed that 'forcibleness' which Sir Philip Sidney judged to be the ultimately distinguishing mark of poetry itself, although it was a forcibleness which revealed itself as unmistakably in the aggravations and affronts of his work as in its triumphs.

So the negative things that can be said about MacDiarmid's poetry do not invalidate his achievement, nor would they have greatly disturbed the poet himself. He was very clear-headed about his productions and in the 1960s wrote to a BBC producer as follows: 'My job, as I see it, has never been to lay a tit's egg, but to erupt like a volcano, emitting not only flame, but a lot of rubbish.' From a person of less abundant capacity and with a less compulsive appetite for overdoing things, this could have sounded like an excuse; from MacDiarmid, however, it emerges as a boast. With him, the speech from the dock is sure to be a roar of defiance. No wonder Norman MacCaig suggested that the anniversary of his death should be marked each year by the observance of two minutes of pandemonium. 'He would walk into my mind,' MacCaig said at the graveside in Langholm in 1978, 'as if it were a town and he a torchlight procession of one, lighting up the streets . . .'

Still, although his vitality was epoch-making, MacDiarmid has probably written more disconcertingly than any other major twentieth-century poet. Anybody who wishes to praise the work has to admit straight away that there is an un-get-roundable connection between the prodigality of his gifts and the prodigiousness of his blather. The task for everybody confronted with the immense bulk of his collected verse is to make a firm distinction between the true poetry and what we might call the habitual printout. And then there are the questions that arise because of his magpie habits of composition (or is it modernist collage?): the silent incorporation into his own text of the texts of others, sometimes of a technical nature, sometimes discursive, sometimes even literary, the most notorious case here being the eight-line lyric entitled 'Perfect', which – depending upon how much of a critical Malvolio you want to be – can be regarded as either a found poem or a plagiarism from a story by Glyn Thomas. Even if all that mileage of earnest, pedantic and notoriously problematic verse does not disqualify him from the league of the major talents, it does prevent him from being regarded as 'a master'. If we call a writer a master, it suggests an oeuvre with a kind of roundedness and finish that MacDiarmid did not even aspire to. He was more devoted to opening salvoes than finishing touches; and even though as a poet he must have approved the idea that every force evolves its form, he was one of those whose faculties rally more naturally to the banner of force.

So the volcanic image he used about himself was entirely appropriate, and, in fact, MacDiarmid the poet was himself the result of an eruption. In 1922 he emerged like a new and fiery form out of the agitated element of Christopher Grieve's imagination; or it could be said with equal justification that he emerged from the awakened energies of the Scots language itself. These had been long dormant as a literary resource until they were stirred into fresh activity when Grieve encountered a learned monograph entitled *Lowland Scotch as Spoken in the Lower Stratheam District of Perthshire* and wrote his first poem in a new version of that old speech. And it was at this moment that he took the pseudonym Hugh MacDiarmid, as if he knew instinctively that he had been born again, as if his boydeeds as a literary figure were now over and he had discovered his heroic name and destiny. MacDiarmid arrived as a fully developed phenomenon, one who both produced and was produced by the language he wrote in, henceforth to be known variously as Synthetic Scots or Vernacular Scots or the Doric. And the first poem of the new language was called 'The Watergaw':

> Ae weet forenicht i' the yow-trummle
> I saw yon antrin thing,
> A watergaw wi' its chitterin' licht
> Ayont the on-ding;
> An' I thocht o' the last wild look ye gied
> Afore ye deed!
>
> There was nae reek i' the laverock's hoose
> That nicht – an' nane i' mine;
> But I hae thocht o' that foolish licht
> Ever sin' syne;
> An' I think that mebbe at last I ken
> What your look meant then.

The poet's biographer, Alan Bold, records how these lines came about, when Grieve focused upon two pages of Sir James Wilson's researches in the book I have just mentioned:

Most of the words in 'The Watergaw' ... came from two pages of Wilson's work. Yow-trummle ('cold weather in July after shearing'), watergaw ('indistinct rainbow') and on-ding ('beating rain or snow') are all on one page; the first phrase of the second stanza 'There was nae reek i' the laverock's hoose / That nicht' appears in Wilson's list of Proverbs and Sayings ... where it is glossed as 'There's no smoke in the lark's house to night (said when the night is cold and stormy).

The use Grieve made of these found elements was a far cry from the kind of busy transcription out of dictionaries and reference books which would disfigure so much of his later work in English. In 1922, however, what the recorded words and expressions did was to stretch a tripwire in the path of Grieve's auditory imagination so that he was pitched headlong into his linguistic unconscious, into a network of emotional and linguistic systems that had been in place since childhood. The common speech of his subcultural life as a youngster in Dumfriesshire was suddenly ratified by the authority of scholarship. His little self, the dialect creature at the core of his adult speech, began to hear itself amplified within a larger historical acoustic. Grieve turned into MacDiarmid when he realized that his writing identity depended for its empowerment upon his securing an ever deepening access to those primary linguistic strata in his own and his country's memory. And this sense of a nascent truth, of a something not quite clearly apprehended but very definitely experienced, is exactly what is embodied in 'The Watergaw'. Its real subject is the uncanny. The watergaw, the faint rainbow glimmering in chittering light, provides a sort of epiphany, and MacDiarmid connects the shimmer and weakness and possible revelation in the light behind the drizzle with the indecipherable look he received from his father on his deathbed. But how the poem sounds is probably more important than what it sees. What constitutes the true originality here is the combined sensation of strangeness and at-homeness which the words create. Each expression, each cadence, each rhyme is as surely and reliably in place as a stone on a hillside. The words themselves are uncanny: whether or not their dictionary meaning is understood, it is hard to resist their phonetic allure, their aura of a meaning which has been intuited but not yet quite formulated. Just as the dying father's look transmitted a definite if mysterious promise of revelation, so, on the verge of its disappearance as a living speech, the old language rallies and delivers a new poetry for the future.

What happened in 'The Watergaw', of course, and in other famous lyrics that followed it such as 'The Eemis Stane' and 'Wheesht, Wheesht' and 'The Bonnie Broukit Bairn', was what typically happens in lyric poetry of the purest sort. Suddenly the thing chanced upon comes forth as the thing predestined: the unforeseen appears as the inevitable. The poem's words seem always to have belonged together and to have enjoyed a distinct existence apart from all other words. Here, for example, is another one of those lyrics upon which MacDiarmid's fame rests, a very short one called 'The Bonnie Broukit Bairn'. The bairn or baby in question is the earth itself, which is distinguished here from other planets by its ability to 'greet', which is to say its ability to weep or cry like an infant. The crimson aura of Mars and the green luminosity of Venus represent one kind of beauty. But earth's beauty is different, since earth is the site of human suffering, and this gives it a more grievous and vulnerable presence in the firmament than any of the other planets. 'Crammasy' means crimson, 'gowden' feathers are golden feathers, 'wheen o' blethers' is a pack of nonsense, 'broukit bairn' is a neglected baby, and the 'haill clanjamfrie' is the whole bloody lot of them.

> Mars is braw in crammasy,
> Venus in a green silk goun,
> The auld mune shak's her gowden feathers,
> Their starry talk's a wheen o' blethers,

Nane for thee a thochtie sparin',
Earth, thou bonnie broukit bairn!
– *But greet, an' in your tears ye'll droun*
The haill clanjamfrie!

When he wrote this poem, Grieve was thirty-one years of age, a working journalist with an intense commitment to cultural and political renewal within Scotland, which for him boiled down to resisting and reversing the influence and impositions of English standards and English ways. Born in 1892 in the town of Langholm in Dumfriesshire, he was the first child of a postman father who had died young in 1910. His mother came from farming stock and had revealed her own gift for the demotic when she described the newborn poet as 'an eaten and spewed lookin' wee thing wi' een like twa burned holes in a blanket.' After being educated locally and having read, by his own account, everything in the local Carnegie Library, Grieve went at the age of sixteen to a teacher training college in Edinburgh, an institution from which he was forced to withdraw because of an escapade involving the theft of the headmaster's books. From then on, he made his living as a migrant journalist, although it has to be admitted that the migrancy was helped along by Grieve's innate gift for falling out with bosses and his rapidly developing capacity as a whisky drinker. Be that as it may, between January 1911 (when he quit college in Edinburgh) and July 1915 (when he joined the British Army and went off to serve with the Medical Corps in Salonika) Christopher Grieve had worked with the *Edinburgh Evening Despatch*, the *Monmouthshire Labour News*, the *Clydebank and Renfrew Press*, the *Fife Herald*, and the *Fife Coast Chronicle*. He had also read voraciously and had contributed articles to the journal which was to be central to his whole intellectual development, A. R. Orage's *The New Age*. Through contact with Orage and his magazine, he was led to read, among others, Nietzsche and Bergson, and was as deeply susceptible to the Nietzschean injunction 'Become what thou art' as he was to Bergson's claim that it was creative urge rather than natural selection which promoted the evolutionary process. But for Grieve to become what he was would mean becoming MacDiarmid, which in turn would mean achieving a Scottish identity long repressed by Anglocentric attitudes and standard English speech: the evolutionary process would have to be creative at both personal and political levels.

He returned from the war with a gradually clarifying pro-gramme and developed into a propagandist for a new Scottish Idea, something that would take off from and reflect in literary terms Whitman's democratic American idea and Yeats's cultural nationalism; whilst in the political sphere, the project for a new Scotland would be fired by Lenin's communism and by a vestig-ial but emotionally decisive predisposition to the Christian way of redemption through self-sacrifice. Grieve, moreover, had been initiated into the rough and tumble of politics during a miners' strike in Wales in 1911, and after that through his contacts with socialist activists in Scotland, people like John MacLean and James Maxton; so naturally he was deeply stirred by the Easter Rising in Dublin in 1916 and the Bolshevik Revolution in Russia the following year, two events which had a powerful impact on the way he would henceforth imagine the future, both nationally and internationally.

There was generosity as well as ferocity in MacDiarmid's es-pousals, and it is well to be reminded that behind his habitual self-promotions there was a constant desire to be of service. As Douglas Sealy observed in a recent review, he had a calling which he served rather than a career which he worked at. By 1922, at any rate, Christopher Grieve had perfected his idiom as a polemicist and propagandist and was ready for pupation into Hugh MacDiarmid, a creature he would later variously describe as the 'stone among the pigeons' and 'the catfish that vitalizes the other torpid denizens of the aquarium.' Here he is, getting into his stride in an editorial in the first number of the *Scottish Chapbook*, a journal edited by Grieve and devoted to the creation of a new movement in Scottish literature:

Scottish literature, like all other literatures, has been *written* almost exclusively by blasphemers, immoralists, dipsomaniacs, and madmen, but, unlike most other literatures, has been *written about* almost exclusively by ministers, with, on the whole, an effect similar to that produced by the statement (of the worthy Dr John McIntosh) that 'as a novelist, Robert Louis Stevenson had the art of rendering his writings interesting', and 'his faculty of description was fairly good'.

This prose was fired off in 1922, and represents Grieve in typically provocative form: zesty, head-on, fiercely devoted to eliciting a response. His polemical writings had all the trouble-making tactics of a dangerman in a bar, stripped to his shirt-sleeves and squaring up to anyone and everyone. Protest and crusade rather than nostalgia and pathos were the hallmarks of his new commitment to the old words. There was nothing backward-looking in the impulse, for MacDiarmid was very consciously organizing a new movement in literature and revealing the ambitions of an experimenter: he could never have been accused of subscribing to some form of arrested linguistic development. Synthetic Scots was not simply meant to give audiences the pleasures of self-recognition, for that could lead to the sentimentality and self-indulgence which MacDiarmid wanted to banish from the culture altogether. Nor was his first purpose to proclaim the superior vitality of the local language over the compromised and compromising idiom of standardized modern English. These things might be incidental to his effort, but central to it was the challenge of jump-starting a language interrupted by history (as Douglas Dunn has called it) and getting it into modern running order. In fact, MacDiarmid's ways with the old words were as revolutionary and self-conscious as the young Ezra Pound's ways with a diction based upon archaism and a translatorese derived from Anglo-Saxon, Latin and Chinese originals. And there was also something in his practice which corresponded to the poetics of Robert Frost, in so far as the thing that MacDiarmid was after in the deep Scottish ear resembled what Frost called 'the sound of sense', a phonetic patterning which preceded speech and authenticated it, a kind of pre-verbal register to which the poetic voice had to be tuned.

What gave these ideas and hopes credibility was not, however, MacDiarmid's forcible personality, but rather the astonishing poem which he published in 1926 called *A Drunk Man Looks at the Thistle*. The title tells all that a reader needs to know before plunging in: this is an encounter between an intoxicated imagination and everything which that imagination can invent by meditation upon the national symbol of Scotland. At one moment, for example, the thistle has a mainly domestic and negative meaning, and is perceived by the drunk man as part and parcel of Scottish kitsch, of a piece with tartan for tourists, Burns suppers, haggises, Harry Lauder and every kind of Caledonian corniness. But at another moment it becomes the *yggdrasil*, the world-tree, a cosmic symbol that allows for poetry that is more visionary than satiric, a poetry of great sweep and intellectual resonance which nevertheless still keeps its ear to the native ground. In these lines towards the end of the poem, for example, you can hear the reassuring democratic measure of the ballad stanza; but you can also hear something more stately and deeply orchestrated. There is a stereophonic scope to the music, as if the *gravitas* of the medieval Scots poet William Dunbar were echoing within the stellar reaches of Dante's *Divine Comedy*. (The word 'hain' here, incidentally, means to keep or preserve, and 'toom' to empty out, but what is more important than these details of sense is the verity of the tone of the whole passage.)

> The stars like thistle's roses floo'er
> The sterile growth o' Space ootour,
> That clad in bitter blasts spreids oot
> Frae me, the sustenance o' its root.
>
> O fain I'd keep my hert entire,
> Fain hain the licht o' my desire,
> But ech, the shinin' streams ascend,
> And leave me empty at the end.

For aince it's toomed my hert and brain
The thistle needs maun fa' again.
– But a' its growth'll never fill
The hole it's turned my life intill! . . .

Yet hae I silence left, the croon o' a'.

Through the deep reach of this poem's music, through its associative range and its inclusion of haunting translations from Russian and French sources, MacDiarmid served notice that his sympathies and concerns were not confined to the local scene, and that his outrage at the condition of Scotland was just an aspect of his longing for a totally transformed life for all human beings on the planet. In other words, if MacDiarmid did have a nostalgia, it was the one which Osip Mandelstam embraced, a 'nostalgia for world culture'.

And yet *A Drunk Man* could hardly be described as a solemn bid in the high-cultural stakes. On the contrary, what distinguishes it is its inspired down-to-earthness. It has a huge improvisational energy and is driven forward by an impetuous anti-Establishment urge. Even though this impetuousness is an effect of the poem's style, it seems paradoxically to manifest an impatience with the very idea of style *per se*. The overriding impression is that the poem has too much business to get through to be bothered with merely literary considerations. It can be as close to doggerel as to Dante – and get away with it. Here, for instance, are a few lines from a rough-and-tumble section where the drunk man has a vision of the great cosmic wheel, where Scotland and the *dramatis personae* of Scottish history are at once set up and cut down within the perspectives of infinity:

I felt it turn, and syne I saw
John Knox and Clavers in my raw,
And Mary Queen o' Scots ana',

And Robbie Burns and Weelum Wallace
And Carlyle lookin' unco' gallus,

And Harry Lauder (to enthrall us).

And as I looked I saw them a',
A' the Scots baith big and sma',
That e'er the braith o' life did draw.

'Mercy o' Gode, I canna thole
Wi sic an orra mob to roll.'
– 'Wheesht! It's for the guid o' your soul!'

*

'But in this huge ineducable
Heterogeneous hotch and rabble
Why am I condemned to squabble?'

'A Scottish poet maun assume
The burden o' his people's doom,
And dee to brak' their livin' tomb.

Mony ha'e tried, but a' ha'e failed.
Their sacrifice has nocht availed.
Upon the thistle they're impaled!'

The mixture of passion and irreverence is everywhere in *A Drunk Man* and relates it to Irish masterpieces like Brian Merriman's *The Midnight Court* and Patrick Kavanagh's *The Great Hunger*, poems which similarly combine the expression of poetic high spirits, personal outrage and social protest. Merriman's metrical vitality and insinuating intelligence remind me of parallel qualities in the MacDiarmid poem; and Kavanagh's rawer expression of personal and social trauma is also akin to much that is going on in the Scottish work. Yet perhaps the main point is that none of these poems is directly confessional; all of them are more than simply therapeutic. They do get something aggrieved out of their authors' systems, but their purpose is as public as it is personal. They act like their society's immunity systems, going to attack whatever unhealthy or debilitating forces are at work in the body politic. And in this, they manifest poetry's high potential, its function as an agent of possible transformation, of evolution towards that more radiant and generous life which the imagination desires.

This poem is MacDiarmid's masterpiece. Even if his political programme failed to materialize, even if the nationalism and socialism which he espoused found themselves unrealized and unpopular, even if his vernacular republic did not attain constitutional status, the fact is that *A Drunk Man Looks at the Thistle* did achieve the redress of poetry. MacDiarmid created a fully realized, imaginatively coherent work, one that contained such life-enhancing satire, such emotional weight and such specific imaginative gravity that it could be placed in the mind's scales as something both equal to and corrective of the prevailing conditions. It was a magnificent intervention by creative power into an historical situation. Its force was the force of the glimpsed alternative and it still gives credence to MacDiarmid's wonderfully stirring affirmation in another context that poetry is human existence come to life. In the year of its publication, it may have sold only ninety-nine copies, but already it was on its way to that most important audience of all, 'the reader in posterity'. It released in the Scots language what MacDiarmid also accurately called a *vis comica*, a capacity for comedy in the widest sense; it was both a deluge and an overflow, so much so that we might say the poem introduced an almost magical element into Scottish life, the kind represented by the crane bag in old Irish mythology.

The crane bag belonged to Manannan, the god of the sea, and contained every precious thing that he possessed. And then 'when the sea was full, all the treasures were visible in it; but when the fierce sea ebbed, the crane bag was empty.' Similarly, *A Drunk Man Looks at the Thistle* contains all the treasures that might or might not become radiant and life-enhancing within the personal and national life of Scotland. Indeed, there are moments when the drunk man himself seems to have intimations that the poem he is speaking relates to the crane bag myth. In the following stanza, for example, he says that his 'harns' or brains respond to the ebb and flow of inspiration as seaweed responds to the ebb and flow of tides. And the poem itself will be forever correspondingly susceptible to the changing capacities of its audience. Like Manannan's marvellous sporran, it will reveal or retain its treasures, depending upon the fullness or emptiness of the imaginative world in which it subsists:

> My harns are seaweed – when the tide is in
> They swall like blethers and in comfort float,
> But when the tide is oot they lie like gealed
> And runkled auld bluid-vessels in a knot.

The tidal wave of MacDiarmid's verse in Vernacular Scots was to keep running long after he completed *A Drunk Man Looks at the Thistle*, and it sustained him through many other astonishing performances, such as 'Water Music' and 'Tarras' and the title poem of the volume in which these appeared in 1932, *Scots Unbound*. In that book, the poet is in his element, hitting the note and holding the tune with all his old resource and exhilaration. But at this point I must take my leave of MacDiarmid, the Scots 'makar' *redivivus*, and turn, too briefly and in conclusion, to the problematic status of MacDiarmid's vast output of verse in English during the remainder of his always amazing writing life.

I was once told about the entry procedures to be followed at a hospital run by a fundamentalist religious group in Tulsa, Oklahoma: incoming patients are asked to fill out a form which requires them to declare, among other things, the date of their birth, and then, the date of their rebirth. For Grieve, there would have been no problem with this: birth, 1892; rebirth, 1922. But the fact of the matter is that MacDiarmid *qua* Mac-Diarmid could have come up with two sets of dates also, in so far as he was born in Synthetic Scots in 1922 and reborn in English some time around 1933.

Personally, I find this period the most moving in the whole of MacDiarmid's life. These were the years when he lived with his second wife Valda Trevlyn and his newborn son Michael on the small island of Whalsay in the Shetlands. In retreat. Over the top and out of sight, so to speak, both physically and psychologically. Drink, the strain of breaking up with his first wife, political hassles, financial troubles, the tension of personal enmities – in the early 1930s, all of these things brought Mac-Diarmid to the stage of nervous breakdown. But he survived, and his survival had to do with his getting down to the bedrock of his own resources, a bedrock which was reinforced at the time by contact with the stoical fishermen of the Shetland Islands and his at-homeness in the bleakness of the actual geological conditions. Racked by the huge ambitions he had imagined for himself, he now endured the beginnings of an ordeal in his poetic being, one in which the megalomaniac and the marvel-worker vied for the voice of the bard; where the blether of William McGonagall sporadically overwhelmed the strains of Hugh MacDiarmid; where the plagiarist too readily gained an upper hand over the poet; where the sureness of tone and dramatic inevitability which pervade his masterpiece deserted him and a disconcerting unreliability entered his poetic voice. This is the MacDiarmid who breaks the heart because he so often and so enragingly fumbles the job, the poet who can at one moment transport a reader's ear and body into a wonderfully sustaining element, a language pure as air or water, a language which carries the reader (as the truest poetry always does) into the sensation of walking on air or swimming free – but then the air fails or the water drains, a disastrous drop occurs in the vocal and metrical pressure; what was fluent become flaccid, what was detail becomes data and what was poetry becomes pedantry and plagiarism. Such let-downs keep happening at crucial turns in poems which are elsewhere full of lovely clarity and temperate, steady wisdom, poems such as 'Island Funeral' or 'Lament for the Great Music' or 'Direadh III'. And the failure derives in the main from three typical aspects of MacDiarmid's later writing: his increasingly propagandist stance, the uncertainty of his ear outside his native Scots, and his more and more compulsive habit of transcription (perhaps in the end a better term than plagiarism, since his habits were by then so well known to his readership and regarded with such indulgence).

When he wrote *A Drunk Man Looks at the Thistle*, Mac-Diarmid was less tied to the Communist Party line than he would be in years ahead, although there was already a strong admixture of Leninism to corroborate his natural sympathy with the underdog. As time went on, however, Lenin's dream of world revolution gradually became associated in MacDiarmid's mind with the boundary-crossing powers of a new world language, one which he took to be foreshadowed in the experimental, meaning-melting ventures of Joyce's *Finnegans Wake*. Joyce's move from the baby-babble of a Dublin infant at the beginning of *A Portrait of the Artist as a Young Man* to the dream-speak of a world-embracing, multilingual consciousness in *Finnegans Wake* was, for MacDiarmid, a pattern of the way local speech could exfoliate into an all-inclusive world idiom, and be fundamental to the evolution of that higher intellectual and imaginative plane which the revolution would promote. In practice, however, these two writers differed greatly in so far as Joyce's linguistic virtuosity was radically pleasure-seeking and absolved of any didactic purpose, whereas MacDiarmid's attempts at philological inclusiveness were doctrinaire and strenuously politically correct. Unfortunately, too, his identification of himself with the great prophets and projects of modernism led to an astounding self-inflation and to a verse that eventually strayed into megalomaniac fantasy. It even attained a certain monstrous dimension in poems like the 'First Hymn to Lenin' where MacDiarmid declares that the murderous activities of the Cheka (the secret police of the USSR) are a fair price to have to pay for the maintenance of that evolutionary momentum which he and his hero prized so much:

> As necessary, and insignificant, as death
> Wi' a' its agonies in the cosmos still
> The Cheka's horrors are in their degree;

And'll end suner! What maitters 't wha we kill
To lessen that foulest murder that deprives
Maist men o' real lives?

Such a doctrinal extremism marred both the nationalist and internationalist strain in MacDiarmid's thinking all through his life. His Anglophobia, for instance, can be both salubrious and strategic, a natural and allowable consequence of opposition to imperialism, and another consequence of his ambition to relocate the focus and idiom of Scottish literature. But unless it is exercised in the service of his more broadly transformative vision of world language and communist order, the Anglophobia only massages a kind of vindictive nativism, the very opposite of the liberated consciousness he intended to promote. And it can, of course, pass beyond the stage of mere prejudice to arrive at the lunacy of something like the following, taken from one of the late poems in English:

So every loveliness that Scotland has ever known
Or will know, flies into me now,
Out of the perilous night of English stupidity,
As I lie brooding on the fact
That perchance the best chance
Of reproducing the ancient Greek temperament
Would be to 'cross' the Scots with the Chinese.

This flawed poetry of the 1930s and 1940s, with all its technical vocabularies, its Joycean revel in the words and ways of other languages, its insistence on the possibility of harnessing a future-oriented dream of Scottish life to the Gaelic and medieval Scots heritages, its ache to produce a seismic poetry that might include every thing and every language and every discipline – this poetry wanted to go so far beyond the proprieties of English literature that it would come right out the other side of orthodox expression. Yet it is only occasionally that the eerily beautiful, deliberately arcane words with which he confronts the reader attain the kind of inevitability which I praised earlier on in the Scots lyrics. Poems such as 'On a Raised Beach' and 'In a Cornish Garden' do surprise by a fine excess, and word by word they possess a unique multitudinous accuracy and psychedelic richness. Even they, however, totter close to self-parody and only get by through the huge appetite their author displays for matching the multiplicity of the phenomena with a correspondingly cornucopic vocabulary. More often, alas, neither MacDiarmid's lavishness nor his originality can move the data across the frontier of writing. Skewed rhythms, egregious diction, encyclopaedic quotation, sheer monotony – MacDiarmid certainly gave his detractors plenty to work with.

Before I end, therefore, I want to suggest very briefly a way of both respecting and admitting the failure of MacDiarmid's immense epic effort, in projects such as 'Cornish Heroic Song' and 'In Memoriam James Joyce'. Historically, it's worth thinking of these works as being all of a piece with the awesome and sometimes terrible projects of twentieth-century Soviet communism; they are like those gigantic dams and steelworks and tyrannically organized communal farms, every one of them the result of cruel effort, every one a breath-taking conception surviving in the world as something both spectacular and uncherished, evidence of actions at once heroic and doomed. If I exaggerate, it is partly to emphasize the huge amount of MacDiarmid's poetry that remains unread and unassimilated. The journalist and the activist in him would not be quieted, and when there was no outlet for them in prose, they invaded the verse without compunction. Sooner or later, however, what happened to Wordsworth will happen to MacDiarmid: the second phase of his career will be rendered down to a series of self-contained, self-sustaining passages of genuine poetry, disentangled at last from the editorials and encyclicals he launched so indefatigably for more than forty years upon the unresponsive world.

Still, MacDiarmid was right to make the leap towards the impossible. With the publication of his short lyrics in the collections called *Sangschaw* and *Penny Wheep* (in 1925 and 1926 respectively), then *A Drunk Man* in 1926, not to mention *To Circumjack Cencrastus* and *Scots Unbound* in the early 1930s – with the publication of all this work he not only had created a language, but within a decade had endowed it with enough literature to be going on with. But then, in poetry, enough is never enough. To find its true measure, creative talent must exert itself beyond the limit. If MacDiarmid were to continue with the exploration and experiment that had characterized his great decade, he had to get through the barrier of the very excellence he had created. He had to find an idiom that would not make a fetish of the local but would rather transpose the parochial into the planetary. He therefore strove for an all-inclusive mode of utterance, and wrote a loose-weave, discursive, digression-filled verse, prone to off-loading miscellaneous information and opinions, constantly punctuated by disconcerting and abrupt shifts of tone. Although his reasons for this were outlined with exhilarating force in 'The Kind of Poetry I Want' – 'Poetry of such an integration as cannot be effected / Until a new and conscious organization of society / Generates a new view / Of the world as a whole' and so on, – it did not work. These later poems in Synthetic English generally don't have the intensity or oddity or uncanny inevitability of the early work in Scots, even if here and there they do manage to create that double sensation of sure-footed homecoming and light-headed expedition which only the highest poetry achieves. It is surely time, for example, that anthologies of twentieth-century verse – which almost invariably print W. H. Auden's 'In Praise of Limestone' – should also carry something from the luminous, almost biblical reveries of 'On a Raised Beach'. Philip Larkin's *Oxford Book of Twentieth Century English Verse* ignores it, and Larkin's *Selected Letters* give us his candid assessment of MacDiarmid in one sentence, as follows: 'I am so averse from his work I can hardly bring my eyes to the page.' That comes in a letter to Dan Davin at the Oxford University Press, and a couple of weeks later Larkin is asking Anthony Thwaite: 'Is there any bit of MacD that's noticeably less morally repugnant and aesthetically null than the rest?' Thwaite may have given him a few tips, but unfortunately he doesn't seem to have directed his attention to lines like these:

> Nothing has stirred
> Since I lay down this morning an eternity ago
> But one bird. The widest door is the least liable to
>   intrusion,
> Ubiquitous as the sunlight, unfrequented as the sun.
> The inward gates of a bird are always open.
> It does not know how to shut them.
> That is the secret of its song,
> But whether any man's are ajar is doubtful.
> I look at these stones and I know little about them,
> But I know their gates are open too,
> Always open, far longer open, than any bird's can be,
> That every one of them has had its gates wide open far
>   longer
> Than all birds put together, let alone humanity,
> Though through them no man can see,
> No man nor anything more recently born than themselves
> And that is everything else on the Earth.
> I too lying here have dismissed all else.
> Bread from stones is my sole and desperate dearth,
> From stones, which are to the Earth as to the sunlight
> Is the naked sun which is for no man's sight.
> I would scorn to cry to any easier audience
> Or, having cried, lack patience to await the response.

This scorning to cry to an easy audience is, of course, the secret of MacDiarmid's best work. When he was at his artistic best, his appeal was made to an imagined authority, a court of higher spiritual attainment and more illuminated understanding than any he could find around him. And in this, he fulfilled a poetic demand which always precedes and survives the demands of technique and artistic skills. This is the demand that the artist sacrifice himself or herself to an envisaged standard, and what such a demand entails was expressed with great eloquence and persuasiveness by Richard Ellmann when he wrote of the good poetic example of W. B. Yeats: according to Ellmann, in much of his work Yeats 'wishes to show how brute fact may be transmogrified, how we can sacrifice ourselves ... to our imagined selves which offer far higher standards than anything offered by social convention. If we must suffer, it is better to create the world in which we suffer, and this is what heroes do spontaneously, artists do consciously, and all [others] do in their own degree.'

For all his intellectual arrogance and poetic megalomania, MacDiarmid was an approachable and companionable man. The exorbitance and wilfulness of his poetic persona were partly self-inflationary, but they did arise from his conception of the large prophetic role which poetry had to fulfil in Scotland, and in the world of the future. He did not, however, confuse the greatness of the office with the dimensions of his own life as a citizen. When I met him in his later years, he and Valda lived modestly in their cottage in Biggar in Lanarkshire. Their hospitality was very moving, and they had attained a composure which seemed right after the buffeting they had both undergone forty years earlier, when their extreme poverty only intensified what was already an emotional and vocational ordeal. But then and always MacDiarmid was sustained by a faith older and simpler than the one he professed in Marxism. Lenin's utopian vision was undeniably inspirational for him, but deep down in the consciousness of this child of the Bible-reading Scottish Borders, Christ's commandment to people to love one another was surely equally powerful.

22 October 1992

Dylan the Durable?:
On Dylan Thomas

Dylan Thomas is by now as much a case history as a chapter in the history of poetry. Mention of his name is enough to turn on a multi-channel set of associations. There is Thomas the Voice, Thomas the Booze, Thomas the Debts, Thomas the Jokes, Thomas the Wales, Thomas the Sex, Thomas the Lies – in fact there are so many competing and revisionist inventions of Thomas available, so many more or less corrective, reductive, even punitive versions of the phenomenon that it is with a certain tentativeness that one asks whether there is still any place on the roll-call for Thomas the Poet.

Yet it was very much Thomas the Poet that my generation of readers and listeners encountered in our teens. He died at the age of thirty-nine in New York, immediately because of a wrongly prescribed dose of morphine, but inevitably because of years of spectacular drinking, and he died at the height of his fame, at the moment when print culture and the electronic media were perfecting their alliance in the promotion of culture heroes. Indeed, to recollect that moment is to have second thoughts about any easy condescension towards the role of the media in these areas. The records of Dylan Thomas reading his own poems, records which were lined up on the shelves of undergraduate flats all over the world, were important cultural events. They opened a thrilling line between the centre and the edges of the Anglophone world. For all of us young provincials, from Belfast to Brisbane, the impact of Thomas's performance meant that we had a gratifying sense of access to something that was acknowledged to be altogether modern, difficult *and* poetry.

Later, of course, there were second thoughts, but Dylan Thomas will always remain part of the initiation of that first

'eleven-plus' generation into literary culture. He was our Swin-
burne, a poet of immediate spellbinding power. And yet
nowadays he has become very much the Doubted Thomas.
In this lecture, therefore, almost forty years after his death, I
want to ask which parts of his *Collected Poems* retain their
force. In the present climate of taste, his rhetorical surge and
mythopoeic posture are unfashionable, and his bohemi-
anism is probably suspect for all kinds of politically correct
reasons, which only makes it all the more urgent to ask if there
is not still something we can isolate and celebrate as Dylan
the Durable.

Dylan Thomas was both a uniquely gifted writer and a recognizable type. Within the sociology of literature, he was a Welsh
version of what Patrick Kavanagh called in the Irish context a
'bucklepper', which is to say, one who leaps like a young buck.
The bucklepper, as you might guess, is somebody with a stereo-
typical sprightliness and gallivanting roguery, insufficiently
self-aware and not necessarily spurious, but still offering himself or herself too readily as a form of spectator sport. Thomas's
Welshness, his high genius for exaggeration and for entertain-
ment, his immense *joie de vivre* and his infectious love of
poetry, the intoxication (in every sense) of his presence – all of
this qualified him as a fully developed specimen of the buck-
lepping tribe, an image of the Celt as perceived by the Saxon, a
principle of disorder and childish irresponsibility complemen-
tary to the earnest, gormless routines and civility of Albion. But
the clamorous spectacle of a writer like Brendan Behan or
Dylan Thomas quickly becomes, according to Kavanagh, a way
of getting credit as an artist without having to produce the art.
In fact, the very conventionality of Thomas's anti-conventional
behaviour contributed to his being too easily slotted and accom-
modated. He was inevitably co-opted by the literary establishment on both sides of the Atlantic as the in-house bohemian,
and no matter how sympathetic we may find his masquerade
as the lord of misrule, no matter how attractive his reckless-
ness and his mockery of fiscal and social rectitude may

at times appear, it is still regrettable to think of his acting out the allotted role so predictably. Indeed, one's big regret about Thomas is that he did not follow the example of a far sturdier interloper from the Celtic realms, the example, that is, of W. B. Yeats. Yeats in the 1890s punted into the scene on the Celtic current, but, once in the swim, he used his mystique to initiate a counter-cultural move within English poetry itself. Thomas, however, never did have that kind of ambition.

In the end, Thomas's achievement rests upon a number of strong, uniquely estranging, technically original and resonant poems, including one of the best villanelles in the language, and it is to these that I am going to direct my attention in this lecture. His 'play for voices', *Under Milk Wood*, is an idyllic romp, as if *The Joy of Sex* were dreamt under the canvas at a Welsh eisteddfod. It will always occupy an honourable place in that genre which Graham Greene usefully christened 'entertainments', as will his many broadcast talks and stories. But the poems are his definitive achievement. They promote his melodramatic apprehension of language as a physical sensation, as a receiving station for creaturely intimations, cosmic process and sexual impulses. But they also manage to transform such unremarkable obsessions into a mighty percussive verse. No history of English poetry can afford to pass them over. Others may have written like Thomas, but it was never vice versa. Call his work Neo-Romantic or Expressionist or Surrealist, call it apocalyptic or overrated or an aberration, it still remains *sui generis*.

Thomas himself was good at recognizing and describing the real thing although he rarely paused to do so. Vernon Watkins, however, brought out the best in him. Here is Thomas, at twenty-three years of age, writing to Watkins about poems which Watkins had shown him:

Poems. I liked the three you sent me. There is something very unsatisfactory, though, about 'All mists, all thoughts' which seems – using the vaguest words – to lack a central strength. All the words are lovely but they seem so *chosen*, not struck out. I can see the sensitive picking of words, but not the strong inevitable pulling that makes a poem an event, a happening, an action perhaps, not a still life or an experience *put down* . . . They [the words] seem, as indeed the whole poem seems, to come out of the nostalgia of literature . . . A motive has been rarefied; it should be made common. I don't ask you for vulgarity, though I miss it; I think I ask you for a little creative destruction, destructive creation.

This is the voice of somebody who knows what the demands are. There's a wonderful sureness about the passage, an authority that comes from the writer's knowing what it feels like to have composed something true and knowing the difference between it and all imitations, however worthy. What Thomas is talking about here is the *élan* which distinguishes the most powerfully articulated metrical verse. Yeats's 'Sailing to Byzantium', Pope's 'Epistle to Arbuthnot', the prologue to Marlowe's *Tamburlaine* – these and other moments of passionate utterance in English poetry do not depend upon what Thomas fondly but critically terms 'the nostalgia of literature'. They are literary, certainly, in that all of them take a self-conscious pleasure in stepping it out correctly, showing their prosodic paces or their rhyming heels; but the poems I mention are not what Thomas calls nostalgic, they are not concerned with 'effects'. Like all definitive poems, they spring into presence and stand there, as Czeslaw Milosz says, blinking and lashing their tails. They break the print-barrier, as it were, and make their sonic boom within the ear. All of which can be said without exaggeration of 'Before I Knocked and Flesh Let Enter', an early Thomas poem about incarnation in both the biological and the theological sense of the term. Eternal life enters and exits from the womb, and in crossing that threshold twice, it double-crosses it, as the poem says. The voice speaks out of what could be either the moment of Christian annunciation or when the sperm fertilizes the ovum and spirit knocks to be admitted through the door of flesh:

Before I knocked and flesh let enter,
With liquid hands tapped on the womb,
I who was shapeless as the water
That shaped the Jordan near my home
Was brother to Mnetha's daughter
And sister to the fathering worm.

I who was deaf to spring and summer,
Who knew not sun nor moon by name,
Felt thud beneath my flesh's armour,
As yet was in a molten form,
The leaden stars, the rainy hammer
Swung by my father from his dome.

I knew the message of the winter,
The darted hail, the childish snow,
And the wind was my sister suitor;
Wind in me leaped, the hellborn dew;
My veins flowed with the Eastern weather;
Ungotten I knew night and day.

As yet ungotten, I did suffer;
The rack of dreams my lily bones
Did twist into a living cipher,
And flesh was snipped to cross the lines
Of gallow crosses on the liver
And brambles in the wringing brains.

My throat knew thirst before the structure
Of skin and vein around the well
Where words and water make a mixture
Unfailing till the blood runs foul;
My heart knew love, my belly hunger;
I smelt the maggot in my stool.

And time cast forth my mortal creature
To drift or drown upon the seas

Acquainted with the salt adventure
Of tides that never touch the shores.
I who was rich was made the richer
By sipping at the vine of days.

I, born of flesh and ghost, was neither
A ghost nor man, but mortal ghost.
And I was struck down by death's feather.
I was a mortal to the last
Long breath that carried to my father
The message of his dying christ.

You who bow down at cross and altar,
Remember me and pity Him
Who took my flesh and bone for armour
And doublecrossed my mother's womb.

Dylan Thomas died long before men landed on the moon, before we saw our planet from that perspective, profiled like the green-webbed X-ray of a foetus's head. But even though he missed those photographs of earth, round and gelid with oceans, translucent like a cell under the microscope, this poem offers a corresponding superimposition of images, of the microcosm and macrocosm. And even if there is something Godawful about the maggot in the stool, there is still something superbly forthright about the verse itself, a sense of somebody going head-on and barehanded at the task in front of him. There is no sense of the poet hovering over a word choice or taking a bow to acknowledge some passing felicity. There are, of course, a number of overt flourishes, yet such high-flown phrases as 'the rainy hammer', 'the vine of days', 'death's feather', 'the fathering worm', and so on go sweeping past like eddies on a big flow. They aren't set out for our admiration: instead, they are sent swiftly about their business. The words, to quote the letter to Watkins, are 'struck out' rather than 'chosen'.

There is, of course, always a temptation to caricature this early poetry as a kind of tumescent fantasia, but to take that line too glibly is to demean a real achievement. One must beware of confusing the subject with what the poet makes of it. At twenty, Thomas knew about art as a making and a discipline and was writing to Charles Fisher: 'I like things that are difficult to write and difficult to understand. I like "redeeming the contraries" with secretive images. But what I like isn't a theory, even if I stabilize into dogma my own personal affections.' We might say, therefore, that in the case of 'Before I Knocked' and 'The Force that through the Green Fuse Drives the Flower' and 'A Process in the Weather of the Heart' and in the early poems generally, affections and impulses have been stabilized not into dogma but into musical form. Work has been done. Imaginative force has moved a load of inchoate obsession into expressed language: something intuited and reached for has had its contours and location felt out and made manifest.

Thomas himself was often given to speaking of the process of composition as one of bringing the dark to light, although for him the creative work of hauling forth the psychic matter and discovering its structure probably had more to do with the story of Caedmon than with the practices of Freud. In his *Ecclesiastical History*, the Venerable Bede recounts the brief and simple tale of the calling of the poet Caedmon, an event that is set near the monastery at Whitby. Caedmon, the cowherd, found it impossible to contribute any improvised verses when it was his turn to take the harp and keep the banquet lively. But he always managed to find a way of dodging these crises by contriving to be at his yard-work when the harp was being passed. He would be out among the cattle, busy being busy. Then, one night when he was in the byre stalls as usual, he fell asleep and an angel appeared and commanded him to sing the creation of the world; and he did so, in the poem known ever since as Caedmon's Hymn, a poem which entered into the language as a marvel and a bewilderment. Caedmon wrote, 'It is meet that we worship the Warden of heaven, / The might of the maker, His purpose of mind' – and I am reminded of that hymn every time I read the last sentence of Thomas's 'Note' to his *Collected Poems*. 'These poems,' Thomas declared there, 'with all their crudities, doubts, and confusions, are written for the love of Man and in praise of God, and I'd be a damn' fool if they weren't.'

To his contemporaries, however, Thomas was not the Caedmon of Cwmdonkin Drive but its Rimbaud, and his status as *enfant terrible* combined with the opacity of his writing to give the nickname a certain appropriateness. He plunged into the sump of his teenage self, filling notebooks with druggy, bewildering lines that would be a kind of fossil fuel to him for years to come. For composition to be successful, Thomas had to be toiling in the element of language like a person in a mudbath: the strain of writing was palpably muscular, the sensation of hydraulic passage through the words paramount and indispensable. 'I think [poetry] should work from words, from the substance of words and the rhythm of substantial words set together, not towards words.' So he wrote to Charles Fisher in the letter I have already quoted, and in doing so played a variation on a theme that was preoccupying him at the time, namely, the difference between working *from* words, as he called it, and working *towards* them. He blames John Clare for working towards them, not out of them, 'describing and cataloguing the objects that met his eyes . . . He could not realize', said Thomas, 'that the word is the object.' How far this is fair to John Clare or how good it is as linguistic theory is not the point: what it does is to clue us in to Thomas's need for an almost autistic enclosure within the phonetic element before he could proceed. Probably the most famous of his utterances about the physicality of writing is in the letter where he tells Pamela Hansford Johnson that the greatest description of the earthiness of human beings is to be found in John Donne's *Devotions*, where the body is earth, the hair is a shrub growing out of the land, and so on. He continues as follows:

All thoughts and actions emanate from the body. Therefore the description of a thought or an action – however abstruse it may be – can be beaten home by bringing it on to a physical level. Every idea, intuitive or intellectual, can be imaged and translated in terms of the body, its flesh, skin, blood, sinews, veins, glands, organs, cells and senses. Through my small bone island I have learnt all I know, experienced all, and sensed all.

There is something about this passage that might be called Egyptian. Thomas, on the evidence here, would have been completely at home in a world where the cycles of life manifested themselves in the mud and floods of the Nile and the god of the dead was Anubis – a doghead, so to speak; and creation myths involving the almost glandular collusion of the elements would have suited him down to the ground. So the Caedmon comparison not only should take in the note of praise in each poet, but should extend to the inescapable physical conditions in which each laboured: the body heat of Thomas's imaginings corresponding to the reek of the Whitby byre and the breath of the beasts. And perhaps the comparison should even extend to the language they both used, in so far as the stress and alliteration of Caedmon's Anglo-Saxon are still clearly audible in the following early creation song by Thomas:

> The force that through the green fuse drives the flower
> Drives my green age; that blasts the roots of trees
> Is my destroyer.
> And I am dumb to tell the crooked rose
> My youth is bent by the same wintry fever.
>
> The force that drives the water through the rocks
> Drives my red blood; that dries the mouthing streams
> Turns mine to wax.
> And I am dumb to mouth unto my veins
> How at the mountain spring the same mouth sucks.
>
> The hand that whirls the water in the pool
> Stirs the quicksand; that ropes the blowing wind
> Hauls my shroud sail.

And I am dumb to tell the hanging man
How of my clay is made the hangman's lime.

The lips of time leech to the fountain head;
Love drips and gathers, but the fallen blood
Shall calm her sores.
And I am dumb to tell a weather's wind
How time has ticked a heaven round the stars.

And I am dumb to tell the lover's tomb
How at my sheet goes the same crooked worm.

When I thought of Dylan Thomas as the subject of this lecture, I intended to stress the positive metrical power of these early poems, and had hoped to find in them an echo still travelling outward from Christopher Marlowe's mighty line. In my recollection, Thomas's poems retained a turning, humming resonance, something that seemed to be generated less by the movement of the iambic pentameter than by the circulation of the blood itself. Remembered fragments conspired to strengthen this impression. 'I see the boys of summer in their ruin / Lay the gold tithings barren . . .' You intoned that and you felt again in your bones and joints a trace of the purchase it had on you at your first reading. The words did indeed 'thud beneath [the] flesh's armour' – so much so that they constituted a kind of Finneg-onan's wake. Still, I wanted to be able to praise a poetry of such fullness, to commend without reservation the heave of positive gesture, to feel that the recurrent obscurity and bravura of the poems were a small price for the authentic power that produced them. What I was wanting, in fact, was a return to poetic Eden. In my mind, Thomas had gradually come to represent a longed-for, prelapsarian wholeness, a state of the art where the autistic and the acoustic were extensive and coterminous, where the song of the self was effortlessly choral and its scale was a perfect measure and match for the world it sang in.

Even if Thomas's poetry cannot quite match these expectations, I would still like to affirm his kind of afflatus as a constant possibility for poetry, something not superannuated by the irony and self-knowing tactics of the art in post-modern times. I would like to stand up for the same kind of fine contrary excess that had preceded Thomas in the poetry of Hart Crane and succeeded him in poems like Geoffrey Hill's 'Genesis' and Sylvia Plath's 'Ariel'. I would like to discover in the largeness of his voice an implicit ethic of generosity that might be worth emulating for its inclusiveness and robustness.

But too often in the *Collected Poems* the largeness of the utterance is rigged. The poet is under the words of the poems like a linguistic body-builder, flexing and profiling. Too often what he achieves is something Martin Dodsworth called 'redundancy' rather than intensity, a theatrical verve, a kind of linguistic hype. The generosity promoted by poems such as 'In the White Giant's Thigh' turns out to be a kind of placebo, and the robustness of 'Lament' turns more and more into loud macho swagger. All in all, what his work begins to lose after the dark 'Egyptian' mode of *Eighteen Poems* is a quality that might be called 'tonal rectitude', taking tone in the radically vindicating sense attributed to it by Eavan Boland in an essay in *PN Review*. Boland is writing there about Elizabeth Bishop, in particular about Bishop's tone, and this leads her to meditate as follows upon the primacy of tone in general:

Poetic tone is more than the speaking voice in which the poem happens; much more. Its roots go deep into the history and sociology of the craft. Even today, for a poet, tone is not a matter of the aesthetic of any one poem. It grows more surely, and more painfully, from the ethics of the art. Its origins must always be in a suffered world rather than a conscious craft.

This last sentence is a wonderful formulation of what we seek from any poet's undermusic. The power of the final chorus of *Doctor Faustus*, or the opening lines of *Paradise Lost* or the whole somnambulant drift of a late Wallace Stevens poem such as 'The River of Rivers in Connecticut' has not to do simply with its author's craft. The affective power in these places comes from a kind of veteran knowledge which has gathered to a phonetic and rhythmic head, and forced an utterance. It is, for example, the undermusic of just such knowledge that makes Emily Dickinson devastating as well as endearing and makes the best of John Ashbery's poetry the common, unrarefied expression of a disappointment that is beyond self-pity.

The gradual withdrawal of a suffered world and the compensatory operations of a conscious craft weaken much of Thomas's poetry and rob it of emotional staying power as well as 'tonal rectitude'. The snowscape of a later poem like 'A Winter's Tale', for example, is meant to be a visionary projection, but it rather suggests a winter-wonderland in the Hollywood mode. It is too softly contoured, too obligingly suffused with radiance and too repetitive – the verbal equivalent of a Disney fantasia:

> It is a winter's tale
> That the snow blind twilight ferries over the lakes
> And floating fields from the farm in the cup of the vales,
> Gliding windless through the hand folded flakes,
> The pale breath of cattle at the stealthy sail,
>
> And the stars falling cold,
> And the smell of hay in the snow, and the far owl
> Warning among the folds, and the frozen hold
> Flocked with the sheep white smoke of the farm house cowl
> In the river wended vales where the tale was told.

This displays a genius for lyricizing, for setting forth to good advantage its own immediacy and naïvety and textures. And as the poem goes sweeping forward for the whole of its twenty-six stanzas, one move forward for every two moves back – in keeping with the swirling motions of its blizzard world – Thomas does rise to the technical occasion. He meets the demands of a difficult rhyme scheme that also involves from time to time the deployment of internal rhyme and the manipulation of end-of-line assonance – and he does it so resourcefully that it almost feels like an injustice to question the poem's excellence and blame it for having just *too* much of the craftsman's effort about it. Yet the demand for more matter, less art, does inevitably arise. The tone is a rhetorical pitch framed for the occasion. The reader is tempted to quote Thomas's letter to Vernon Watkins against Thomas himself and to say, 'All the words are lovely but they seem so *chosen* . . . I can see the sensitive picking of words, but not the strong, inevitable pulling . . .' For example, in the second stanza above, in those lines about 'the frozen hold / Flocked with the sheep white smoke of the farm house cowl', there is a little too much winsomeness about the oddity of 'hold' where we might expect 'fold', and there is a little too much self-regard about the submerged pun on the word 'flocked' which has the sense of white fluff as well as of a herd of sheep – all the more regrettable when the adjective 'sheep white', with its own double-take on 'snow white', comes along immediately in the same line:

> and the frozen hold
> Flocked with the sheep white smoke of the farm house cowl
> In the river wended vales . . .

It may be a bit smart-assed to see this more as a case of 'vended Wales' than 'wended vales', but the poet's own verbal opportunism encourages the reader to indulge in just such a nifty put-down. Indeed, I have the impression that negative criticism of Dylan Thomas's work is more righteous and more imbued with this kind of punitive impulse than is usual. Even a nickname like 'The Ugly Suckling' has an unusual animus behind it. It often seems less a matter of the poet's being criticized than of his being got back at, and my guess is that on these occasions the reader's older self is punishing the younger one who hearkened to Thomas's oceanic music and credited its promise to bring the world and the self into cosmic harmony.

I count myself to some extent among this disappointed group – but not always. Not, for example, when I re-encounter a poem like 'Do Not Go Gentle into That Good Night', which fulfils its promise precisely because its craft has not lost touch with a suffered world. The villanelle form, turning upon itself, advancing and retiring to and from a resolution, is not just a line-by-line virtuoso performance. Through its repetitions, the father's remoteness – and the remoteness of all fathers – is insistently proclaimed, yet we can also hear, in an almost sobbing counterpoint, the protest of the poet's child-self against the separation:

> Do not go gentle into that good night,
> Old age should burn and rave at close of day;
> Rage, rage against the dying of the light.
>
> Though wise men at their end know dark is right,
> Because their words had forked no lightning they
> Do not go gentle into that good night.
>
> Good men, the last wave by, crying how bright
> Their frail deeds might have danced in a green bay,
> Rage, rage against the dying of the light.
>
> Wild men who caught and sang the sun in flight
> And learn, too late, they grieved it on its way,
> Do not go gentle into that good night.
>
> Grave men, near death, who see with blinding sight
> Blind eyes could blaze like meteors and be gay,
> Rage, rage against the dying of the light.
>
> And you, my father, there on the sad height,
> Curse, bless, me now with your fierce tears, I pray.
> Do not go gentle into that good night.
> Rage, rage against the dying of the light.

This poem was written at a late moment in Thomas's life, when he was thirty-seven, almost twenty years after 'Before I Knocked'. The year before, in 1950, he had worked on the too deliberate raptures of 'In the White Giant's Thigh' and the never-to-be-completed 'In Country Heaven'. And all the while, on and off, he was fiddling with the genial dream-scape of *Under Milk Wood*. But now, in 1951, at a time when his father was dying from cancer and his relationship with his wife Caitlin was in a kind of deep freeze because of his affair with the American woman whom biographers call 'Sarah', Thomas came through with a poem in a single, unfumbled movement, one with all the confidence of a necessary thing, one in which again at last the fantasy and extravagance of imagery and diction did not dissipate themselves or his theme. Words forking 'lightning', frail deeds dancing 'in a green bay', blind eyes blazing 'like meteors' – these defiant and lavishly affirmative phrases could conceivably have appeared in the windier ambience of a piece like 'Lament', but within the genuinely desperate rhetoric of the villanelle they are informed with an urgency which guarantees their immunity from the virus of rant and posturing.

'Do Not Go Gentle' is obviously a threshold poem about death, concerned with the reverse of the process which occupied Thomas in 'Before I Knocked'. In that earlier poem, the body was about to begin what Thomas calls elsewhere its 'sensual strut', here the return journey out of mortality into ghosthood is about to be made, so in fact the recurrent rhymes of the villanelle could as well have been 'breath' and 'death' or 'womb' and 'tomb' – but what we have instead are 'night' and 'light'. And the night is a 'good night'. But, for once, a characteristic verbal tic has become an imaginative strength and not just an irritating cleverness. 'Good night' is a pun which risks breaking the decorum of the utterance but which turns out in the end to embody its very complexity and force. The mixture of salutation and farewell in the phrase is a perfect equivalent for the balance between natural grief and the recognition of necessity which pervades the poem as a whole.

This is a son comforting a father; yet it is also, conceivably, the child poet in Thomas himself comforting the old ham he had become; the neophyte in him addressing the legend; the green fuse addressing the burnt-out case. The reflexiveness of the form is the right correlative for the reflexiveness of the feeling. As the poem proceeds, exhortation becomes self-lamentation; the son's instruction to the disappointed father to curse and bless him collapses the distance between the sad height of age and physical decay in the parent and the equally sad eminence of poetic reputation and failing powers in the child. 'Do Not Go Gentle' is a lament for the maker in Thomas himself as well as an adieu to his proud and distant schoolteacher father. The shade of the young man who once expressed a fear that he was not a poet, just a freak user of words, pleads for help and reassurance from the older, sadder literary lion he has become, the one who apparently has the world at his feet.

Not that Thomas intended this meaning, of course. One of the poem's strengths is its outwardly directed address, its escape from emotional claustrophobia through an engagement with the specifically technical challenges of the villanelle. Yet that form is so much a matter of crossing and substitutions, of back-tracks and double-takes, turns and returns, that it is a vivid figure for the union of opposites, for the father in the son, the son in the father, for life in death and death in life. The villanelle, in fact, both participates in the flux of natural existence and scans and abstracts existence in order to register its pattern. It is a living cross-section, a simultaneously open and closed form, one in which the cycles of youth and age, of rise and fall, growth and decay find their analogues in the fixed cycle of rhymes and repetitions.

Indeed, there is something Rilkean in the tendency of 'Do Not Go Gentle', for we are here in the presence of knowledge transformed into poetic action, and the extreme claims that

Rilke made for poetry are well enough matched by Thomas on this occasion. The following, which comes from a Rilke letter about his *Duino Elegies*, seems relevant and worth quoting:

Death is a *side of life* that is turned away from us . . . the true figure of life extends through both domains, the blood of the mightiest circulation drives through *both: there is neither a here nor a beyond, but a great unity*, in which those creatures that surpass us, the 'angels', are at home.

In its canvassing of the idea of a great unity and its employment of the bodily image of circulating blood, this statement by Rilke is reminiscent of the murkier, more biological statements of the young Thomas. Yet in 'Do Not Go Gentle', I would suggest that the old murkiness has been worked through and a new set of angelic rather than Egyptian words has been worked towards. I would also suggest that the mighty vaunt of 'A Refusal to Mourn the Death, by Fire, of a Child in London' has now been made good, and its operatic, death-defying strains have modulated into something even more emotionally persuasive. In fact, in the light of Rilke's statement we can begin to discern the mistake which Thomas made during his twenties and thirties when he confined himself to the repetition of his own early procedures and convictions as a poet.

Eliot once diagnosed the problem of a younger contemporary as being a case of technical development proceeding ahead of spiritual development. What this suggests is that there should be a correspondence between the maturation of a sensibility and its methods of expression at different stages. Thomas's methods as a teenager, bogged in masturbatory claustrophobia, desperately seeking in language the fulfilment of clandestine sexual needs, the kind of thing that the old Yeats mysteriously called 'a blurred touch through a curtain' – those methods were suited to the phallocentric, percussive, short-circuited poetry proper to his situation then, but they were not what he needed later as a sexually mature, world-scarred and world-skilled outsider at the literary centre. Thomas's anti-intellectualism, for example, is a bad boy's habit wastefully prolonged and this doctrinaire immaturity, which was at once tedious and entertaining in life, was finally retrograde for his art. But 'Do Not Go Gentle' is a positively magnificent achievement. This poem does not begin with words, as the young Thomas too simply insisted that poetry should, but it moves towards them. And it is exactly the sensation of language on the move towards a destination in knowledge which imbues 'Do Not Go Gentle' with a refreshing maturity. 'The Force that through the Green Fuse Drives the Flower' gained its power from a language entrapped and certified by its obsessions, and was the kind of poem that an eighteen-year-old of genius could properly and prodigiously deliver. But as long as he kept too rigidly to those bodily, earthy, Egyptian imperatives, it was not possible for Thomas to admit into his poetry the presence of that which Rilke calls the angels. The jurisdiction of the bone-bound island, to which he had pledged his loyalty, forbade the necessary widening of scope. The poems of his twenties and thirties pursued a rhetorical magnificence that was in excess of and posthumous to its original, vindicating impulse. They mostly stand like elaborately crenellated fabrications, great gazebos built to the extravagant but finally exhibitionist specifications of their inventor.

Thomas did recognize the need to open and seek what Rilke calls 'that great unity which is neither here nor beyond', but when he did so, time and again what failed him was the tone. The suffered world peels away from the proffered idiom. The great first gift, which enabled him to work instinctively at the deep sound-face and produce a poetry where the back of the throat and the back of the mind answered and supported each other – this did, alas, weaken. His original ability to discover a path for the poem's progress by means of a sixth sense – what he called 'creative destruction, destructive creation' – began to atrophy: the enigmas of 'Altarwise by Owl-Light' seem to be contrived rather than discovered. 'After the Funeral' even goes so far as to diagnose the problem and to suggest a way out of it by admitting into the high-pressure conditions of the poem the sweet, uninflated particulars of the world such as 'a stuffed fox and a stale fern' and fern seeds 'on the black sill'. But the problem of harmonizing rhetorical pitch and emotional content remained and was only overcome when Thomas opened the texture of his language and allowed the affirmative strains of 'Poem in October' and 'Fern Hill' to rise into the higher, less bodily and more 'angelic' registers:

And honoured among foxes and pheasants by the gay house
Under the new made clouds and happy as the heart was long,
   In the sun born over and over,
     I ran my heedless ways,
    My wishes raced through the house high hay
And nothing I cared, at my sky blue trades, that time allows
In all his tuneful turning so few and such morning songs
   Before the children green and golden
    Follow him out of grace.

Nothing I cared, in the lamb white days, that time would take me
Up to the swallow thronged loft by the shadow of my hand,
   In the moon that is always rising,
    Nor that riding to sleep
   I should hear him fly with the high fields
And wake to the farm forever fled from the childless land.
Oh as I was young and easy in the mercy of his means,
    Time held me green and dying
   Though I sang in my chains like the sea.

'Fern Hill' is buoyant upon memories of a sensuously apprehended world and is suffused by them. Its poetry is admirably and bewitchingly candid, held out at an unclammy distance between poet and reader. It is far from Egyptian. Its green singing spaces are swept by less breathy airs than the too artfully pleasing landscape of 'A Winter's Tale' and one has the gratifying sense of the poet completely absorbed in his very own subject. Yet its dimensions as a poem of loss become plainer if we set it beside Wordsworth's 'Immortality Ode'. The comparison is unfair, of course, but it makes clear that what 'Fern Hill' lacks is precisely an intonation arising from the 'years that bring the philosophic mind', being more concerned to over-whelm its sorrows in a tidal wave of recollection than to face what Rilke calls 'a *side of life* that is turned away from us'. It is as if Orpheus, grown older, had reneged on his larger task, that of testing the power of his lyre against the gods of the under-world and wresting life back out of death, and had gone back instead to his younger, happier if less world-saving task of cast-ing musical spells upon the whole of nature.

My quotations from Rilke are taken from a study of the myth of Orpheus by the distinguished classicist Charles Segal, and I want to conclude by considering both the excitements and limitations of Dylan Thomas's poetry in the light of Segal's read-ing of that particular myth. According to his understanding, Orpheus, in his early manifestations within Greek culture, is 'the oral poet par excellence. He sings outside, under an open sky, accompanying himself on his famous lyre. His fabled effect upon wild beasts, stones and trees generalizes to the animal world that mimetic response that an oral audience feels in the situation of the performance ... This compulsive, incantatory power of oral song ... the animal magnetism with which it holds its hearers spellbound, all find mythical embodiment in Orpheus.' And so, in turn, I would want to find in the undimin-ished incantatory power of early Dylan Thomas poems on the page, and in the spellbinding memory of his oral performance of poems from all periods of his career, a continuing aspect of the Orphic principle and an example of the survival of rhapsodic poetry of the most ancient kind.

Yet this is the kind of poetry which Plato describes and disa-vows in his *Ion*. He suspects it in much the same way as critics have suspected Dylan Thomas, and he is against what Segal calls its 'magical, quasi-hypnotic effect, emotional response, power to move and compel large audiences'. As far as Plato is concerned, the way in which this poetry works bodily, through the agency of the senses, is a limitation. He underrates it because it is powerless to know reality through the intellect. In the *Symposium*, for example, he tells a version of the story of Orpheus which is clearly meant to indicate that Orphic power operates only in the realm of illusion. According to Plato, when Orpheus goes to the underworld and sues for the return of Eurydice, he is given only a *phasma*, a wraith or shadow, a phantom woman.

But this pejorative version of Orpheus as an energy absorbed in the unconscious flux of nature and exemplifying a process which it cannot know – this is only a beginning. Subsequent poets, from Virgil to Rilke, seek to outflank Plato's objections by developing and extending other parts of the myth besides the musical, spellbinding gift of the singer. Their treatments emphasize the truth-to-life-and-death in the story and they abstract meanings from the drama of Eurydice that are variously sombre or symbolic. Thus, from one perspective, Orpheus's trip to the land of the dead and his initially successful bid to have Eurydice released from the underworld can represent the ability of art – poetry, music, language – to triumph over death; yet from another perspective, Orpheus's fatal backward look must equally represent 'the failure of art before the ultimate reality of death' – or, to put it in Charles Segal's more drastic formulation, the loss of Eurydice expresses 'the intransigence of reality before the plasticity of language'.

To make the final application of all this, then, to Dylan Thomas: we can say that he continued to place a too unenlightened trust in the plasticity of language, that he emphasized unduly the romantic, positive side of the story and overrated the lyre's ability to stay or reverse the course of nature. The backward look of 'Poem in October' or 'Fern Hill', however radiant and understandable, becomes, in this reading, like the backward look of Orpheus himself. These poems avert their eyes from the prospect of necessity. 'Do Not Go Gentle into That Good Night', on the other hand, keeps its gaze firmly fixed on the upward path, and works against the gradient of relapse. Its verbal elaborateness is neither otiose nor merely ornamental.

On the contrary, its art is as straightforward and homely as Caedmon's, and as extremely engaged as that of Orpheus in the underworld. In the telling of its rhymes and repetitions, the litany of Dylan the Durable will always be credible and continuing.

21 November 1991

Joy or Night: Last Things
in the Poetry of W. B. Yeats
and Philip Larkin

To begin with, I want to read a poem by the Czech poet Miroslav Holub. This describes two characters who are like allegorical representations of the different poetic postures adopted by W. B. Yeats and Philip Larkin, not only towards last things, but towards nearly everything. It has all the clarity of a blackboard diagram and makes an excellent introduction to my concerns in this lecture:

The Dead

After the third operation, his heart
pierced like an old carnival target,
he woke in his bed and said,
'Now I'll be fine,
like a sunflower, and by the way
have you ever seen horses make love?'

He died that night.

And another one plodded on for eight
milk and water years
like a long-haired waterplant
in a sour creek,
as if he stuck his pale face out
on a skewer from behind the graveyard wall.
Finally his face disappeared.

In both cases the angel of death
stamped his hob-nailed boot
on their *medulla oblongata*.

I know they died the same death
but I don't think they died
in the same way.

As Philip Larkin once said, readability is credibility: because of the truth-to-life in Holub's presentation of the different ways the two men lived, there is great cogency in his claim that there was a difference in the way they died. Indeed, it's because of this thoroughly persuasive quality that I want to set Holub's poem beside one by Larkin which takes an opposing view and contains the line 'Death is *no* different whined at than withstood' (my italics). Larkin's 'Aubade' is the poem where this dark observation appears and it constitutes a direct contradiction of Holub, in that it treats as mystification any imaginative or rhetorical ploy which might mask the facts of the body's dissolution and the mind's disappearance after death. Religion, courage, philosophy, drink, the routines of work and leisure – all these are regarded by Larkin as placebos. As he aged, his vision got arrested into a fixed stare at the inexorability of his own physical extinction. Human wisdom, therefore, seemed to him a matter of operating within the mortal limits, and of quelling any false hope of transcending or outfacing the inevitable. The poet in Larkin, in other words, was entirely sympathetic to living as a long-haired waterplant in a sour creek, and the persona he created for himself in the last two decades of his life bore a definite resemblance to that pale face on a skewer sticking out from behind the graveyard wall. So what I want to do in this lecture is to consider the implications for poetry of Larkin's attitude, and to ask whether his famous rejection of Yeats's more romantic stance has not been too long and too readily approved of.

Consider Yeats's extraordinary visionary exclamation 'The Cold Heaven'. He once described it as a poem about the mood produced in him by looking at the sky in wintertime, but the poem carries things far beyond mood and atmosphere. It is as much about metaphysical need as it is about the meteorological conditions:

Suddenly I saw the cold and rook-delighting heaven
That seemed as though ice burned and was but the more ice,

And thereupon imagination and heart were driven
So wild that every casual thought of that and this
Vanished, and left but memories, that should be out of season
With the hot blood of youth, of love crossed long ago;
And I took all the blame out of all sense and reason,
Until I cried and trembled and rocked to and fro,
Riddled with light. Ah! when the ghost begins to quicken,
Confusion of the death-bed over, is it sent
Out naked on the roads, as the books say, and stricken
By the injustice of the skies for punishment?

This is an extraordinarily vivid rendering of a spasm of consciousness, a moment of exposure to the total dimensions of
what Wallace Stevens once called our 'spiritual height and
depth'. The turbulence of the lines dramatizes a sudden apprehension that there is no hiding place, that the individual human life
cannot be sheltered from the galactic cold. The spirit's vulnerability, the mind's awe at the infinite spaces and its bewilderment at
the implacable inquisition which they represent – all of this is
simultaneously present. The poem could be described in Hopkins's phrase as 'the swoon of a heart . . . trod / Hard down
with a horror of height', for Yeats has clearly received what
Hopkins in another context called a 'heaven-handling'. He too
has gone through his ordeal on the mind's mountains, on those
'cliffs of fall / Frightful, sheer, no-man-fathomed.' But the difference is that, in Hopkins, the terror has its given co-ordinates; the
Deity, doubted though He may be, does provide a certain theological longitude and latitude for what is unknown and unknow-
able. In 'The Wreck of the Deutschland' and 'The Terrible
Sonnets', Hopkins's intensity is the intensity of dialogue, of blame
and beseeching: a 'thou' is being addressed, a comforter is being
called upon (or else a false comforter is being rejected, the car-
rion comfort, Despair). In Yeats, on the other hand, this personal God has disappeared and yet Yeats's poem still conveys a
strong impression of direct encounter. The spirit still suffers
from a sense of answerability, of responsibility, to a something

out there, an intuited element that is as credible as the 'rook-delighting heaven' itself.

There is, for example, this marvellous sense of both physical visitation and intellectual apprehension in the phrase 'riddled with light'. Light as strobing rays and light as spiritual illumination are here indistinguishable. The 'I' of the poet as a first person singular, a self-knowing consciousness, is brilliantly and concretely at one with the eye of the poet as a retina overwhelmed by the visual evidence of infinity and solitude. And this is only one of several instances where the poem's stylistic excellence and its spiritual proffer converge. When, in one place, the verb 'to quicken' is rhymed with the participle 'stricken' and still manages to hold its own against it; and when, in another, the rhyme word 'season' sets its chthonic reliability against the potentially debilitating force of 'reason' – when such things occur, the art of the poem is functioning as a corroboration of the positive emotional and intellectual commitments of the poet. To put it in yet another and perhaps provocatively simple way, 'The Cold Heaven' is a poem which suggests that there is an overall purpose to life; and it does so by the intrinsically poetic action of its rhymes, its rhythms, and its exultant intonation. These create an energy and an order which promote the idea that there exists a much greater, circumambient energy and order within which we have our being.

The ghost upon the road, the soul's destiny in the afterlife, the consequences in eternity of the individual's actions in time – traditional concerns like these are profoundly relevant to 'The Cold Heaven' and they are also, of course, typical of the things which preoccupied Yeats for the whole of his life. Whether it was fairy lore in Sligo or Buddhism with the Dublin Hermetic Society or spiritualist séances or Noh dramas which imagined the adventures of Cuchulain's shade in the Land of the Dead, Yeats was always passionately beating on the wall of the physical world in order to provoke an answer from the other side. His studies were arcane, his cosmology was fantastic and yet his intellect remained undeluded. Rational objections were often rationally allowed by him, if only to be imaginatively and rhetorically overwhelmed. Yeats's embrace of the supernatural, in other words, was not at all naïve; he was as alive as Larkin to the demeaning realities of bodily decrepitude and the obliterating force of death, but he deliberately resisted the dominance of the material over the spiritual. He was, moreover, as complicated as the rest of us when it came to the nature of his beliefs in a supernatural machinery, and nowhere more engagingly so than in his introduction to *A Vision*, that thesaurus of arcane information and speculation which was in part dictated to him by beings whom he liked to call his 'ghostly instructors'.

Some will ask whether I believe in the actual existence of my circuits of sun and moon ... To such a question I can but answer that if sometimes, overwhelmed by miracle as all men must be when in the midst of it, I have taken such periods literally, my reason has soon recovered; and now that the system stands out clearly in my imagination I regard them as stylistic arrangements of experience comparable to the cubes in the drawing of Wyndham Lewis and to the ovoids in the sculpture of Brancusi. They have helped me to hold in . single thought reality and justice.

This is both sonorous and moving, but I would like to supplement it with another, very different illustration of the provisional nature of Yeats's thinking about last things. This comes from Lady Dorothy Wellesley's recollection of the poet's conversation in old age, and is an almost deadpan account of one of their sessions:

I once got Yeats down to bed-rock on these subjects and we talked for hours. He had been talking rather wildly about the after life. Finally I asked him: 'What do you believe happens to us immediately after death?' He replied, 'After a person dies, he does not realize that he is dead.' I: 'In what state is he?' W. B. Y.: 'In some half-conscious state.' I said: 'Like the period between waking and sleeping?' W. B. Y.: 'Yes.' I: 'How long does this state last?' W. B. Y.: 'Perhaps some twenty years.' 'And after that,' I asked, 'what happens next?' He replied, 'Again a period which is Purgatory. The length of that period depends upon the sins of the man when he was upon this earth.' And then again I asked:

'And after that?' I do not remember his actual words, but he spoke of the return of the soul to God. I said, 'Well, it seems to me that you are hurrying us back into the great arms of the Roman Catholic Church.' He was of course an Irish Protestant. I was bold to ask him, but his only retort was his splendid laugh.

The laugh was not really evasive. The laugh, in fact, established a conversational space where the question could move again. It was the social expression of that frame of mind which allowed the venturesomeness of a supernatural faith to co-exist with a rigorously sceptical attitude. It was the comic expression of the tragic perception which Richard Ellmann attributed to Yeats in his important essay entitled 'W. B. Yeats's Second Puberty'. Ellmann wrote that the poet, in his old age, 'was obliged by his inner honesty to allow for the possibility that reality was desolation and justice a figment. 'The image of life as cornucopia,' Ellmann continued, 'was relentlessly undermined by the image of life as empty shell.' Yet it is because of Yeats's fidelity to both perceptions and his refusal to foreclose on either that we recognize in him a poet of the highest attainment. Towards the middle of the twentieth century, he continued to hold the tune which 'the darkling thrush' announced to Thomas Hardy at its very beginning. The thrush's song proclaimed that the basis of song itself was irrational, that its prerogative was to indulge impulse in spite of the evidence; and Hardy, in spite of his temperamental inclination to focus his attention upon the dolorous circumstances, for once allowed his heart in hiding to stir for that particular bird:

> So little cause for carolings
>   Of such ecstatic sound
> Was written on terrestrial things
>   Afar or nigh around,
> That I could think there trembled through
>   His happy good-night air
> Some blessed Hope, whereof he knew
>   And I was unaware.

We might say that Hardy, at this moment, experienced what Yeats says he experienced in the writing of *A Vision*: he too was simply overwhelmed by miracle whilst in the midst of it. But this, for sure, is not the Hardy to whom Larkin was converted after the strong enchantments of Yeats had failed for him. At that crucial point in his artistic development, Larkin turned to Hardy, the poet of human sadness, rather than to Hardy, the witness of irrational hope. It was the 'neutral tones' rather than the 'ecstatic carolings' that attracted him; the disenchantment of Hardy's 'God-curst sun, and a tree / And a pond edged with greyish leaves' carried far more weight and cut more emotional ice with Larkin than any illumination that a positively 'rook-delighting heaven' could offer. At any rate, it is surely a God-curst sun that creates the glassy brilliance at the end of his poem 'High Windows'. Certainly it is the opposite of whatever illuminates the scene where Yeats's protagonist 'cried and trembled and rocked to and fro'. Yeats's cold heaven, as I have tried to demonstrate, is neither frigid nor negative. It is, on the contrary, an image of superabundant life, whereas Larkin's sun-struck distances give access to an infinity as void and neuter as those 'blinding windscreens' which flash randomly and pointlessly in 'The Whitsun Weddings'. 'High Windows' concludes:

> And immediately
>
> Rather than words comes the thought of high windows:
> The sun-comprehending glass,
> And beyond it, the deep blue air, that shows
> Nothing, and is nowhere, and is endless.

When Larkin lifts his eyes from nature, what appears is a great absence. Neither justice nor injustice is to be sought in the skies; space offers neither illumination nor terminus. Out there, no encounter is possible. Out there is not our business. And all we have to protect us against these metaphysically Arctic conditions is the frail heat-shield generated by human kindness. Larkin is to be taken very seriously when he writes, in his late poem 'The Mower', 'we should be careful / Of each other, we

should be kind / While there is still time.' But this minimal
shield is insufficient to ward off the enormous *No* which reality
pronounces constantly into the face of human life. Naturally,
we would like him to answer back with the enormous *Yes*
which love and art might generate, but he is unable to do it
because he insists on taking full account of the negative evidence and this finally demoralizes the affirmative impulse. The
radiance of a poem like 'Solar' is always going to be qualified
by the pallor of one like 'Sad Steps'.

And this, of course, is why Larkin's poetry at its best is read
with such gratitude. It too is sensitive to the dialectic between
the cornucopia and the empty shell, obliged to try to resolve the
imagination's stalemate between the death-mask of nihilism and
the fixed smile of a pre-booked place in paradise. As Czeslaw
Milosz has observed, no intelligent contemporary is spared the
pressure exerted in our world by the void, the absurd, the
anti-meaning, all of which are part of the intellectual atmosphere we subsist in; and yet Milosz notices this negative pressure only to protest against a whole strain of modern literature
which has conceded victory to it. Poetry, Milosz pleads, must
not make this concession but maintain instead its centuries-old
hostility to reason, science and a science-inspired philosophy.
These views were recorded by Milosz in an article published
in 1979 in *Poetry Australia*, and they are intrinsically challeng-
ing; but the challenge is all the more pointed because they were
made in conjunction with remarks about Larkin's 'Aubade', the
poem to which I've already alluded and which I would now like
to consider in more detail. Milosz praises the poem as 'a high
poetic achievement', yet even that approbation may seem mild
to those who remember coming upon it in the *TLS*, two days
before Christmas, 1977:

> I work all day, and get half-drunk at night.
> Waking at four to soundless dark, I stare.
> In time the curtain-edges will grow light.
> Till then I see what's really always there:

Unresting death, a whole day nearer now,
Making all thought impossible but how
And where and when I shall myself die.
Arid interrogation: yet the dread
Of dying, and being dead,
Flashes afresh to hold and horrify.

The mind blanks at the glare. Not in remorse
– The good not done, the love not given, time
Torn off unused – nor wretchedly because
An only life can take so long to climb
Clear of its wrong beginnings, and may never;
But at the total emptiness for ever,
The sure extinction that we travel to
And shall be lost in always. Not to be here,
Not to be anywhere,
And soon; nothing more terrible, nothing more true.

This is a special way of being afraid
No trick dispels. Religion used to try,
That vast moth-eaten musical brocade
Created to pretend we never die,
And specious stuff that says *No rational being*
Can fear a thing it will not feel, not seeing
That this is what we fear – no sight, no sound,
No touch or taste or smell, nothing to think with,
Nothing to love or link with,
The anaesthetic from which none come round.

And so it stays just on the edge of vision,
A small unfocused blur, a standing chill
That slows each impulse down to indecision.
Most things may never happen: this one will,
And realization of it rages out
In furnace-fear when we are caught without
People or drink. Courage is no good:
It means not scaring others. Being brave

Lets no one off the grave.
Death is no different whined at than withstood.

Slowly light strengthens, and the room takes shape.
It stands plain as a wardrobe, what we know,
Have always known, know that we can't escape,
Yet can't accept. One side will have to go.
Meanwhile telephones crouch, getting ready to ring
In locked-up offices, and all the uncaring
Intricate rented world begins to rouse.
The sky is white as clay, with no sun.
Work has to be done.
Postmen like doctors go from house to house.

It would be hard to think of a poem more opposed than this one to the life-enhancing symbolism of the Christ child in the Christmas crib. It is as if the mid-winter gleam and promise of medieval carols had been obliterated completely by the dread and dolour of a medieval morality play like *Everyman*. In fact, Larkin's terror here is very reminiscent of the terror suffered by the character Everyman; and Everyman's summoner, the presence whom Larkin calls 'unresting death', stalks the poem every bit as menacingly as he stalks the play. There is, furthermore, a specially vindictive force to the figure of death in 'Aubade' because the adjective 'unresting' had been employed most memorably by Larkin in an earlier poem celebrating the opulence and oceanic vitality of leafy trees, their lush power to revivify both themselves and us, year after year. The last stanza of 'The Trees' reads:

> Yet still the unresting castles thresh
> In fullgrown thickness every May.
> Last year is dead, they seem to say,
> Begin afresh, afresh, afresh.

In this stanza, the word 'unresting' embodies an immense luxuriance and deep-rootedness, but in 'Aubade' it has the rangy hungry speed and relentlessness of a death hound: Larkin unleashes it at line five and then for the next forty-five lines it beats the bounds of our mortality, forcing its borders to shrink farther and farther away from any contact with consoling beliefs. Also in 'Aubade', the word 'afresh' (so joyful in 'The Trees') is relocated in a context of horror, the word 'dread' comes to an almost catatonic confrontation with its full meaning as it rhymes with 'dead', and 'die' is forced to live with its own emotional consequences in the verb 'horrify'.

> Unresting death, a whole day nearer now,
> Making all thought impossible but how
> And where and when I shall myself die.
> Arid interrogation: yet the dread
> Of dying, and being dead,
> Flashes afresh to hold and horrify.

One could go on praising the technical aspects of this poem, such as the rhyming of 'vision' with 'indecision', a piece of undercutting that is characteristically Larkinesque in its implicit refusal of the spiritual upbeat of Yeats's rhymes. Instead of any further detailed commentary, however, I shall confine myself to the observation that this, for me, is the definitive post-Christian English poem, one that abolishes the soul's traditional pretension to immortality and denies the Deity's immemorial attribute of infinite personal concern. Moreover, no matter how much or how little readers may at the outset be in sympathy with these views, they still arrive at the poem's conclusion a little surprised at how far it has carried them on the lip of its rhetorical wave. It leaves them like unwary surfers hung over a great emptiness, transported further into the void than they might have expected to go. It arrives at a place where, in Yeats's words, 'cold winds blow across our hands, upon our faces, the thermometer falls.'

Yeats, however, considered these things to be symptoms not of absence but of the ecstatic presence of the supernatural. Writing near the end of his life, in 'A General Introduction for My Work', Yeats told of his aspiration to a form of utterance in which imagination would be 'carried beyond feeling into the

aboriginal ice'. Which ice, needless to say, was the antithesis of
the stuff to be found under the mortuary slabs. It represented not
so much a frigid exhaustion as an ultimate attainment. It was
an analogue of that cold heaven where it 'seemed as though ice
burned and was but the more ice'; an analogue also of Yeats's
rejection of the body heat of the pathetic and the subjective in
art, for his embrace of the dramatic and the heroic, his determina-
tion to establish the crystalline standards of poetic imagination
as normative for the level at which people should live. For Yeats,
there was something both enviable and exemplary about the
enlargement of vision and the consequent histrionic equanimity
which Shakespeare's heroes and heroines attain at the moment
of their death, 'carried beyond feeling into the aboriginal ice.'
He wanted people in real life to emulate or at least to internal-
ize the fortitude and defiance thus manifested in tragic art.
Where Larkin was all for human beings huddling together in
kindness, like refugees from the injustice of the skies, Yeats was
all for flourish and theatrical challenge. Larkin might declare:

> Courage is no good:
> It means not scaring others. Being brave
> Lets no one off the grave.
> Death is no different whined at than withstood.

Yeats absolutely disagreed. 'No actress', he maintained, 'has
ever sobbed when she played Cleopatra, even the shallow brain
of a producer has never thought of such a thing.' Which
amounts to saying that death withstood is indeed very different
from death whined at; and that it is up to poets and actresses to
continue to withstand.

So we must imagine Yeats as the reader in eternity who resists
Philip Larkin's 'Aubade', high poetic achievement though it may
be; and resists it for the same reason as Czeslaw Milosz, who,
having conceded the integrity of 'Aubade' as a work that copes
with the eternal subject of death 'in a manner corresponding
to the sensibility of the second half of the twentieth century',
goes on to protest:

And yet the poem leaves me not only dissatisfied but indignant, and I wonder why myself. Perhaps we forget too easily the centuries-old mutual hostility between reason, science and science-inspired philosophy on the one hand and poetry on the other? Perhaps the author of the poem went over to the side of the adversary and his ratiocination strikes me as a betrayal? For, after all, death in the poem is endowed with the supreme authority of Law and universal necessity, while man is reduced to nothing, to a bundle of perceptions, or even less, to an interchangeable statistical unit. But poetry by its very essence has always been on the side of life. Faith in life everlasting has accompanied man in his wanderings through time, and it has always been larger and deeper than religious or philosophical creeds which expressed only one of its forms.

Still, when a poem rhymes, when a form generates itself, when a metre provokes consciousness into new postures, it is already on the side of life. When a rhyme surprises and extends the fixed relations between words, that in itself protests against necessity. When language does more than enough, as it does in all achieved poetry, it opts for the condition of overlife, and rebels at limit. In this fundamentally artistic way, then, Larkin's 'Aubade' does not go over to the side of the adversary. But its argument does add weight to the negative side of the scale and tips the balance definitely in favour of chemical law and mortal decline. The poem does not hold the lyre up in the face of the gods of the underworld; it does not make the Orphic effort to haul life back up the slope against all the odds. For all its heartbreaking truths and beauties, 'Aubade' reneges on what Yeats called the 'spiritual intellect's great work'.

This phrase comes from Yeats's poem 'The Man and the Echo', with which I am going to conclude. In it, the theme so playfully treated by Holub in the lines I read at the beginning is orchestrated into something far more sombre and vigorous. Both poets present their characters at death's door, but whereas Holub's spunky surrealist affirms his faith in life with a whimsical vision of horses making love, Yeats's seer endures a more strenuous ordeal and is rewarded with a vision of reality that is at once more demanding and more fulfilling. Indeed, what 'The

Man and the Echo' implies is something that I have repeatedly tried to establish through several different readings and remarks in the course of these lectures: namely, that the goal of life on earth, and of poetry as a vital factor in the achievement of that goal, is what Yeats called in 'Under Ben Bulben' the 'profane perfection of mankind'.

In order to achieve that goal, therefore, and in order that human beings bring about the most radiant conditions for themselves to inhabit, it is essential that the vision of reality which poetry offers should be transformative, more than just a print-out of the given circumstances of its time and place. The poet who would be most the poet has to attempt an act of writing that outstrips the conditions even as it observes them. The truly creative writer, by interposing his or her perception and expression, will transfigure the conditions and effect thereby what I have been calling 'the redress of poetry'. The world is different after it has been read by a Shakespeare or an Emily Dickinson or a Samuel Beckett because it has been augmented by their reading of it. Indeed, Beckett is a very clear example of a writer who is Larkin's equal in not flinching from the ultimate bleakness of things, but who then goes on to do something positive with the bleakness. For it is not the apparent pessimism of Beckett's world-view that constitutes his poetic genius: his excellence resides in his working out a routine in the playhouse of his art which is both true to the depressing goings-on in the house of actuality and – more important – a transformation of them. It is because of his transformative way with language, his mixture of word-play and merciless humour, that Beckett the writer has life and has it more abundantly than the conditions endured by Beckett the citizen might seem to warrant.

We go to poetry, we go to literature in general, to be forwarded within ourselves. The best it can do is to give us an experience that is like foreknowledge of certain things which we already seem to be remembering. What is at work in this most original and illuminating poetry is the mind's capacity to conceive a new plane of regard for itself, a new scope for its own activity. Which is why I turn in conclusion to 'The Man and the Echo', a poem where human consciousness is up against the cliff-face of mystery, confronted with the limitations of human existence itself. Here the consciousness of the poet is in full possession of both its creative impulse and its limiting knowledge. The knowledge is limiting because it concedes that pain necessarily accompanies the cycles of life, and that failure and hurt – hurt to oneself and to others – persist disablingly behind even the most successful career. Yet in the poem the spirit's impulse still remains creative and obeys the human compulsion to do that 'great work' of spiritual intellect.

The situation of the man in 'The Man and the Echo' is that of somebody *in extremis*, somebody who wants to make his soul, to bring himself to wholeness, to bring his mind and being into congruence with the divine mind and being. He therefore goes to consult the oracle, not at Delphi, but in a glen on the side of Knocknarea in County Sligo, at a place called Alt; but this rock face does not issue any message from the gods – all it does is give back an echo. And what the echo communicates, of course, is the man's own most extreme and exhausted recognitions. The echo marks the limits of the mind's operations even as it calls the mind forth to its utmost exertions, and the strenuousness of this dialectic issues in a poem that is as shadowed by death as Larkin's 'Aubade' but is far more vital and undaunted. 'The Man and the Echo' tries to make sense of historical existence within a bloodstained natural world and an indifferent universe. It was written near the end of Yeats's life, when he was reviewing his involvement with the historical events in Ireland over a previous half-century: events such as the founding of the Abbey Theatre and its political impact in the lead-up to the 1916 Rising; the Irish War of Independence and the destruction of many of the big houses belonging to the Anglo-Irish gentry; and other, more private, guilt-inducing events, such as the nervous breakdown of a young poet and dancer, Margot Collis, with whom Yeats felt himself half-culpably implicated:

Joy or Night

The Man and the Echo

Man

In a cleft that's christened Alt
Under broken stone I halt
At the bottom of a pit
That broad noon has never lit,
And shout a secret to the stone.
All that I have said and done,
Now that I am old and ill,
Turns into a question till
I lie awake night after night
And never get the answers right.
Did that play of mine send out
Certain men the English shot?
Did words of mine put too great strain
On that woman's reeling brain?
Could my spoken words have checked
That whereby a house lay wrecked?
And all seems evil until I
Sleepless would lie down and die.

Echo

Lie down and die.

Man

That were to shirk
The spiritual intellect's great work,
And shirk it in vain. There is no release
In a bodkin or disease,
Nor can there be a work so great
As that which cleans man's dirty slate.
While man can still his body keep
Wine or love drug him to sleep,
Waking he thanks the Lord that he
Has body and its stupidity,
But body gone he sleeps no more,

161

And till his intellect grows sure
That all's arranged in one clear view
Pursues the thoughts that I pursue,
Then stands in judgement on his soul,
And, all work done, dismisses all
Out of intellect and sight
And sinks at last into the night.

Echo

Into the night.

Man

    O Rocky Voice,
Shall we in that great night rejoice?
What do we know but that we face
One another in this place?
But hush, for I have lost the theme
Its joy or night seem but a dream;
Up there some hawk or owl has struck
Dropping out of sky or rock,
A stricken rabbit is crying out.
And its cry distracts my thought.

This is a far cry from the experience of illumination and visitation that Yeats wrote about in 'The Cold Heaven': here he is not so much riddled with light as with dark. And much, much more could be said about the poem – about, for example, the resilience of the man and the vigor of the metre in face of the echo's intransigence. I shall confine myself, however, to one detailed comment and one brief concluding reflection. The detail is the final rhyme, which yokes together the words 'crying out' and 'thought'. It is not a perfect rhyme, nor should it be, for there is no perfect fit between the project of civilization represented by thought and the facts of pain and death represented by the rabbit's 'crying out'. What holds the crying out and the thought together is a consciousness which persists in trying to make sense of a world where suffering and violence are more evi-

dently set to prevail than the virtue of being 'kind'. The rhyme –
and the poem in general – not only tell of that which the spirit
must endure; they also show *how* it must endure, by pitting
human resource against the recalcitrant and the inhuman, by
pitting the positive effort of mind against the desolations of
natural and historical violence, by making 'rejoice' answer back
to the voice from the rock, whatever it says:

> O Rocky Voice,
> Shall we in that great night rejoice?
> What do we know but that we face
> One another in this place?
> But hush, for I have lost the theme
> Its joy or night seem but a dream;
> Up there some hawk or owl has struck
> Dropping out of sky or rock,
> A stricken rabbit is crying out.
> And its cry distracts my thought.

There is a strong sense, at the conclusion of this poem, that
the mind's options are still open, that the mind's constructs are
still vital and reliable, even though its functions may for the
moment be suspended. Where Larkin's 'Aubade' ended in entrapment, 'The Man and the Echo' has preserved a freedom, and
manages to pronounce a final *Yes*. And the *Yes* is valuable because we can say of it what Karl Barth said of the enormous
Yes at the centre of Mozart's music, that it has weight and
significance because it overpowers and contains a *No*. Yeats's
poetry, in other words, gives credence to the idea that courage
is *some* good; it shows how the wilful and unabashed activity of
poetry itself is a manifestation of 'joy' and a redressal, in so far
as it fortifies the spirit against assaults from outside and temptations from within – temptations such as the one contained
in Larkin's attractively defeatist proposition that 'Death is no
different whined at than withstood'.

30 April 1990

Counting to a Hundred:
On Elizabeth Bishop

About a third of the way through Elizabeth Bishop's autobiographical story 'In the Village', the small girl who narrates the tale is sent by her grandmother and her aunts on an errand to the village dressmaker. The dressmaker has already visited their house earlier in the day and is due to return, but the message brought by the child is that this second visit will have to be postponed. And then:

> Mysteriously enough, poor Miss Gurley – I know she is poor – gives me a five-cent piece. She leans over and drops it in the pocket of the red-and-white dress that she has made herself. It is very tiny, very shiny. King George's beard is like a little silver flame. Because they look like herring- or maybe salmon-scales, five-cent pieces are called 'fish scales'. One heard of people's rings being found inside a fish, or their long-lost jackknives. What if one could scrape a salmon and find a little picture of King George on every scale?
>
> I put my five-cent piece in my mouth for greater safety on the way home, and swallowed it. Months later, as far as I know, it is still in me, transmuting all its precious metal into my growing teeth and hair.

There is a wonderful lyric freshness about the way this narrator sees things, but the way she announces that she simply 'swallowed' the five-cent piece shows that she also possesses what the poet Marianne Moore would later recognize in Elizabeth Bishop as 'a flicker of impudence'. The narrator, in other words, is manifestly the little self of the young poet whom Moore knew in the 1930s, as she is also the precursor of the mature poet who wrote to Anne Stevenson in the 1960s, 'Although I think I have a prize "unhappy childhood", almost good enough for the text-books – please don't think I dote on it.' And furthermore, this narrator bears a definite resemblance to the Elizabeth Bishop whose mind the novelist Mary McCarthy once said she envied, a mind 'hiding in her words, like an "I" counting up to a hundred'.

Hiding in the words of the paragraph I just quoted is the whole story of that un-doted-upon childhood unhappiness. Miss Gurley's gift of the five-cent piece may have been mysterious to the child, but to the adults in the village and to the reader of the story it is clear that the child is an object of sympathy because she is virtually an orphan. Her father has died, and ever since then her mother has been intermittently absent because of her recurrent nervous breakdowns. In fact, this tremulous mother figure was the person being fitted by the dressmaker earlier in the day when she gave the scream which rent the child's world for ever and set up an echo of pain that was potentially unsilenceable.

The scream, of course, had happened in Bishop's life as well, just before her own mother was finally and permanently committed to an insane asylum in 1916. The actual village was called Great Village and the poet-to-be had come there with her mother from Massachusetts in the aftermath of the father's death in 1911 – the year of Elizabeth Bishop's birth. For the rest of her life, these original hurts and absences would also hide and count and multiply within her like fish scales multiplying out of a single five-cent coin: indeed, Elizabeth Bishop's supreme gift was to be able to ingest loss and to transmute it. She would count to a hundred by naming the things of the world, one after another, like the coins and scales and rings and jackknives in her story; and with each of these things she would mark a point on the scale of memory, a mark which both proclaimed and contained the forces that it took the measure of.

Ever since the publication in 1946 of her first volume, *North & South*, Bishop's place in American poetry has been consolidating. The terms of that title are in one way strictly geographic and indicate the points between which her life would keep taking her, but they represent also the emotional extremes she

navigated in her art, in subsequent books with equally suggestive titles – *A Cold Spring* (1955), *Questions of Travel* (1965)
and *Geography III* (1976). Early and late, she was something of
a migrant. To begin with, there had been her move north to
Canada as an infant, but more important, there was the subsequent removal south when she felt as if she had been kidnapped
by her father's side of the family and carried away from the
secure village life of Nova Scotia into an uneasy adolescence
among her more sedate, less emotionally nurturing relatives in
Massachusetts. Later on, her north and south became the north
and south of the United States themselves: as a young woman
just out of Vassar College, Bishop lived for an important forma-
tive period in the literary milieu of 1930s New York before
making a happy retreat to Key West in Florida, spending five
years there in a house with her Vassar contemporary, Louise
Crane, and enjoying the richly textured local life which inspired
many of her most famous poems, notably 'Roosters' and 'The
Fish'. But the most decisive and long-lasting of these shifts of
address occurred in the 1950s when Bishop domiciled herself in
Brazil, with her beloved companion Lota de Macedo Soares, in
a house in the mountains north of Rio de Janeiro. She spent
sixteen years there, sometimes in Rio, sometimes on great trips
up the Amazon, but always at a remove from the literary life of
the States, until that particular arrangement also came to an
end, and Bishop returned to live again in Massachusetts in an
apartment on Lewis Wharf in Boston; and in that apartment, at
the comparatively early age of sixty-eight, she died suddenly on
6 October 1979.

Much of this is documented in a book by the late David
Kalstone about Bishop's friendships with two other important
American poets. Entitled *Becoming a Poet*, this is one of the
best studies of the process to be found and focuses upon 'the
mystery of affinity' and influence. The affinity was more obvious in the case of Bishop's relationship with Marianne Moore,
the influence more palpable in the effect she (Bishop) had upon
Robert Lowell, but the book is constantly illuminating in the

way it treats both of these relationships. Robert Lowell was, of course, the clamorous poet-challenger of his generation, a champion who galloped into the lists, sought confrontation, created an uproar and made magnificent bother for himself and everybody close to him. He was exorbitant in his demands from poetry and in his exercise of its prerogatives, and he was in the end rebuked for it all by Elizabeth Bishop, both by her manners as a person and by her example as a poet. In contrast to Lowell, there was something wonderfully Cordelia-like in Bishop, a reticence which gave her work its attractive steadiness, a reticence which was also fortified by something that Marianne Moore described with characteristic acumen as 'a certain satisfactory doughtiness'. And these qualities of reticence and doughtiness are evident also in the child narrator of the story 'In the Village', who is a vigilant, self-reliant little spirit, already familiar (as the story tells us) with 'an immense, sibilant, glistening loneliness'.

If the family drama which Bishop experienced was less catastrophic than the one Cordelia faced, it still seems to have been suffered by her as a kind of test. Each measured her spirit and her allowable words against the circumstances, and each found that an early apprenticeship to reticence rendered both herself and her words a capable match for disaster. 'In the Village', for example, ends with a sound which matches and acknowledges and bears away the sound of the mother's scream with which the story begins: this second sound has been underneath the story all along, counting its meaning stroke by stroke like the author's mind counting up to a hundred; it is the sound of the blacksmith's anvil coming from the forge behind the house:

Clang.
Clang.
Nate is shaping a horseshoe.
Oh, beautiful pure sound!
It turns everything else to silence.
But still, once in a while, the river gives an unexpected gurgle. '*Slp*', it says, out of glassy-ridged brown knots sliding along the surface.

Clang.

And everything except the river holds its breath.

Now there is no scream. Once there was one and it settled slowly down to earth one hot summer afternoon; or did it float up, into that dark, too dark, blue sky? But surely it has gone away, forever.

It sounds like a bell buoy out at sea.

All those other things – clothes, crumbling postcards, broken china; things damaged and lost, sickened or destroyed; even the frail almost-lost scream – are they too frail for us to hear their voices long, too mortal?

Nate!

Oh, beautiful sound, strike again!

Both the reader and the writer of this story might revise Keats's exclamation in his 'Ode to a Nightingale' and say instead 'Brightling I listen', because it is in the daylight clarity of Bishop's writing that its unique virtue resides. Things as they are seem to be even more themselves once she has written them. In the above passage, for example, the little *slp* of the river says in perfect riverspeak what Bishop then says in English: "everything except the river holds its breath". And yet, of course, it is precisely Bishop's linguistic virtuosity which creates the delightful illusion of access to a pristine, pre-linguistic state. As readers, we had not known that we ached for this fulfilment in language until it was proffered; we had not known that the givens of experience could be raised to this sweet, new power.

There is nothing spectacular about Bishop's writing, even though there is always something transformative about it. One has a sense of justice being done to the facts of a situation even as the situation is being re-imagined into poetry. She never allows the formal delights of her art to mollify the hard realities of her subjects. For example, in one of her two sestinas – the one she calls, with typical plain-spokenness, 'Sestina' – the six end-words have a thoroughly domestic provenance and in the first instance they seem all set to keep the poem within comforting emotional bounds. House, grandmother, child, stove, almanac, tears. They imply a little drama of youth and age, even perhaps of instruction and correction. A Victorian genre piece, almost. A decorous domestic interior, at any rate, in terms both of the setting and of the emotions. The end-words, at one level, do keep bringing to mind a conventional home situation where we would naturally expect to find a father and a mother as well as a child and a grandparent. But gradually and insistently a second realization is forced into consciousness by the inexorable formal recurrences within the poem itself. Gradually, the repetition of grandmother and child and house alerts us to the significant absence from this house of a father and a mother:

> September rain falls on the house.
> In the failing light, the old grandmother
> sits in the kitchen with the child
> beside the Little Marvel Stove,
> reading the jokes from the almanac,
> laughing and talking to hide her tears.

> She thinks that her equinoctial tears
> and the rain that beats on the roof of the house
> were both foretold by the almanac,
> but only known to a grandmother.
> The iron kettle sings on the stove.
> She cuts some bread and says to the child,

> *It's time for tea now*; but the child
> is watching the teakettle's small hard tears
> dance like mad on the hot black stove,
> the way the rain must dance on the house.
> Tidying up, the old grandmother
> hangs up the clever almanac

> on its string. Birdlike, the almanac
> hovers half open above the child,
> hovers above the old grandmother
> and her teacup full of dark brown tears.
> She shivers and says she thinks the house
> feels chilly, and puts more wood in the stove.

It was to be, says the Marvel Stove.
I know what I know, says the almanac.
With crayons the child draws a rigid house
and a winding pathway. Then the child
puts in a man with buttons like tears
and shows it proudly to the grandmother.

But secretly, while the grandmother
busies herself about the stove,
the little moons fall down like tears
from between the pages of the almanac
into the flower bed the child
has carefully placed in the front of the house.

Time to plant tears, says the almanac.
The grandmother sings to the marvellous stove
and the child draws another inscrutable house.

Like any successful sestina, this has a touch of virtuosity about it, but its virtuosity is not what engages one's attention. Its immediate effect is as emotionally direct as a fairytale. Just as Dylan Thomas's villanelle 'Do Not Go Gentle into That Good Night' comes across as a dramatic cry rather than a formal set-piece, so the narrative and dramatic interest of Bishop's sestina very quickly deflects attention from its master-class excellence as a technical performance. The poem circles unspoken sorrows, and as it circles them, it manages to mesmerize them and make them obedient to creative will. The resolution of the poem is therefore like the resolution of 'In the Village'; each of these works confounds its elaborately articulated and indirectly stated grief in an art within its art. In the story, the scream is transposed and modulated into the anvil-song of the shape-making blacksmith; and in the poem, the short-circuited pain within the grandmother's house, a pain to which the almanac imparts a fatal inevitability, is shut up for the time being inside the inscrutable house which the child draws. In so far as it echoes old tales where the wicked spirit is

imprisoned in some box or tree or rock, this conclusion represents a victory over the negative conditions. But viewed from
another perspective, it simply returns the situation to its original configuration, where the entrapment is ongoing and resolution is something attainable only in imagination.

In fact, 'Sestina', with its inscrutable house, performs the
same reflexive but ultimately salubrious function as the monument performs in an early Bishop poem called (with equal plain-
ness) 'The Monument'. This monument is made of wood, of
boxes placed upon boxes; like the sestina it is both enigmatic
and entirely satisfactory. It promises nothing beyond what it
exhibits, and yet it seems to be standing over something which
it also stands *for*. Once again, a withdrawn pressure, an inscrutable purpose or missing element is what the resulting structure
exists to express or shelter. In fact, the final lines of the poem
declare that the monument commemorates something unde-
clared, something embodying and maintaining a meaning it
feels no need to proclaim:

> It is an artifact
> of wood. Wood holds together better
> than sea or cloud or sand could by itself,
> much better than real sea or sand or cloud.
> It chose that way to grow and not to move.
> The monument's an object, yet those decorations,
> carelessly nailed, looking like nothing at all,
> give it away as having life, and wishing;
> wanting to be a monument, to cherish something.
> The crudest scroll-work says 'commemorate',
> while once each day the light goes around it
> like a prowling animal,
> or the rain falls on it, or the wind blows into it.
> It may be solid, may be hollow.
> The bones of the artist-prince may be inside
> or far away on even drier soil.
> But roughly but adequately it can shelter

> what is within (which after all
> cannot have been intended to be seen).
> It is the beginning of a painting,
> a piece of sculpture, or poem, or monument,
> and all of wood. Watch it closely.

This monument to something which 'cannot have been intended to be seen' finds itself menaced by the very light which goes around it 'like a prowling animal'. Yet in spite of the guardedness which these conditions induce, it still does want 'to cherish something'. And if we watch it closely, as we are counselled to, we shall find that in being an object which has life and 'can shelter / what is within', it resembles the work of the poet who imagined it into being in the first place. For the gratifying thing about Elizabeth Bishop's poetry is that in the end it too overcomes the guardedness of its approach. It may be an observant poetry but it does not finally, in the colloquial sense of the term, 'watch it', even though the inclination to caution is persistently felt as a condition of the poet's style. Qualification is her natural habit of mind, but even so, the poetry continually manages to go out to greet what is there, to salute what Louis MacNeice called 'the drunkenness of things being various'. And it justifies itself *as* poetry by the thoroughness of its assistance. At its most ardent, it wants to give itself entirely to what it discovers, as when her poem 'Over 2000 Illustrations and a Complete Concordance' concludes by asking 'Why couldn't we have ... looked and looked our infant sight away'?

This is to say that Bishop's famous gift for observation is more than a habit of simply watching; it represents rather a certain self-conquest, the surmounting of a definite temperamental wariness. She is more naturally fastidious than rhapsodic. If she is well enough disposed towards the phenomena, she is still not exultant. Her detachment is chronic, and yet the combination of attentiveness and precision which she brings to bear upon things is so intense that the detachment almost evaporates. What Bishop does is to scrutinize and interrogate things

as they are before giving her assent to them. She does not immediately or necessarily glorify them, being more of a sympathetic
adjudicator than a born cheer-leader, but neither does she refuse
them their just measure of praise. Her sense of reality, to put it
another way, is more earth-bound than angelic. Her early
poem 'Anaphora', for example, is a morning song in which
Bishop does indeed conceive of an angelic creature, one who
represents a part of us that is potentially equal to the brilliant
promises of the morning and the day; yet she is constrained to
acknowledge that this creature is also the one whose possibilities we nevertheless actually and repeatedly fail to realize. And
so he

> suffers our uses and abuses,
> sinks through the drift of bodies,
> sinks through the drift of classes
> to evening to the beggar in the park
> who, weary, without lamp or book
>> prepares stupendous studies:
>> the fiery event
>> of every day in endless
>> endless assent.

But there is, after all, something marvellous about a beggar
assenting to things as they are. For him, the fiery event of every
day, be it the dawn or the sunset, has to be its own reward,
since there is nothing else in it for him; and it is in similar acts
of outstripping one's own deprivation, in not doting upon it, so
to speak, but proceeding instead into freely offered celebration
– it is in such acts and attainments of the spirit that Bishop's
poetry redresses the scales that were loaded against her from
the start.

The move is not so much from delight to wisdom, although
both of these things figure importantly in the poems; in her
case, the characteristic shift might be more precisely described
as being from self-containment to an acknowledgement of the
mystery of the other, with the writing functioning as an enact-

ment of all the bittersweet deferrals in between. 'The Fish' is an obvious instance of this, the whole poem hypnotically suspended between the two definite actions reported in the first and the last lines: 'I caught a tremendous fish', 'And I let the fish go'. In between, what the poem offers is a slow-motion replay, sensation by sensation, of the process by which the fish is recognized as a harbinger of what Hopkins calls 'the glory of God', of that dearest freshness that lives deep down in things, all that which the poem itself finally calls 'rainbow, rainbow, rainbow'. For once, Bishop seems to go beyond assent, yet in fact the action of releasing the fish is simply the deepest form which assent can take, and, in a Cordelia-like way, it speaks more loudly than the superlative words. The fish is recognized as a kindred spirit, one of the swimming as opposed to the walking wounded, one who takes things in but prefers to keep his counsel:

> I looked into his eyes
> which were far larger than mine
> but shallower, and yellowed,
> the irises backed and packed
> with tarnished tinfoil
> seen through the lenses
> of old scratched isinglass.
> They shifted a little, but not
> to return my stare.
> – It was more like the tipping
> of an object toward the light.
> I admired his sullen face,
> the mechanism of his jaw,
> and then I saw
> that from his lower lip
> – if you could call it a lip –
> grim, wet, and weaponlike,
> hung five old pieces of fish-line,
> or four and a wire leader

with the swivel still attached,
with all their five big hooks
grown firmly in his mouth.

One can imagine this fish and the poet who writes about him
recognizing the truth in the reply of the old Eskimo woman
who, when asked why all the songs sung by her tribe were so
short, answered simply: 'Because we know so much.'

Similarly, the cost of Bishop's composure in her poems
should not be underestimated. The rainbow effect is not attained without some expense of spirit. No writer is more positive in registering the detailed marvels of the world, yet no
writer is more scrupulous in conceding that there are endanger-
ing negative conditions which must equally and simultaneously
be accounted facts of life. I would like, therefore, to concentrate
for a few minutes on a poem which reveals these characteristic
motions of Bishop's mind, both in art and in life, one which
also has about it a touch of comedy and a hint of self-
portraiture. This is her poem about the sandpiper:

> The roaring alongside he takes for granted,
> and that every so often the world is bound to shake.
> He runs, he runs to the south, finical, awkward,
> in a state of controlled panic, a student of Blake.
>
> The beach hisses like fat. On his left, a sheet
> of interrupting water comes and goes
> and glazes over his dark and brittle feet.
> He runs, he runs straight through it, watching his toes.
>
> – Watching, rather, the spaces of sand between them,
> where (no detail too small) the Atlantic drains
> rapidly backwards and downwards. As he runs,
> he stares at the dragging grains.
>
> The world is a mist. And then the world is
> minute and vast and clear. The tide
> is higher or lower. He couldn't tell you which.

His beak is focused; he is preoccupied,

looking for something, something, something.
Poor bird, he is obsessed!
The millions of grains are black, white, tan, and gray,
mixed with quartz grains, rose and amethyst.

'The roaring alongside he takes for granted', we are told right
away; and if we think of that roaring as the noise of the public
world as well as the noise of the sea, we can say much the same
thing about Elizabeth Bishop. She does not go in for the epic
panorama, for large historical treatments, for the synoptic view
of cultures and crises so typical of other major twentieth-century poets. She is, of course, deeply aware that every so often
the world is bound to shake, and not only with the thunder of
waves, but also with the thunder of war or of earthquake or the
merciless death of a parent or the untimely and guilt-inducing
suicide of a beloved friend. In such circumstances, panic is a
natural enough reaction, a reflex impulse to escape from the
scene altogether. And yet since one cannot escape one's times or
one's destiny, such panic has to be controlled, and to control is
to set limits, to map a defined space within which one will
operate. In the case of the sandpiper, this space is a shifting
space of sand, between the tide and the land: it is here that the
sandpiper naturally becomes a student of Blake, since William
Blake is the poet who urged in 'Auguries of Innocence':

> To see a World in a Grain of Sand,
> And a Heaven in a Wild Flower,
> Hold Infinity in the palm of your hand,
> And Eternity in an hour.

Blake's poem is visionary and prophetic, but even as zealous a
student as the sandpiper can never possess its immense bardic
confidence. The poor bird is 'finical', a word whose very sound
and texture suggest nervousness, primness, petulance; a finical
creature will never be in command of the situation, and so,
instead of standing his ground, the sandpiper runs:

Counting to a Hundred

He runs, he runs to the south, finical, awkward.

Nevertheless, the poet is instinctively drawn to the bird, and cannot blame him for his twitchiness. There is something detached and concerned in her attitude to his fretful busy scurrying which is not unlike her own attitude to herself as she expressed it in a speech in 1976. 'Yes,' she said then, 'all my life I have lived and behaved very much like that sandpiper – just running along the edges of different countries, "looking for something".' But it's not just Bishop's migrant impulse that links her to the sandpiper. There is also her vigilant, hesitant, yet completely fascinated attention to detail, and her habitual caution in the face of the world. The phrase 'watching his toes', for example, applies in an exact and jokey way to both the bird and the poet. It echoes, obviously, the phrase 'watch your step' while putting a spin on the phrase 'keep on your toes', and in its double encompassing of alertness and caution, of being menaced and being ready, it is consonant both with Elizabeth Bishop's habitual attitudes and with the tiny plight of the sandpiper.

I say 'tiny' plight. But part of the purpose of this writing is to blur the distinction between what is vast and what is tiny. The student of Blake, after all, will see a world in a grain of sand. So this poem will see to it that vast words like 'Atlantic' and 'world' and indeed the word 'vast' itself are matched and balanced and equalled by small words like 'toes' and 'beak' and 'grains'. No detail is too small, as the parenthesis in line ten insists. 'The world is a mist. And then the world is / minute and vast and clear.' We might in fact go so far as to say that the poem is about the way in which obsessive attention to detail can come through into visionary understanding; the way in which an intense focus can amplify rather than narrow our sense of scope. The last two lines of the poem do transform what is tiny and singular and project it on a cosmic screen. They make radiant and marvellous that which is in danger of being overlooked and disregarded. Again, the small and the great are brought into contact, and the small brings the great into question:

> looking for something, something, something.
> Poor bird, he is obsessed!
> The millions of grains are black, white, tan, and gray,
> mixed with quartz grains, rose and amethyst.

'The millions of grains': we see a pepper-and-salt of grains. A yard of sand is first a gritty texture and then a glittering marvel. And all this is effected without any straining of linguistic muscle. The poem does not raise its voice or overstretch its vocabulary. The words are usual and plain and available to everybody. Yet the poet does to words what she does to details: she makes them beckon us into hitherto unsuspected spaces. Quartz, rose, amethyst: all three of them are now ashimmer, 'minute and vast and clear', as if they had escaped from the light-drenched empyrean of Dante's *Paradiso*. The student of Blake has found not only a world but a whole system of heavens in the grains of sand.

'Sandpiper' is a poem of immense discretion and discreet immensity, and if I appear to be talking it up in excess of its merits, then all I can say is that appearances are deceptive. It is a perfect achievement, one that brings itself and its reader into a renewed awareness of that mysterious otherness of the world. And it brings us to that threshold by following its nose – or its beak – through the old crazy-paving and matter-of-fact of detail. And the same is true of many of Bishop's acknowledged triumphs, especially her great meditative *excursus*, 'At the Fish-houses'. But since I have written at length about that poem in the title essay of *The Government of the Tongue*, I want to draw attention here briefly instead to those two longish late poems, 'The Moose' and 'Crusoe in England'. Each of them is a memory poem, each gives access to a marvellous thing, but neither of them treats the marvellous as other than an achievement of the imagination. When the moose comes out of the woods, when Crusoe remembers the aura which his jackknife

once possessed for him, the world does shimmer in a transformed light; and yet both of these poems, in Auden's words,
find the mortal world enough. Their characteristic strength
comes from Bishop's old gift for raising the actual to a new
linguistic power. Their triumph is the redundancy of that power,
its capacity to be more than enough. Here is Crusoe, remembering waterspouts:

> And I had waterspouts. Oh,
> half a dozen at a time, far out,
> they'd come and go, advancing and retreating,
> their heads in cloud, their feet in moving patches
> of scuffed-up white.
> Glass chimneys, flexible, attenuated,
> sacerdotal beings of glass . . . I watched
> the water spiral up in them like smoke.
> Beautiful, yes, but not much company.

And here is the almost beautiful moose appearing out of the
night as the passengers on a bus talk and talk intimately among
themselves on the long journey south out of Nova Scotia, a
journey which follows a scheduled bus-route and at the same
time retraces in memory the path the poet once took from the
pre-reflective world of her childhood:

> Talking the way they talked
> in the old featherbed,
> peacefully, on and on,
> dim lamplight in the hall,
> down in the kitchen, the dog
> tucked in her shawl.
>
> Now, it's all right now
> even to fall asleep
> just as on all those nights.
> – Suddenly the bus driver
> stops with a jolt,
> turns off his lights.

A moose has come out of
the impenetrable wood
and stands there, looms, rather,
in the middle of the road.
It approaches; it sniffs at
the bus's hot hood.

Towering, antlerless,
high as a church,
homely as a house
(or, safe as houses).
A man's voice assures us
'Perfectly harmless . . .'

Some of the passengers
exclaim in whispers,
childishly, softly,
'Sure are big creatures.'
'It's awful plain.'
'Look! It's a she!'

Taking her time,
she looks the bus over,
grand, otherworldly.
Why, why do we feel
(we all feel) this sweet
sensation of joy?

'Curious creatures,'
says our quiet driver,
rolling his *r*'s.
'Look at that, would you.'
Then he shifts gears.
For a moment longer

by craning backward,
the moose can be seen
on the moonlit macadam;

> then there's a dim
> smell of moose, an acrid
> smell of gasoline.

Something that the American poet Charles Simic has written in relation to the work of the artist Joseph Cornell – an artist, incidentally, to whom Elizabeth Bishop was also devoted – seems worth quoting at this juncture. 'There are really three kinds of images,' Simic writes:

First, there are those seen with eyes open in the manner of realists in both art and literature. Then there are images we see with eyes closed. Romantic poets, surrealists, expressionists and everyday dreamers know them. The images Cornell has in his boxes are, however, of the third kind. They partake of both dream and reality, and of something else that doesn't have a name. They tempt the viewer in two opposite directions. One is to look and admire ... and the other is to make up stories about what one sees ... Neither [way] by itself is sufficient. It's the mingling of the two that makes up the third image.

Simic entitles his short meditation 'The Gaze We Knew as a Child,' which again seems apposite to Bishop's images, for they too strike us as being both preternaturally immediate and remotely familiar. Their attraction partakes of 'something that doesn't have a name', as if things known once upon a time in a pre-literate security were reappearing among the destabilizations of the post-modern. Her images call consciousness towards recollection. And it is surely Bishop's successful effort to become utterly receptive in face of the phenomena and to give a just account of the reactions, both positive and negative, which they induce – it is surely this peculiar honest gaze, both level and brimming, which has drawn so many readers to her work over the last couple of decades. Naturally, as a woman poet whose laconic sense of her relegation through gender was matched only by her sense of entitlement through achievement, Bishop has rightly gained the advocacy of feminist critics. Her quietude was a far cry from quietism, and poems like 'Roosters', dating from the early 1940s, were a clear-eyed and

deeply creative response to the impositions of a militaristic, patri-
archal world. Yet she always resisted the pressures to connect
herself politically with activist feminist politics. She was by temperament and choice too much of a loner to subscribe even to
the most urgent of solidarities.

Within recent American poetry, Bishop occupies a position
analogous to that long occupied on the other side of the ocean
by Philip Larkin. In an era of volubility, she seems to demonstrate that less is more. By her sense of proportion and awareness of tradition, she makes what is an entirely personal and
contemporary style seem continuous with the canonical poetry
of the past. She writes the kind of poem that makes us want to
exclaim with admiration at its professional thoroughness, its
technical and formal perfections, and yet at the same time she
tempts us to regard technical and formal matters as something
of a distraction, since the poem is so candidly *about* something,
engaged with its own business of observing the world and discovering meaning.

All of which is immediately manifest in the poem I want to
read and comment upon by way of conclusion. This is a villanelle entitled 'One Art', and, since its publication sixteen
years ago in Bishop's last volume, it has become one of the
most admired examples of her work. This last volume,
Geography III, was published in 1976 and contains a number
of extraordinary poems of summation and benediction – including 'The Moose' and that other hide-and-seek, count-to-a-
hundred dramatic monologue, 'Crusoe in England'. These
poems arise from a mind that is unembittered but still unap-
peased, like the sandpiper still 'looking for something, something, something'. They come near the end of a life which
Bishop had long contemplated both with regard to its penalties
and its blessings. They represent the effort of a memory observing its own contents, a consciousness squaring up to itself and
taking the measure of its own strengths and weaknesses. And
this reflexive strain, this compulsion of her intelligence to keep
standing at an angle to her predicament, finds its natural form

in the villanelle. With its repetitions and revisions and nuancings, its shifts and refinements and siftings of what has already been finely sifted, the villanelle is the perfect mould for Bishop's habitual method of coming at a subject in little renewed attempts and sorties. But each little attempt falls short of stating the big sorrow or sorrows which occasioned the poem. Anybody familiar with the outlines of the poet's biography will know that there are plenty of specific occasions from which the poem's general preoccupation with loss could have arisen, but the lines can be read without any special knowledge of the facts of Bishop's life:

> The art of losing isn't hard to master;
> so many things seem filled with the intent
> to be lost that their loss is no disaster.
>
> Lose something every day. Accept the fluster
> of lost door keys, the hour badly spent.
> The art of losing isn't hard to master.
>
> Then practice losing farther, losing faster:
> places, and names, and where it was you meant
> to travel. None of these will bring disaster.
>
> I lost my mother's watch. And look! my last, or
> next-to-last, of three loved houses went.
> The art of losing isn't hard to master.
>
> I lost two cities, lovely ones. And, vaster,
> some realms I owned, two rivers, a continent.
> I miss them, but it wasn't a disaster.
>
> – Even losing you (the joking voice, a gesture
> I love) I shan't have lied. It's evident
> the art of losing's not too hard to master
> though it may look like (*Write* it!) like disaster.

In this poem, Bishop's ability to write plainly and at the same time reticently manifests itself *in extremis*. This is wonderful lyric writing; it is impossible to separate the poem's reality as a made thing from its effect as a personal cry. It is in one way, of course, entirely formal, preoccupied with its technical procedures, taking delight in solving the challenges of rhyme, in obeying (and disobeying) the rules of the highly constraining villanelle form. At the same time, it is obviously the whimper of a creature who has been hard done by; or, to be more exact, it is a choked-off whimper, the learnt behaviour of somebody who, without the impersonal demands of an art and an ethic of doughty conduct, might have submitted to self-pity. In fact, the conquest of a temptation to self-pity is what the poem manages to effect: wit confronts hurt and holds a balance that deserves to be called wisdom. The writing itself could be called deadpan-ironical or whimsical-stoical, but it is not exactly either. It is, to quote another famous line of Bishop's, 'like what we imagine knowledge to be.' By its trust in poetic form and its abnegation of self, it bears a recognizable relationship to the work of that seventeenth-century English poet-priest whom Elizabeth Bishop so admired, George Herbert. Like Herbert, Bishop finds and enforces a correspondence between the procedures of verse and the predicaments of the spirit. She makes rhyme an analogy for self-control. The first time 'master' and 'disaster' occur, in stanza one, they are tactfully, elegantly, deprecatingly paired off. It wasn't a disaster. The speaker is being decorous, good-mannered, relieving you of the burden of having to sympathize, easing you out of any embarrassed need to find things to say. The last time the rhyme occurs, however, the shocking traumatic reality of what happened almost overbrims the containing form. It *was* a disaster. It was devastatingly and indescribably so. And yet what the poem has just managed to do, in the nick of time, is to survive the devastation. The verb 'master' places itself in the scales opposite its twin noun, 'disaster', and holds the balance. And the secret of the held balance is given in the parenthesis '(*Write* it!)'. As so often in Bishop's work, the parenthesis (if you have ears to hear) is the place to hear the real truth. And what the parenthesis in

'One Art' tells us is what we always knew in some general way, but now know with an acute pang of intimacy, that the act of writing is an act of survival:

> I lost two cities, lovely ones. And, vaster,
> some realms I owned, two rivers, a continent.
> I miss them, but it wasn't a disaster.
>
> – Even losing you (the joking voice, a gesture
> I love) I shan't have lied. It's evident
> the art of losing's not too hard to master
> though it may look like (*Write* it!) like disaster.

The pun in that nick-of-time imperative – '*Write* it!' – is in deadly earnest. The redress of poetry is called upon by one of poetry's constant votaries; the poem is asked to set the balance *right*. Losses of all sorts have caused the mind's scales to tilt drastically and so they desperately need to be evened out by a redistribution of the mind's burdens – and the act of writing is depended upon to bring that redistribution about. The throwaway tone of the thing is recognizably the tone that accompanies a throw that risks all. In the pun on the word 'write', therefore, and in the harmony which prevails momentarily in the concluding rhyme, we experience the resolving power of deliberately articulated sound in much the same way as the narrator of the story 'In the Village' experienced it. There the scream was subsumed in the anvil note; here the 'disaster' is absorbed when it meets its emotional and phonetic match in the word 'master'. Bishop's 'one art' does not after all fail her. For all her caution about over-stating its prerogatives and possibilities, she does continually manage to advance poetry beyond the point where it has been helping us to enjoy life to that even more profoundly verifying point where it helps us also to endure it.

2 December 1992

Frontiers of Writing

In Oxford, in May 1981, I was a guest at a college dinner, one of those annual celebrations held to commemorate the largesse of a benefactor. My sense of occasion would have been high anyhow, but it was increased by the knowledge that I was to spend the night in a fellow's room in the college, and it was further abetted by a faint pleasurable sense of transgression. Earlier that evening, after all, I, a Northern Irish Catholic from a nationalist background, had attended Evening Prayer in an Anglican chapel in the company of a former Lord Chancellor of the realm; and later on I learnt that the room I was to sleep in belonged to a minister in the then Tory Cabinet. Yet piquant as all these circumstances were, they were not the real reason for my heightened feelings during that quintessentially Oxford event.

What raised the pressure was the fact that a quintessentially Irish event was coinciding with this Oxford one. Earlier that day, only a week after the death of the hunger striker Bobby Sands, another hunger striker had died in the Maze Prison, the second in a death toll that would mount to ten over the next three months. The young man who had just died belonged to a neighbour's family in Co. Derry. Although I had never known him personally, our families had been friends for a couple of generations and I had grown up friendly with his older brothers and sisters. So, because of all those ties of memory, affection and community, my mind kept turning towards that corpse house in Co. Derry. Even as I circulated with my glass of sherry, I could imagine the press of a very different crowd outside and inside the house in mid-Ulster, the movement of people from one room to the next, the protocols of sympathy, the hush as members of the bereaved family passed, and so on. What was in the eyes of the world at large the death of an IRA hunger striker was in the eyes of a smaller, denser world the death of a son and neighbour. And so, the imagined reality of that confusing wake – confusing because for some it was necessarily a domestic rite of mourning, whilst for others it was inevitably a show of political solidarity – that imagined event from which I was absent shadowed and questioned my presence at an otherwise perfectly jocund college feast.

But then, even if I had been at home in Dublin, I still would not have travelled the hundred miles north to the wake. Because some country habits have remained more or less second nature to me, I would have been susceptible to the traditional sense of obligation, but I would have been wary of the political implication of attendance. Suffice it to say that the handling of the 1981 hunger strike by the British government of the day had created a moment of entrapment for everybody. Whether you were Irish or English, Northern Catholic or Northern Protestant, activist or audience, the spectacle of a fast to the death being used as a weapon in what was by then essentially a propaganda war was intensely emotive – distressing for some, enraging for others. And those who so totally chose the role of victim in order to expose the total intransigence of those in power had no recourse when the government refused to relent but to follow the fatal logic of their choice. There was a terrible sadness about their plight that could be appreciated even by those who deplored their affiliations. As the Thatcher administration remained unmoved in the face of the deaths, and the cortèges kept winding from the prison gates to the local graves, there began to be something almost unseemly about the scruple which prevented a show of support for the hunger strikers' immediate claims – a support withheld because logically it would have been taken as an endorsement of the violent means and programmes of the Provisional IRA. Such caution had produced only silence, and now the silence was by default appearing like assent to the triumphalist, implacable handling of the affair by the Thatcher cabinet.

It was a classic moment of conflicting recognitions, self-division, inner quarrel, a moment of dumbness and inadequacy when it felt like a betrayal to be enjoying the hospitality of an Establishment college and occupying, if only accidentally, the room of a British minister. And yet the bind in which I found myself mirrored exactly the classic bind of all of Northern Ireland's constitutional nationalists. Constitutional nationalists find themselves constantly wrong-footed or are forced to wrong-foot themselves because of a conflict between on the one hand their commitments to cultural and political ideals which are fundamentally Ireland-centred – a conflict between this on the one hand and on the other hand their disavowal of support for the violent means of the Irish Republican Army, an army which operates with pre-emptive and atrocious force in order to further similar cultural and political ideals. In consorting with Westminster, for example, John Hume has for years been subject to taunts of shoneenism and sell-out by the Republican movement. In seeking to moderate the Republican Army's campaign by negotiation with Sinn Fein, he has been assailed by accusations of collusion in violence from the loyalist side. Neither his long record of political probity nor his large peace-seeking purpose was sufficient to constitute the political equivalent of a golden bough that would guarantee him a safe return from the underground of secret talks into the daylight of the old banal repetitions.

Not, of course, that there is anything new about all of this. The Irish political leader operating between two systems of loyalty, the Irish writer responsive to two cultural milieux, the Irish place invoked under two different systems of naming – we can recognize the syndrome in all its different manifestations from Hugh O'Neill to Mr Hume, from Oliver Goldsmith to Edna O'Brien, from Londonderry to Derry Colmcille. The problem is familiar and one of its unignorable causes is the border in Ireland, a frontier which has entered the imagination definitively, north and south, and which continues to divide Britain's Ireland from Ireland's Ireland. And I use these terms rather than British

Ireland and Irish Ireland because in the north there is a minority who prefer not to think of themselves as British although they do live in Britain's Ireland, and in the republic there is a section of the population, quite vocal at the present time, who would regard the phrase 'Irish Ireland' as reactionary, triumphantly nationalistic and part of an historical baggage which they would prefer to shed. But whether the north and the south are to be regarded as monolithic or pluralist entities, the fact of the border, of partition, of two Irelands on one island, remains the salient fact.

Several years ago, in a essay called 'Place and Displacement', I talked about what this division and bilocation entailed for the Northern Irish writer and at the time I found an English literary parallel which nicely illuminated the typical case of the poet from the minority in Ulster. When England declared war upon Revolutionary France in 1791, the young William Wordsworth suffered a dislocation which corresponded to much that still happens in the Irish situation. Here was this revolutionary sympathizer whose political ideals were French but whose nation was England, caught upon the horns of a dilemma. Wordsworth dramatizes the predicament by recollecting the sense of alienation and traitorous disaffection which he experienced in church during the prayers for the success of the English armies. No shock before or since, Wordsworth says, no blow administered to what he calls his moral nature equalled the disorienting force of this sudden fissure that had opened in his loyalties. And, of course, the poem in which Wordsworth reports the trauma is the very poem whose composition was part of the process of healing the trauma. *The Prelude* is about a consciousness coming together through the effort of articulating its conflict and crises. And the same could be said of much poetry from Northern Ireland. For the best efforts there have been evident in writing that is a mode of integration, of redistributing the whole field of cultural and political force into a tolerable order.

I shall come back to Northern Irish writing in a while, but

before leaving the subject I should emphasize that it is not just the writers and politicians who must make the effort I'm talking about: the whole population are adepts in the mystery of living in two places at one time. Like all human beings, of course, they would prefer to live in one, but in the meantime they make do with a constructed destination, an interim place whose foundations straddle the areas of self-division, a place of resolved contradiction, beyond confusion. A place, slightly to misquote Yeats, that does not exist, a place that is but a dream, since this promised land of durable coherence and perpetual homecoming is not somewhere that is ultimately attainable by constitutional reform or territorial integration. Or perhaps one could say that it exists as a state of resolved crisis which Ulster people don't quite admit as an immediate realistic expectation but don't quite deny as a deferred possibility. Poetically, it is an aspect of the place to which the quester in Robert Frost's poem 'Directive' is guided, and of the place in which the speaker of Thomas Hardy's poem 'Afterwards' arrives – an elsewhere beyond the frontier of writing where 'the imagination presses back against the pressure of reality'.

I quoted those words of Wallace Stevens in my first lecture on 'The Redress of Poetry', and in another preliminary lecture during my second year I gave some account of the Frost and Hardy poems. And when I took up the theme of redress in the Michaelmas Term of 1989, I was every bit as clear in my mind then as I am now that the theme is in fact an aspect or consequence of my autobiography. Indeed, I included the story of that 1981 Oxford visit in an early draft of my first lecture because I wanted to suggest that poetry represented a principle of integration within such a context of division and contradiction. But on second thoughts I decided to drop it because it seemed unduly loaded with political promise and would have suggested – wrongly – that my contributions at Oxford were going to be concerned with the exacerbations and entrapments of Northern Ireland's politics. Still, even though I removed the parable from my text and even though the subjects of the lectures have been for the most part poets from the English and American canons, the unspoken background has been a Northern Irish one. And because that background has recently, tragically and urgently become foreground, I think it is now worthwhile making explicit what was implicit and reaffirming the words of George Seferis, which I also quoted in the inaugural lecture. Writing about the Greek poet Makriyannis, at a time of world crisis and personal crisis, Seferis said that poetry was 'strong enough to help'.

Seferis did not mean that Makriyannis's poetry had the kind of strength that is supposed to come from reading books of an uplifting nature. It was rather that he found in it an adequate response to conditions in the world at a moment when the world was in crisis and Greece was *in extremis*. And that idea of poetry as an answer, and the idea of an answering poetry as a responsible poetry, and the idea of poetry's answer, its responsibility, being given in its own language rather than in the language of the world that provokes it, that too has been one of my constant themes. Early on, for example, I quoted Robert Pinsky's wise observation that an artist

needs not so much an audience, as to feel a need to answer, a promise to respond. The response may be a contradiction, it may be unwanted, it may go unheeded . . . but it is owed and the sense that it is owed is a basic requirement for the poet's good feeling about the art.

This is well said, and it is well supplemented by Pinsky's further statement that 'the artist must answer the received cultural imagination of the subject with something utterly different'. The artist, the poet must in some sense set the world free to have a new go at its business. As I also said in that first lecture, if our given experience is a labyrinth, then its impassability is countered by the poet's imagining some equivalent of the labyrinth and bringing himself and the reader through it.

Of course, in order that this salubrious effect be achieved, the poet need not be working with any specifically improving end in mind. To effect the redress of poetry, it is not necessary for the poet to be aiming deliberately at social or political change. Hugh MacDiarmid might make a transcendent effort on behalf of Scottish cultural nationalism and achieve a masterpiece like *A Drunk Man Looks at the Thistle*; and Oscar Wilde might admit a propagandist motive and produce 'The Ballad of Reading Gaol', a work intended to have an immediate effect upon the penal code, but in these cases MacDiarmid and Wilde are still appealing to an imagined standard as well as to an empirical audience. And the same is true when John Clare makes the field called 'Swordy Well' lament its post-enclosure fate in the voice of an early-nineteenth-century parish pauper, or when Brian Merriman makes his bailiff in *The Midnight Court* deplore the state of late-eighteenth-century Ireland. In other words, even when the redress of poetry is operative in the first sense in which I employed it – poetry, that is, being instrumental in adjusting and correcting imbalances in the world, poetry as an intended intervention into the goings-on of society – even then, poetry is involved with supreme fictions as well as actual conditions. What it is offering is a glimpsed alternative, a world to which 'we turn incessantly and without knowing it'.

But I also intended these lectures to be concerned with the redress of poetry in another sense, where the meaning of redress was 'to set (a person or thing) upright again, to raise again to an erect position ... to restore, re-establish.' I have been intent upon treating poetry as an answer given in terms of metre and syntax, of tone and musical trueness; an answer given also by the unpredictability of its inventions and its need to go emotionally and artistically 'above the brim', beyond the conventional bounds. To redress poetry in this sense is to know it and celebrate it for its forcibleness as itself, as the affirming spiritual flame which W. H. Auden wanted to be shown forth. It is to know and celebrate it not only as a matter of proffered argument and edifying content, but as a matter of angelic potential, a motion of the soul. And this is why I have tried to profess the pleasure and surprise of poetry, its rightness and thereness, the way it is at one moment unforeseeable and at the next indispensable, the way it arrives as something unhindered and self-directing, sweeping ahead into its full potential. In effect, I have talked about the work of my chosen writers as a 'vehicle of world harmony', a phrase which Nadezhda Mandelstam used in the course of her discussion of the poet's role in *Hope Against Hope.*

The work of the poet, as a vehicle of world harmony, has a social character – that is, it is concerned with the doings of the poet's fellow men, among whom he lives and whose fate he shares. He does not speak 'for them', but with them, nor does he set himself apart from them: otherwise he would not be a source of truth.

To be a source of truth and at the same time a vehicle of harmony: this expresses what we would like poetry to be and it takes me back to the kinds of pressure which poets from Northern Ireland are subject to. These poets feel with special force a need to be true to the negative nature of the evidence and at the same time to show an affirming flame, the need to be both socially responsible and creatively free. Among poets of my own generation in the 1960s there was a general feeling of being socially called upon which grew as the polarization grew and the pressure mounted upon the writers not only to render images of the Ulster predicament, but also perhaps to show solidarity with one or other side in the quarrel. Even if they preferred to avoid the redemptive stance, the writers could not altogether escape the myth of their own importance in an ongoing work of definition and transformation. We all experienced a need to get certain unique and almost subcultural realities of Ulster life into words, and we all learnt something from each other and from the example of other generations. I learnt from John Hewitt and John Montague and Patrick Kavanagh special confidences and orientations which I could not have got from Gerard Manley Hopkins or Dylan Thomas. Michael Longley and Derek Mahon learned different things from Louis MacNeice and again from Patrick Kavanagh. And much of this learning went towards getting down in words what it was we grew up with, establishing cultural and literary credentials, being able to say to ourselves with some satisfaction, well, there's a bit of psycho-political matter that has been got into the language, there's something new on the page which this audience will recognize as something old.

Certainly, when I wrote about a Presbyterian farmer standing in the yard at night, not going in to his Catholic neighbours' house until he heard them finish their prayers, part of my pleasure was in thinking that the subject had not, as far as I knew, been treated in a poem. And this was fundamentally a literary pleasure, a feeling that the work answered not only in Pinsky's terms but also in the colloquial Ulster sense of the word: if you say in Northern Ireland that a thing answers, it means that it is up to the mark, fit for the job, has passed itself. So in that way the poem answered well enough; even if it showed Protestant and Catholic in harmony, it was not fundamentally intended as a contribution to better community relations. It had come out of creative freedom rather than social obligation, it was about a moment of achieved grace between people with different allegiances rather than a representation of a state of constant goodwill in the country as a whole, and as such it was not presuming to be anything more than a momentary stay against confusion.

I shall read another of my poems today by way of conclusion, but before that I am going to talk some more about the way certain poets have answered the conditions in Northern Ireland and about the adequacy of those answers. I want to go back to a lecture I gave here in 1991 on the poetry of Louis MacNeice. In it I discussed MacNeice's bilocation in Ireland and England, the subsequent relegation of his importance in England and the resistance to his inclusion within the *echt*-Irish canon in Ireland. I said then that it was inevitable that a category of Irishness which left no room for the complicated colonial relationship of Northern Protestants to the island of Ireland was going to run into trouble. The political arrangement which incorporated Northern Ireland into the United Kingdom of Great Britain and Northern Ireland was not one allowed for in the envisaging minds of the writers of the Irish Literary Revival. Yeats, Synge and Lady Gregory constructed an imagined place that gave eternal life to Gaelic country people of the west and their Anglo-Irish lords and ladies, while Joyce made a divine comedy out of the urban tumult of Dublin. So, both Joyce and the Revivalists, in their different ways, prepared cultural paths for the political fact of Irish independence; and indeed when that independence came it included only those constituencies whom the writers of genius at the turn of the century had written into the imaginative record. The Irish Free State was from the start coterminous as a demographic and geographic entity with the textual Ireland of Joyce and the Revivalists – the Ireland, that is, of urban Catholicism, rural peasantry and those of the Protestant ascendancy and professional classes who were prepared to stay on after the Union Jack came down.

North of the border, of course, and still under the Union Jack, there dwelt what was now a Unionist majority, resistant and defensive, and what was suddenly a nationalist minority, an enclave of frustrated, distrusted Catholics. Then, beginning in the 1930s and 1940s, John Hewitt attempted to write into the imaginative record the Ulster Planters' sense of difference and entitlement by deliberately recognizing and affirming the colonial nature of the Ulster Protestant experience. Hewitt settled upon the region of Ulster itself as the first unit of his world, in the hope that a place that was both a *provincia* of the British imperium and an area of the ancient Irish province of Uladh or Ulster could command the allegiance of both Unionists *and* Nationalists. Hewitt's move was original and epoch-making, a significant extension of the imagining faculty into the domain of politics, but it could not wholly reconcile the Unionist mystique of Britishness with the Irish Nationalist sense of the priority of the Gaelic inheritance.

Hewitt's regionalism suited the feeling of possession and independence of the empowered Protestants with their own Parliament and fail-safe majority at Stormont more than it could ever suit the sense of dispossession and political marginalization of the Catholics. The poet was personally a man of the deepest tolerance and sympathy, principled in his sense of diversity, passionate for social justice; but in his imagining he could not include the Irish dimension in anything other than an under-privileged way. The pre-eminence, as he saw it, of the British intellectual tradition, the obscurantism, as he saw it, of the Roman Catholic Church and the logic of his colonial trope which naturally validated the culture of the colonizing power over that of the native – all this meant that he stood his ground in the north as a resolute democrat, with a vision of the just society based on regional loyalties, but a vision that was slightly Nelson-eyed, as it were, more capable of seeing over the water than over the border.

Hewitt, for example, allied his regional approach with that of Hugh MacDiarmid in Scotland; but Hewitt's vision of the re-deemed region was significantly less inclusive than MacDiar-mid's. There was nothing in the Irish poet's concerns which corresponded to MacDiarmid's effort to include the Gaelic inher-itance of Scottish life within his total imagining. In poems like the 'Lament for the Great Music' and 'Island Funeral' the Scot-tish poet made a big space for that whole other mode of Scot-tish belonging. His cradle culture was that of the Dissenters and his hearth language the Lallans Scots, but that did not preclude a sympathy for the Gaelic, Catholic culture of the Highlands and Islands. It did not matter to MacDiarmid that the Gaelic life was marginal or in decline. What mattered was its meaning, its necessity as part of the whole diverse Scottish possibility; it was only through acknowledging it and embracing it that a totally inclusive future could be prefigured. Hewitt was, of course, sympathetic to the older culture and literature of Ire-land, but its incorporation was not part of his intellectual project. The fact that Gaelic was a dying language was enough for Hewitt to absolve himself of any imaginative obligation to the Gaelic order. He was predisposed to write out rather than write in the native inheritance and his identification of his point of view with that of the voice in Robert Frost's poem 'The Gift

Outright' is telling in this respect. Frost's poem is about the transition the New Englanders made between the seventeenth century and the twentieth century from being colonists with loyalties to England to being Americans in their own right in their own land, given over to the place, surrendered to it:

> Such we were, we gave ourselves outright
> (The deed of gift was many deeds of war)
> To the land vaguely realizing westward,
> But still unstoried, artless, unenhanced,
> Such as she was, such as she would become.

When Hewitt quoted the poem in a *Lagan* article in 1945, he dropped the line about the deed of gift being many deeds of war, an understandable and tactful suppression of the conquest element behind the planters' at-homeness. But he kept the line about the land being 'unstoried, artless, unenhanced' until the colonists surrendered to it, and in doing so he participated in Frost's unconscious erasure of native American stories and arts and enhancements, and made a similar colonial erasure of the original native culture of *Uladh*.

What I am saying does not take away from the artistic and historic strength of Hewitt's poetic achievement. It merely questions the adequacy in present circumstances of his particular regional planter's myth. That myth, indeed, was as personal as it was public, born as much out of his own solitude as out of his strong sense of social obligation; it was an accounting, in terms of historical pattern, for a sense of displacement Hewitt felt in himself. Poems like 'The Colony' and 'The Search' have the feel of work that springs from an ache in need of appeasement. They are not diagrams of a political bind but ventures of an imagination simultaneously seeking a way out and a way in. In fact, while I have been emphazing the Hewitt effort as a way of retaining an ancestral bond with the mother culture of England, it is equally true that his insistence on the English link is a compensation for the new displacement within Ireland which his northern planter people suffered in 1921. Until then, diversity was the norm within the Union. From Belfast to Brandon, everybody, whether Gaelic speakers from Ballyferriter or Scots speakers from Braid, everybody had the one home under the Crown; if they were not quite at ease within an old dispensation, they were at any rate held equally in place by it. But partition created crisis. It kept the Protestant majority out of Ireland's Ireland every bit as effectively as it kept the Catholic minority within Britain's, and it created the conditions with which Hewitt's peculiar mixture of lyric tenderness and secular tough-mindedness had to cope. His poems are best read as personal solutions to a shared crisis, momentary stays against confusion. At a political and cultural level, the region he envisaged failed to establish itself. It just might have come into being, had the gerrymandered statelet of Brookeborough's era been transformed through the administrations of Lord O'Neill and Brian Faulkner (with the help of agitation by the Civil Rights Movement) into an opener, more tolerant democracy. But that transition was not to happen, and what did happen jumped the political disposition of both minority and majority back into a renewed and desolate defensiveness.

But if Hewitt was the projector of a Northern Ireland that failed to develop, Louis MacNeice is the sponsor of one struggling to be born, one in which allowances for the priority of some of its citizens' Irishness would not prejudice the rights of others' Britishness. I talked two years ago about MacNeice's bifocal vision and about how it is, as they say, 'part of the solution'. MacNeice explored his bilocated extraterritorial fidelities in the poem 'Carrick Revisited', a poem written out of a need to straddle his areas of self-division, and to bring his inherited and acquired characteristics into congruence. It was as if MacNeice combined within himself both the Yankee and the native American. He saw his Northern Ireland nativity – his given destiny, his bridgehead into reality – as something that was to be neither cancelled nor defensively fortified. Like Hewitt, he grew up in pre-partition Ireland, but, unlike Hewitt, he did not allow the border to enter into his subsequent imaginings: his sense of cultural diversity and historical consequence within the country never congealed into a red and green map. In MacNeice's mind, the colours ran – or bled – into each other. His ancestry in Mayo gave him a native dream-place in the south which complemented his actual birthplace in the north, while his dwelling in England gave him a critical perspective on the peculiar Britishness of that first northern environment. And what it all means can be represented, I suggested, by the figure of the quincunx, and my suggestion was no more than another attempt to bring the frontiers of the country into alignment with the frontiers of writing, an attempt to sketch the shape of an integrated literary tradition.

I sketched that tradition in terms of five towers, with first, at the centre, the tower of prior Irelandness, the round tower of original insular dwelling, located perhaps upon what Louis MacNeice called 'the pre-natal mountain'. With this at the centre, I then placed at the southern point of a diamond shape Kilcolman Castle, Edmund Spenser's tower, as it were, the tower of English conquest and the Anglicization of Ireland, linguistically, culturally, institutionally. Then, on the left of the diamond's shoulder, in the west of the country, at Ballylee, there is the Norman tower occupied by W. B. Yeats as a deliberate symbol of *his* poetic effort, which was to restore the spiritual values and magical world-view that Spenser's armies and language had destroyed. The fourth tower, on the eastern edge, is Joyce's Martello tower, on Dublin Bay, the setting of the opening chapter of *Ulysses* and symbol of Joyce's attempt to 'Hellenize the island', his attempt to marginalize the imperium which had marginalized him by replacing the Anglocentric Protestant tradition with a newly forged apparatus of Homeric correspondences, Dantesque scholasticism and a more or less Mediterranean, European, classically endorsed world-view. So: we can say that Spenser's tower faces in to the round tower of the mythic first Irish place and sees popery, barbarism and the Dark Ages; Yeats's tower faces it and sees a possible unity of being, an Irish nation retrieved and enabled by a repossession of its Gaelic heritage; Joyce's tower faces it and sees an archetypal symbol, the *omphalos*, the navel of a reinvented order, or maybe the ivory tower from which the chaste maid of Irish Catholic provincialism must be liberated into the secular freedoms of Europe.

Enter then, from the north, Carrickfergus Castle – MacNeice's keep, shall we say. And this tower, where William of Orange once landed on his way to secure the Protestant Settlement and where the British Army was garrisoned for generations, this tower, once it is sponsored by MacNeice's vision, no longer only looks with averted eyes back towards the Glorious Revolution and the Mother of Parliaments, but is capable of looking also towards that visionary Ireland whose name, to quote MacNeice, 'keeps ringing like a bell / In an underwater belfry.' MacNeice, I suggested, by his English domicile and his civil learning is an aspect of Spenser, by his ancestral and affectionate links with Connemara an aspect of Yeats and by his mythic and European consciousness an aspect of Joyce. And by writing his castle into the poetic annals, he has completed the figure. He can be regarded as an Irish Protestant writer with Anglocentric attitudes who managed to be faithful to his Ulster inheritance, his Irish affections and his English predilections. As such, he offers a way in and a way out not only for the northern Unionist imagination in relation to some sort of integral Ireland but also for the southern Irish imagination in relation to the partitioned north. It may be that there is not yet a political structure to reflect this poetic diagram, but the admission of MacNeice in this way within the symbolic ordering of Ireland also admits a hope for the evolution of a political order, one tolerant of difference and capable of metamorphoses within all the multivalent possibilities of Irishness, Britishness, Europeanness, planetariness, creatureliness, whatever.

'Whatever is given', I wrote in one of my own poems, 'Can always be reimagined, however four-square, / Plank-thick, hull-stupid and out of its time / It happens to be.' And I have been greatly reinforced in that belief by the experience of reading and thinking about poetry in the course of my duties here at

Oxford. It has been a great privilege to have had such a faithful audience throughout the whole five years: the friendliness of your attention is something I cherished from the beginning, and it will always confirm the possibility of a new commonwealth of art, one wrested out of the old dramas of conquest and liberation, of annexation and independence, one that I wrote about ten years ago in *An Open Letter* to the editors of *The Penguin Book of Contemporary British Poetry*. This took up the whole question of naming, what it means to call oneself or another person British or Irish, and in the course of it I alluded to different reviewers who had touched upon the duality:

> Under a common flag, said Larkin.
> Different history, said Haughton.
> Our own fastidious John Jordan
>   Raised an eyebrow:
> How British were these Ulstermen?
>   He'd like to know.
>
> Answer: as far we are part
> Of some new commonwealth of art,
> Salute with independent heart
>   And equally
> Doff and flourish in the court
>   Of poesie.

In that same letter, I wrote that my passport was green, although nowadays it is a Euro-, but not an imperial, purple. I wrote about the colour of the passport, however, not in order to expunge the British connection in Britain's Ireland but to maintain the right to diversity *within* the border, to be understood as having full freedom to the enjoyment of an Irish name and identity within that northern jurisdiction. Those who want to share that name and identity in Britain's Ireland should not be penalized or resented or suspected of a sinister motive because they draw cultural and psychic sustenance from an elsewhere supplementary to the one across the water. Unresented, they could more easily stop resenting. For they, in turn, must not penalize or resist the at-homeness of their neighbours who cherish the primacy of the British link. The Unionists' refusal to be 'outcast on the world', in Hewitt's poetic formulation, expresses itself politically as a refusal to be included in an integral Ireland. And that refusal has to be imaginatively comprehended as well as constitutionally respected. As Professor Roy Foster writes in the introduction to his recent book of essays on the ways that British and Irish history have intersected: 'We need not give up our own claims on Irishness in order to conceive of it as a flexible definition. And in an age of exclusivist jihads to east and west, the notion that people can reconcile more than one cultural identity may have much to recommend it.'

There is nothing extraordinary about the challenge to be in two minds. If, for example, there was something exacerbating, there was still nothing deleterious to my sense of Irishness in the fact that I grew up in the minority in Northern Ireland and was educated within the dominant British culture. My identity was emphasized rather than eroded by being maintained in such circumstances. The British dimension, in other words, while it is something that will be resisted by the minority if it is felt to be coercive, has nevertheless been a given of our history and even of our geography, one of the places where we all live, willy-nilly. It's in the language. And it's where the mind of many in the republic lives also. So I would suggest that the majority in Northern Ireland should make a corresponding effort at two-mindedness, and start to conceive of themselves within – rather than beyond – the Irish element. Obviously, it will be extremely difficult for them to surmount their revulsion against all the violence that has been perpetrated in the name of Ireland, but everything and everybody would be helped were they to make their imagination press back against the pressure of reality and re-enter the whole country of Ireland imaginatively, if not constitutionally, through the northern point of the quincunx.

At any rate, what I have been saying in these lectures has

been somewhat analogous to Professor Foster's proposition. In other words, whatever the possibilities of achieving political harmony at an institutional level, I wanted to affirm that within our individual selves we can reconcile two orders of knowledge which we might call the practical and the poetic; to affirm also that each form of knowledge redresses the other and that the frontier between them is there for the crossing. All of which is implicit in this short poem that formed part of a sequence called 'Lightenings' and appeared in my book *Seeing Things* in 1991:

The annals say: when the monks of Clonmacnoise
Were all at prayers inside the oratory
A ship appeared above them in the air.

The anchor dragged along behind so deep
It hooked itself into the altar rails
And then, as the big hull rocked to a standstill,

A crewman shinned and grappled down the rope
And struggled to release it. But in vain.
'This man can't bear our life here and will drown,'

The abbot said, 'unless we help him.' So
They did, the freed ship sailed, and the man climbed back
Out of the marvellous as he had known it.

23 November 1993

Notes

Introduction

Page

xiv 'needs not so much' Robert Pinsky, *Poetry and the World*, Ecco Press, New York, 1988, p. 85.

xviii 'external testimony but' William Wordsworth, Preface to *Lyrical Ballads*, 1805, reprinted in *Lyrical Ballads 1805*, edited by Derek Roper, Collins, London, 1968, p. 33.

The Redress of Poetry

1 'is a violence' Wallace Stevens, *The Necessary Angel*, Faber and Faber, London, 1984, p. 36.
'In our time' epigraph (by Thomas Mann) to W. B. Yeats's poem 'Politics' in *Collected Poems of W. B. Yeats*, Macmillan, London, 1961, p. 392.

2 'creates the world' Stevens, op. cit., p. 31.

3 'If we know' Simone Weil, *Gravity and Grace*, Routledge, London, 1963, p. 151.
'Obedience to the' ibid., pp. 2–3.

4 'a state of mind' Václav Havel, *Disturbing the Peace*, Faber and Faber, London, 1990, p. 181.

6 'to write short' W. B. Yeats, 'A General Introduction for my Work', in *Essays and Introductions*, Macmillan, London, 1961, p. 521.

8 'The taste of' Jorge Luis Borges, *Selected Poems 1923–1967*, edited, with an Introduction and Notes, by Norman Thomas Giovanni, Dell, New York, 1973, p. 272.
'If in the' ibid., p. 269.

9 'strong enough to help' George Seferis, *A Poet's Journal, Days of 1945–51*, Cambridge, Mass., 1974, p. 134.

11 'The Pulley' and all quotations from George Herbert's poems are from *A Choice of George Herbert's Verse*, Faber and Faber, London, 1967.

13 'a poet's words' Stevens, op. cit., p. 32.

Extending the Alphabet: On Christopher Marlowe's 'Hero and Leander'

17   'Cut is the branch' All quotations from Marlowe's plays are from
      Marlowe's Plays and Poems, edited and introduced by M. R.
      Ridley, J. M. Dent, London, 1955.
23   'The wild O'Neill' *Marlowe's Plays and Poems*, p. 250.
      'had done rough work' H. S. V. Jones, *A Spenser Handbook*, Bell
      & Sons, New York, 1930, p. 33.
24   'the grand elementary principle' William Wordsworth and
      Samuel Taylor Coleridge, *Lyrical Ballads*, ed. Derek Roper,
      Collins, London, 1968, p. 33.
      'the thing that matters' Ezra Pound, *Literary Essays of Ezra
      Pound*, edited with an introduction by T. S. Eliot, Faber and
      Faber, London, 1954, p. 49.
26   'She fell on her' All quotations from 'Hero and Leander' are
      taken from Christopher Marlowe, *The Complete Poems and
      Translations*, edited by Stephen Orgel, Penguin Books,
      Harmondsworth, 1971.
28   'the South African writer' See André Brink, *Writing in a Time of
      Siege*, Summit Books, New York, 1986, pp. 164–5.
      'rhetoric of enticement' Harry Levin, *Christopher Marlowe, The
      Overreacher*, Faber and Faber, London, 1956, p. 172.
29   'a powerful and passionate' W. B. Yeats, *Essays and
      Introductions*, Macmillan, London, 1961, pp. 521–2.
32   'The reader, if' Pound, op. cit., p. 235.
      'there's nothing ails' See 'The Fascination of What's Difficult' in
      W. B. Yeats, *Collected Poems*, Macmillan, London, 1961, p. 104.
33   'In a poem' Introduction to Aleksandr Kushner, *Apollo in the
      Snow*, Farrar, Straus & Giroux, New York, 1991, pp. xi–xii.
36   'since our erected wit' Sir Philip Sidney, 'The Defence of Poesy' in
      Sir Philip Sidney, Oxford Poetry Library, 1994, p. 106.
37   'This is how poems' revised stanza from 'To Sorley Maclean' in
      Somhairle, Dàin is Deilth, Acair, Isle of Lewis, 1991, p. 60.
      'forcibleness or *Energia*' Sidney, op. cit., p.138.

Orpheus in Ireland: On Brian Merriman's *The Midnight Court*

38   'profane perfection of' W. B. Yeats, *Collected Poems of W. B.
      Yeats*, Macmillan, London, 1961, p. 399.
      'the spiritual intellect's great' ibid., p. 394 ('The Man and the
      Echo').
      'a poem written' see *Cúirt an Mheán-Oíche*, Liam P. O Murchu a
      chuir in eagar, Baile Atha Cliath, An Clochomhar Tta, 1982.

39 'his inaugural lecture' See Peter Levi, *The Art of Poetry*, Yale University Press, New Haven, 1991, pp. 5–26.
41 'what [he] witnesses' T. S. Eliot, *Collected Poems 1904–1962*, Faber and Faber, London, 1963, p. 82.
42 'And there (I' Unless otherwise indicated, quotations from *The Midnight Court* are taken from my *The Midnight Verdict*, The Gallery Press, Loughcrew, 1993.
44 'We should picture' Quoted by Sean O'Tuama in 'Brian Merriman and his Court', *Irish University Review*, Vol. 11, No. 2, Dublin, Autumn 1981, p. 160.
'My hair was washed' reprint of first edition of Frank O'Connor's translation of *The Midnight Court*, The O'Brien Press, Dublin, 1989, pp. 32–4.
46 'Now tell us the truth' ibid., pp. 37–8.
51 'in French, Italian' O'Tuama, op. cit., p. 154.
52 'a new demonic' O'Tuama, op. cit., p. 158.
'engross the present' W. B. Yeats, op. cit., p. 392.
'the stylistic arrangements of' W. B. Yeats, *A Vision*, 2nd edition, Macmillan, London, 1962, p. 25.
53 'gave his account' See Daniel Corkery, *The Hidden Ireland*, Gill & Macmillan, Dublin, n.d., pp. 222–39.
54 'cannot write intelligently' quoted in Alan Titley in 'An Breithiunas ar Cúirt an Mheán-Oíche', *Studia Hibernica*, No. 25, Dublin, 1989–90, p. 107. Titley's article is a spirited account (in Irish) of a whole range of scholarly and critical responses to the poem.
55 'As always, when' O'Connor, op. cit., p. 11.
56 'the basic, healthy' quoted in Titley, op. cit., p. 120.
57 'The sun passed' Seamus Heaney, 'Orpheus and Eurydice', in *After Ovid: New Metamorphoses*, edited by Michael Hofmann and James Lasdun, Faber and Faber, London, 1994, p. 225.
58 'It is quite probable' O'Tuama, op. cit., p. 161.
60 'They circled him' Heaney, 'Death of Orpheus', in *After Ovid*, op. cit., p. 227.

John Clare's Prog

63 Epigraph from Michael Traynor, *The English Dialect of Donegal: A Glossary*, Royal Hibernian Academy, Dublin, 1956.
65 'I found a ball' Unless otherwise indicated, all quotations from Clare's poetry are taken from the Oxford Authors' *John Clare*,

edited by Eric Robinson and David Powell, Oxford University
Press, Oxford, 1984.

72 'There's Doctor Bottle' *John Clare: Selected Poetry*, edited by
Geoffrey Summerfield, Penguin, London, 1990, p. 220.

73 'stating some truth' Keith Douglas, *Collected Poems*, Faber and
Faber, London, 1964, p. 148.
'the nugget of harmony' Nadezhda Mandelstam, *Hope Against
Hope*, Penguin Books, Harmondsworth, 1975, p. 225.

74 'a narrow ascendancy' Hugh MacDiarmid, *Selected Prose*, edited
by Alan Riach, Carcanet, Manchester, 1992, p. 67.

80 'The restored texts' *The Faber Book of Vernacular Verse*, edited
by Tom Paulin, Faber and Faber, London, 1990, p. xix.

82 'nostalgia for world' Mandelstam, op. cit., p. 295. John Bayley
refers to this phrase in his review of Valentina Polukhina's
Brodsky through the Eyes of his Contemporaries in *TLS*, 25
September 1992.

Speranza in Reading: On 'The Ballad of Reading Gaol'

83 'Once read, it' Richard Ellmann, *Oscar Wilde*, Knopf, New
York, 1987, p. 532. The biographical details included here are all
taken from Ellmann's study of Wilde.

84 'These poems' *A Book of Old Ballads*, selected by Beverley
Nichols, Hutchinson, London, 1934, p. xiii.
'He did not' Oscar Wilde, *De Profundis and Other Writings*,
Penguin, London, 1986, p. 231. All quotations from 'The Ballad
of Reading Gaol' are taken from this edition.

86 'I object to' Terry Eagleton, *Saint Oscar*, Field Day, Derry, 1989,
p. 46.

87 'Wilde saw that' Declan Kiberd, *Anglo-Irish Attitudes*, reprinted
in *Ireland's Field Day*, Hutchinson, London, 1985, p. 88.

88 'The poem suffers' *Selected Letters of Oscar Wilde*, edited by
Rupert Hart-Davis, Oxford University Press, Oxford, 1979,
p. 311.
'now that I' *The Oxford Book of Modern Verse*, edited by W. B.
Yeats, Oxford University Press, Oxford, 1936, p. vii.

89 'I have stood' ibid., p. vii.
'the finished man' W. B. Yeats, *Collected Poems*, Macmillan,
London, 1961, p. 266.

97 'Lying, the telling' Wilde, *De Profundis and Other Writings*,
p. 87.

98 'As regards these' Michael J. O'Neill, 'Irish Poets of the

Nineteenth Century: Unpublished Lecture Notes of Oscar
Wilde', *University Review*, Vol. 1, No. 4, Dublin, Spring
1955, p. 30.

99 'one / With Davis' W. B. Yeats, *Collected Poems*, Macmillan,
London, 1961, p. 57.
'Of the quality' O'Neill, op. cit., p. 32.

100 'I made them' *The Poems of Speranza (Lady Wilde)*, James
Duffy & Co., Dublin, 1864.
'They are pale' ibid., p. 2.

102 'image of fingerprints' Ellmann, op. cit., p. 552.

A Torchlight Procession of One: On Hugh MacDiarmid

104 'lapsed or unrealized' Hugh MacDiarmid, *Selected Prose*, edited
by Alan Riach, Carcanet, Manchester, 1992, p. 11.

105 'My job, as' Quoted in Alan Bold, *MacDiarmid: Christopher
Murray Grieve, A Critical Biography*, Paladin, London, 1990,
p. 478.
'two minutes of pandemonium' See 'After his Death' in Norman
MacCaig, *Collected Poems*, Chatto, London, 1985, pp. 240–1.
'He would walk' Bold, op. cit., p. 494.

106 'Ae weet forenicht' Hugh MacDiarmid, *Complete Poems,
1920–1976*, edited by Michael Grieve and W. R. Aitken, in two
volumes, Martin, Brian & O'Keefe, London, 1978, Vol. 1, p. 17.
'Most of the words' Bold, op. cit., p. 35.

108 'Mars is braw' MacDiarmid, *Complete Poems*, Vol. 1, p. 17.

109 'an eaten and' Bold, op. cit., p. 35.

111 'Scottish literature, like' MacDiarmid, *Selected Prose*, p. 3.
'a language interrupted' *The Faber Book of Twentieth-Century
Scottish Poetry*, edited by Douglas Dunn, Faber and Faber,
London, 1992, p. xx.

112 'The stars, like' MacDiarmid, *Complete Poems*, Vol. 1, p. 166.

113 'nostalgia for world' See note to p. 82.
'I felt it' MacDiarmid, *Complete Poems*, pp. 164–5.

115 'the reader in posterity' Osip Mandelstam's phrase, quoted in
Robert Tracy's Introduction to his translation of Mandelstam's
Stone, Collins Harvill, London, 1991, p. 40.
'*vis comica*' MacDiarmid, *Selected Prose*, p. 20.
'when the sea' *The Crane Bag Book of Irish Studies*, edited by
Richard Kearney and Mark Patrick Hedermann, Blackwater
Press, Dublin, 1982, p. 10.

116 'My harns are' *Complete Poems*, Vol. 1, p. 95.

201 'Under a common' from 'An Open Letter', reprinted i[...]
    Field Day, Hutchinson, London, 1985, p. 25.
202 'outcast on the world' John Hewitt, *The Collected Poem[...]*
    by Frank Ormsby, The Blackstaff Press, Belfast, 1991, p. [...]
    'We need not' Roy Foster, *Paddy & Mr. Punch*, Allen Lan[e]
    London, 1993, pp. xvi–xvii.
203 'The annals say' Heaney, op. cit., p. 62.

118 'As necessary, and' ibid., p. 298.
119 'So every loveliness' ibid., Vol. 2, p. 1190.
121 'Poetry of such' ibid., p. 1025.
    'I am so' *Selected Letters of Philip Larkin*, edited by Anthony
    Thwaite, Faber and Faber, London, 1992, p. 436.
    'Is there any' ibid., p. 437.
122 'Nothing has stirred' MacDiarmid, *Complete Poems*, Vol. 1,
    pp. 423–4.
123 'wishes to show' Richard Ellmann, *The Identity of Yeats*, 2nd
    edition, Faber and Faber, London, 1964, p. xxiv.

Dylan the Durable? On Dylan Thomas

126 'Poems. I liked' *The Collected Letters of Dylan Thomas*, edited
    by Paul Ferris, Macmillan, New York, 1986, p. 278.
128 'Before I knocked' All poems by Dylan Thomas quoted from
    Collected Poems 1934–1952, Dent, London, 1954.
130 'I like things' *Collected Letters*, ed. Ferris, pp. 181–2.
131 'These poems' Thomas, *Collected Poems*, p. vi.
    'I think [poetry]' *Collected Letters*, ed. Ferris, p. 182.
    'describing and cataloguing' quoted by Paul Ferris in *Dylan
    Thomas*, Penguin Books, Harmondsworth, 1978, p. 109.
    'All thoughts and' *Collected Letters*, ed. Ferris, p. 39.
134 'Poetic tone is' Eavan Boland, 'Time, Memory and Obsession',
    PN Review, Vol. 18, No. 2, p. 22.
138 'sensual strut' Thomas, *Collected Poems*, p. vi.
140 'Death is a' Quoted by Charles Segal in *Orpheus, The Myth of
    the Poet*, Johns Hopkins University Press, Baltimore, 1989,
    p. 216.
    'a blurred touch' *Letters on Poetry from W. B. Yeats to Dorothy
    Wellesley*, Oxford University Press, 1940, p. 110.
141 'creative destruction' See p. 127, above.
143 'the oral poet' Segal, op. cit., p. 15.
    'magical, quasi-hypnotic effect' ibid., p. 16.
144 'intransigence of reality' ibid., p. 3.

Joy or Night: Last Things in the Poetry of W. B. Yeats and
    Philip Larkin

146 'After the third' Miroslav Holub, *Interferon, or On Theater*,
    translated by Dana Habova and David Young, Field Translation
    Series 7, Oberlin, 1982, pp. 42–3.

147 'Suddenly I saw' All quotations from Yeats's poems come from *Collected Poems of W. B. Yeats*, Macmillan, London, 1961.

148 'spiritual height and depth' Wallace Stevens, *The Necessary Angel*, Faber and Faber, London, 1984, p. 34.
'the swoon of a heart' *The Poems of Gerard Manley Hopkins*, edited by W. H. Gardner and N. H. MacKenzie, Oxford University Press, 1970, p. 52.
'heaven-handling' ibid., p. 100.
'cliffs of fall' ibid., p. 100.

150 'Some will ask' W. B. Yeats, *A Vision*, 2nd edition, Macmillan, London, 1962, pp. 24–5.
'I once got' *Letters on Poetry from W. B. Yeats to Dorothy Wellesley*, Oxford University Press, Oxford, 1940, p. 195.

151 'was obliged by' Richard Ellmann, *Four Dubliners*, Hamish Hamilton, London, 1987, p. 48.
'was relentlessly undermined' ibid., p. 50.
'the darkling thrush' *The Complete Poems of Thomas Hardy*, edited by James Gibson, Macmillan, London, 1976, p. 150.

152 'God-curst sun' ibid., p. 12.
'And immediately/Rather' All quotations from Larkin's poetry come from his *Collected Poems*, edited with an introduction by Anthony Thwaite, Marvell Press / Faber and Faber, London, 1988.

156 'cold winds blow' W. B. Yeats, *Essays and Introductions*, Macmillan, London, 1961, p. 523.

157 'carried beyond feeling' ibid., p. 523.
'No actress has' ibid., p. 523.
'in a manner' Czeslaw Milosz, 'The Real and the Paradigms', *Poetry Australia*, No. 72, October 1979, pp. 18–24.

163 'Karl Barth said' See John Updike's discussion of Barth on Mozart in *Odd Jobs, Essays and Criticism*, Penguin, London, 1992, p. 229.

Counting to a Hundred: On Elizabeth Bishop

164 'Mysteriously enough, poor' Elizabeth Bishop, *The Collected Prose*, The Hogarth Press, London, 1984, p. 259.
'a flicker of impudence' quoted in David Kalstone, *Becoming a Poet*, Farrar Straus & Giroux, New York, 1989.
'Although I think' ibid., p. 24.

165 'hiding in her words' ibid., p. 31.

166 'the mystery of affinity' James Merrill's phrase in his Afterw[ord] to *Becoming a Poet*, op. cit., p. 251.

167 'a certain satisfactory' Kalstone, op. cit., p. 41.
'Clang./*Clang.*/Nate' *The Collected Prose*, pp. 252–3.

169 'September rain falls' Elizabeth Bishop, *Complete Poems*, T[he] Hogarth Press, London, 1991, pp. 123–4. All quotations fro[m] Elizabeth Bishop's poems come from this edition.

172 'the drunkenness of things' from 'Snow' in Louis MacNeice[,] *Collected Poems*, Faber and Faber, London, 1966, p. 30.

177 'Yes, all my life' Elizabeth Bishop in *World Literature Toda[y]*, Winter 1977.

181 'First, there are' Charles Simic, *Dime-Store Alchemy*, The [] Press, New York, 1992, p. 60.

184 'like what we imagine' Bishop, 'At the Fishhouses': see *Co[]Poems*, op. cit.

Frontiers of Writing

189 'Place and Displacement' The Pete Laver Memorial Lectur[e,] Grasmere, 2 August 1984, published as a pamphlet by the [] Trustees of Dove Cottage, Grasmere, 1985.

190 'the imagination presses' Wallace Stevens, *The Necessary []* Faber and Faber, London, 1984, p. 36.
'Frost and Hardy poems' See Introduction, pp. xiii–xiv.

191 'strong enough to help' See note to page 9.
'needs not so much' Robert Pinsky, *Poetry and the World[]* Press, New York, 1988, p. 85
'the artist must' Pinsky, op. cit., p. 85.

192 'we turn incessantly' Stevens, op. cit., p. 31.

193 'The work of the poet' Nadezhda Mandelstam, *Hope Aga[inst] Hope*, Penguin Books, Harmondsworth, 1975, pp. 225–6[]

197 'a *Lagan* article' 'The Bitter Gourd', reprinted in John Hewitt, *Ancestral Voices*, Blackstaff Press, Belfast, 1987, [] 120–1.

199 'the pre-natal mountain' see 'Carrick Revisited' in Louis [] MacNeice, *Collected Poems*, Faber and Faber, London, 1966, p. 225.

200 'keeps ringing like' Louis MacNeice, op. cit., p. 132.
'Whatever is given' Seamus Heaney, *Seeing Things*, Fabe[r and] Faber, London, 1991, p. 29.

118 'As necessary, and' ibid., p. 298.
119 'So every loveliness' ibid., Vol. 2, p. 1190.
121 'Poetry of such' ibid., p. 1025.
'I am so' *Selected Letters of Philip Larkin*, edited by Anthony Thwaite, Faber and Faber, London, 1992, p. 436.
'Is there any' ibid., p. 437.
122 'Nothing has stirred' MacDiarmid, *Complete Poems*, Vol. 1, pp. 423–4.
123 'wishes to show' Richard Ellmann, *The Identity of Yeats*, 2nd edition, Faber and Faber, London, 1964, p. xxiv.

Dylan the Durable? On Dylan Thomas

126 'Poems. I liked' *The Collected Letters of Dylan Thomas*, edited by Paul Ferris, Macmillan, New York, 1986, p. 278.
128 'Before I knocked' All poems by Dylan Thomas quoted from *Collected Poems 1934–1952*, Dent, London, 1954.
130 'I like things' *Collected Letters*, ed. Ferris, pp. 181–2.
131 'These poems' Thomas, *Collected Poems*, p. vi.
'I think [poetry]' *Collected Letters*, ed. Ferris, p. 182.
'describing and cataloguing' quoted by Paul Ferris in *Dylan Thomas*, Penguin Books, Harmondsworth, 1978, p. 109.
'All thoughts and' *Collected Letters*, ed. Ferris, p. 39.
134 'Poetic tone is' Eavan Boland, 'Time, Memory and Obsession', PN Review, Vol. 18, No. 2, p. 22.
138 'sensual strut' Thomas, *Collected Poems*, p. vi.
140 'Death is a' Quoted by Charles Segal in *Orpheus, The Myth of the Poet*, Johns Hopkins University Press, Baltimore, 1989, p. 216.
'a blurred touch' *Letters on Poetry from W. B. Yeats to Dorothy Wellesley*, Oxford University Press, 1940, p. 110.
141 'creative destruction' See p. 127, above.
143 'the oral poet' Segal, op. cit., p. 15.
'magical, quasi-hypnotic effect' ibid., p. 16.
144 'intransigence of reality' ibid., p. 3.

Joy or Night: Last Things in the Poetry of W. B. Yeats and Philip Larkin

146 'After the third' Miroslav Holub, *Interferon, or On Theater*, translated by Dana Habova and David Young, Field Translation Series 7, Oberlin, 1982, pp. 42–3.

147 'Suddenly I saw' All quotations from Yeats's poems come from *Collected Poems of W. B. Yeats*, Macmillan, London, 1961.

148 'spiritual height and depth' Wallace Stevens, *The Necessary Angel*, Faber and Faber, London, 1984, p. 34.
'the swoon of a heart' *The Poems of Gerard Manley Hopkins*, edited by W. H. Gardner and N. H. MacKenzie, Oxford University Press, 1970, p. 52.
'heaven-handling' ibid., p. 100.
'cliffs of fall' ibid., p. 100.

150 'Some will ask' W. B. Yeats, *A Vision*, 2nd edition, Macmillan, London, 1962, pp. 24–5.
'I once got' *Letters on Poetry from W. B. Yeats to Dorothy Wellesley*, Oxford University Press, Oxford, 1940, p. 195.

151 'was obliged by' Richard Ellmann, *Four Dubliners*, Hamish Hamilton, London, 1987, p. 48.
'was relentlessly undermined' ibid., p. 50.
'the darkling thrush' *The Complete Poems of Thomas Hardy*, edited by James Gibson, Macmillan, London, 1976, p. 150.

152 'God-curst sun' ibid., p. 12.
'And immediately/Rather' All quotations from Larkin's poetry come from his *Collected Poems*, edited with an introduction by Anthony Thwaite, Marvell Press / Faber and Faber, London, 1988.

156 'cold winds blow' W. B. Yeats, *Essays and Introductions*, Macmillan, London, 1961, p. 523.

157 'carried beyond feeling' ibid., p. 523.
'No actress has' ibid., p. 523.
'in a manner' Czeslaw Milosz, 'The Real and the Paradigms', *Poetry Australia*, No. 72, October 1979, pp. 18–24.

163 'Karl Barth said' See John Updike's discussion of Barth on Mozart in *Odd Jobs, Essays and Criticism*, Penguin, London, 1992, p. 229.

Counting to a Hundred: On Elizabeth Bishop

164 'Mysteriously enough, poor' Elizabeth Bishop, *The Collected Prose*, The Hogarth Press, London, 1984, p. 259.
'a flicker of impudence' quoted in David Kalstone, *Becoming a Poet*, Farrar Straus & Giroux, New York, 1989.
'Although I think' ibid., p. 24.

165 'hiding in her words' ibid., p. 31.
166 'the mystery of affinity' James Merrill's phrase in his Afterword to *Becoming a Poet*, op. cit., p. 251.
167 'a certain satisfactory' Kalstone, op. cit., p. 41.
    'Clang./*Clang.*/Nate' *The Collected Prose*, pp. 252–3.
169 'September rain falls' Elizabeth Bishop, *Complete Poems*, The Hogarth Press, London, 1991, pp. 123–4. All quotations from Elizabeth Bishop's poems come from this edition.
172 'the drunkenness of things' from 'Snow' in Louis MacNeice, *Collected Poems*, Faber and Faber, London, 1966, p. 30.
177 'Yes, all my life' Elizabeth Bishop in *World Literature Today*, Winter 1977.
181 'First, there are' Charles Simic, *Dime-Store Alchemy*, The Ecco Press, New York, 1992, p. 60.
184 'like what we imagine' Bishop, 'At the Fishhouses': see *Complete Poems*, op. cit.

Frontiers of Writing

189 'Place and Displacement' The Pete Laver Memorial Lecture, at Grasmere, 2 August 1984, published as a pamphlet by the Trustees of Dove Cottage, Grasmere, 1985.
190 'the imagination presses' Wallace Stevens, *The Necessary Angel*, Faber and Faber, London, 1984, p. 36.
    'Frost and Hardy poems' See Introduction, pp. xiii–xiv.
191 'strong enough to help' See note to page 9.
    'needs not so much' Robert Pinsky, *Poetry and the World*, Ecco Press, New York, 1988, p. 85
    'the artist must' Pinsky, op. cit., p. 85.
192 'we turn incessantly' Stevens, op. cit., p. 31.
193 'The work of the poet' Nadezhda Mandelstam, *Hope Against Hope*, Penguin Books, Harmondsworth, 1975, pp. 225–6.
197 'a *Lagan* article' 'The Bitter Gourd', reprinted in John Hewitt, *Ancestral Voices*, Blackstaff Press, Belfast, 1987, pp. 120–1.
199 'the pre-natal mountain' see 'Carrick Revisited' in Louis MacNeice, *Collected Poems*, Faber and Faber, London, 1966, p. 225.
200 'keeps ringing like' Louis MacNeice, op. cit., p. 132.
    'Whatever is given' Seamus Heaney, *Seeing Things*, Faber and Faber, London, 1991, p. 29.

201 'Under a common' from 'An Open Letter', reprinted in *Ireland's Field Day*, Hutchinson, London, 1985, p. 25.
202 'outcast on the world' John Hewitt, *The Collected Poems*, edited by Frank Ormsby, The Blackstaff Press, Belfast, 1991, p. 79.
'We need not' Roy Foster, *Paddy & Mr. Punch*, Allen Lane, London, 1993, pp. xvi–xvii.
203 'The annals say' Heaney, op. cit., p. 62.